How They Survived and Why We Lost

Central Intelligence Agency Analysis, 1966: The Vietnamese Communists' Will to Persist

Introduction by

Thomas Fensch

New Century Books

Copyright 2019 Thomas Fensch

New Century Books
8821 Rockdale Rd.
N. Chesterfield, Va., 232136-2150
newcentbks@gmail.com

ISBN 978-1-7333293-1-6 (paperback)
ISBN 978-1-7333293-2-3 (ebook)

Cover image courtesy Pixabay. (No date, location or photographer indicated.)

Note: Documents in this book, insofar as possible, are reprinted from original sources. Type styles and sizes differ from the Introduction and analysis.

Contents

Introduction
by Thomas Fensch — 1

Central Intelligence Agency Analysis, 1966:
The Vietnamese Communists' Will to Persist — 8

Unpopular Pessimism:
Why CIA Analysts Were So Doubtful About Vietnam — 332
by Harold P. Ford

Annotated Bibliography — 337

Notes — 338

About Thomas Fensch — 339

Introduction

It was a tragic prophecy: The Central Intelligent Agency's 1966 evaluation, "The Vietnamese Communists' Will to Persist."

And later, the 2007 essay by Harold P. Ford, a former CIA official, "Unpopular Pessimism: Why CIA Analysts Were So Doubtful About Vietnam"—equally prophetic.

Both were published in secret by the CIA; the Vietnamese Communists analysis was not declassified until 40 years later —in 2006. (With some redactions; another declassified version, released ten years later in 2016 had even more redactions. This volume consists of the first version. Why the C.I.A. made even more redactions and issued the second version in 2016 is unknown.)

Both the C.IA. analysis and the Ford essay were both ultimately accurate.

The timeline of the Vietnam war is now commonly known:

May 7, 1954. Viet Minh troops under General Vo Nguyen Giap overrun the French base at Dien Bien Phu. The stunning victory by Vietnamese forces bring an end to nearly a century of rule by the French in Indochina.

June 1, 1954. The Saigon Military Mission, a covert operation to conduct psychological warfare and paramilitary actives in South Vietnam, is launched under the command of U.S. Air Force Col. Edward Landsdale. This marks the beginning of the Vietnam War. Many of the mission's ongoing efforts are directed at supporting the regime of South Vietnamese President Ngo Dinh Diem.

July 21, 1954. The Geneva Accords effectively divide Vietnam in two at the 17th parallel. Although the accords explicitly state that the 17th parallel should not in any way be interpreted as constituting a political or territorial boundary, it is quickly accorded exactly that status.

November 2, 1963. Ngo Dinh Diem is assassinated by his own generals as part of a coup d'etat that is carried out with the tacit support of U.S. officials. Ngo's autocratic and violent excesses when dealing with South Vietnam's majority Buddhist population led the U.S. to withdraw its patronage of him. At this point approximately 16,000 U.S. military personnel are in Vietnam and 200 have been killed.

August 5, 1964. After commanders reported a North Vietnamese torpedo boat attack on the U.S. destroyers Maddox and Turner Joy in the Gulf of Tonkin, U.S. President Lyndon Johnson submits the Gulf of Tonkin Resolution to Congress. The resolution authorizes the president to "take all necessary measures to repel any armed attack against the forces of the United States." Although the captain of the Maddox urged caution, suggesting that the August 4 attack had been conjured by the imaginations of overeager or inexperienced sonar operators (an assessment that will ultimately prove correct.) Congress overwhelmingly passes the resolution. Approximately 23,000 U.S. troops are in Vietnam and roughly 400 have been killed.

March 1, 1966. "A Program for the Pacification and Long-Term Development of Vietnam," (PROVN), a study commissioned by the U.S. Army Chief of Staff, General Harold K. Johnson, is published. Its findings suggest the strategy of attrition being pursued by U.S. commander General William Westmoreland is counterproductive, and it recommends that more U.S. effort should redirected at ensuring the security and stability of South Vietnam's rural population. PROVN is largely dismissed by U.S. commanders. There are approximately 185,000 U.S. Service members in Vietnam and more than 2,700 have been killed.

August 26, 1966. The C.I.A. completes its analysis ""The Vietnamese Communists Will To Persist," but it is classified secret and only declassified in 2006. A second version, with even more redactions was declassified and released 10 years later, December 22, 2016.

January 30, 1968. During the Vietnamese New Year holiday of Tet, North Vietnamese and Viet Cong forces began an offensive that will eventually hurl some 85,000 troops against five major cities, dozens of military installations, and scores of towns and villages throughout South Vietnam. The attacks which eschew the guerrilla tactic traditionally employed by North Vietnamese forces, play directly to American and South Vietnamese strengths. The North Vietnamese suffer casualty rates approaching 60 percent and Westmoreland saw the Tet offensive as a sign desperation on the part of the North. This view is dramatically at odds with those of the American public. There are approximately 485,000 U.S troops in Vietnam and over 20,000 have been killed.

February 27, 1968. CBS news anchor Walter Cronkite, widely viewed as "the most trusted man in America," who had just returned from a fact-finding mission to Vietnam, tells his nightly viewers, "It seems now more than certain than ever that the bloody experience is to end in a stalemate. To say we are closer to victory today is to believe, in the face of the evidence, the optimists who have been wrong in the past." President Lyndon Johnson is said to have replied, "If I've lost Cronkite, I've lost middle America."

March 16, 1968. As many as 500 unarmed villagers are killed by U.S. Army troops in the hamlet of My Lai. Groups of women, children and elderly men are shot at close range by elements of Charlie Company of the 1st Battalion, 20th Infantry Regiment, 11th Infantry Brigade. Attempts to cover up the massacre began almost immediate before the shooting stops, and only one American, Charlie Company's 1st Platoon commander, Lieutenant William Calley, will be found guilty of any crime in connection with My Lai. In November, 1974, Calley will be released on parole after serving just three and one half years under house arrest.

March 31, 1968. In a televised address to the nation, President Lyndon Johnson announced he would not be a candidate for re-election, knowing that the Vietnam war had split the country and forever stained his presidency.

November 15, 1969. Millions of Americans across the United States take to the streets to protest the continued U.S. involvement in Vietnam. The antiwar demonstrations represent the largest public protests in U.S. history.

April 30, 1970. Richard Nixon announces the invasion to Cambodia, an escalation of the war.

May 4, 1970. Members of the Ohio National Guard open fire on unarmed college students at Kent State University, killing four and wounding one. The incident catalyzes the growing antiwar movement. Roughly 335,000 U.S. troops are in Vietnam, and approximately 50,000 have been killed.

January 27, 1973. Representatives of South Vietnamese communist forces, North Vietnam, South Vietnam and the United States conclude the Agreement on Ending the War and Restoring Peace in Vietnam, in Paris. US troops are to be withdrawn within 60 days and the 17th parallel will remain the dividing line until the country can be reunited by "peaceful means."

March 29, 1973. The last U.S. military unit leaves Vietnam; eventually some 58,318 U.S. troops had been killed. Vietnamese causalities include more than 800,000 South Vietnamese troops and more than 1,000,000 North Vietnamese soldiers and Viet Cong irregulars. Civilian deaths total as many as 2,000,000.

April 29, 1975. Shortly before 11:00 a.m. the American Radio Service network beings to broadcast a prerecorded message that the temperature in Saigon is "105 degrees and rising," follow by a 30-second excerpt from the song "White Christmas." This signaled the start of Operation Frequent Wind, the emergency evaluation of Saigon. American personnel begin converging on more than a dozen assembly points throughout the city. Over the next 24 hours, some 7,000 American and South Vietnamese are flown to safety. The following morning North Vietnamese troops enter downtown Saigon and the South Vietnamese government surrenders unconditionally.

2007. The essay "Unpopular Pessimism: Why CIA Analysts Were So Doubtful About Vietnam," by Harold P. Ford, is published in the the C.I.A.'s internal secret journal, "Studies in Intelligence."

If Richard Nixon, as President, had seen the 1966 Central Intelligence Agency evaluation, he would have read:

So long as the U.S. air offensive remains at present levels, it is unlikely to diminish North Vietnam's continued ability to provide material support to the war in the south. North Vietnam is taking punishment on its own territory, but at a price it can afford and one it probably considers acceptable in light of the political objectives it hopes to achieve.

. . . and ...

Consideration of world popular opposition to U.S. policy would certainly enter into any eventual Vietnamese Communist decision on whether to revise present strategy but would most certainly not be a decisive factor.

. . . and...

The Vietnamese Communists pay close attention to evidence of opposition to current U.S. policy arising within the United States itself. The outcome of their previous struggle with the French almost certainly predisposes them to draw invalid parallels to French domestic opposition in the Indochina war and to look for signs of American domestic political pressures capable of forcing policy changes on Washington.

In short, continued bombings by American air forces would be unlikely to force North Vietnam to end the conflict.

However, previously, in the administration of Lyndon Johnson, was Operation Rolling Thunder, 1965 to 1968. This was the code name for a sustained bombing campaign against North Vietnam by the U.S. Air Force and the Navy, which began March 2, 1965 and ended November 11,1968.

It began with selective targets and when that technique didn't work, the goals became destroying North Vietnam's will to fight by destroying its industrial base, transportation network and its air defenses. More than one million air sorties were flown and three-quarters of a million of bombs were dropped. Eventually, Richard Nixon, as president, decided that the U..S. must take the air fight to North Vietnam and Cambodia, as supply trails from Cambodia led into North Vietnam. He announced this during a national televised speech, April 30, 1970, just several days before the tragedy at Kent State and another at Jackson State.

"This is not an invasion of Cambodia," he said in a classic statement.

"I say tonight: all the offers and approaches made previously remain on the conference table. Whenever Hanoi is ready to negotiate seriously. But if the enemy response to our most conciliatory offers for peaceful negation continues to be to increase its attacks and humiliate and defeat us, we shall react accordingly.

"My fellow Americans, we live in an age of anarchy, both abroad and at home. We see mindless attacks on all the great institutions which have been created by free civilizations in the last 500 years. Even here in the United States, great universities are being systematically destroyed. Small nations all over the world find themselves imder attack from within and from without.

"If, when the chips are down, the world's most powerful nation, the United States of America, acts like a pitiful, helpless giant, the forces of totalitarianism and anarchy will threaten free nations and free institutions throughout the world."

That only led to more protests throughout the country.

Less than three years later —an eternity during those times — representatives of the south Vietnamese Communist forces, South Vietnam, North Vietnam, and the United States met January 27, 1973 and agreed to end the war. On March 29, 1973, the last U.S. military unit left Vietnam.

What did the Central Intelligence Agency learn — or decide — years earlier?

The following list, from Harold P. Ford's essay, "Unpopular Pessimism: Why CIA Analysts Were So Doubtful About Vietnam," is only a partial analysis of what the Agency knew in 1966, the how and why the Central Intelligence Agency believed the United States could not win the war in Vietnam. (Ford's entire essay is reprinted at the end of this volume.)

1) Do not underestimate the enemy's strength, ruthlessness, nationalist appeal, and pervasive undercover assets throughout South Vietnam.
2) Do not underestimate the enemy's resilience and staying power power. He is in for the long run and is confident that US morale will give way before his will. He will keep coming despite huge casualties. If we escalate, he will too.
3) Do not overestimate the degree to which airpower will disrupt North Vietnam's support of the VC or will cause Hanoi to back off from such support.
4) Do not overestimate the military and political potential of our South Vietnamese ally/creation.
5) The war is essentially a political war that cannot be won by military means alone. It will have to be won largely by the South Vietnamese in the villages of South Vietnam.
6) The war is essentially a civil war, run from Hanoi, not a Communist bloc plot to test the will of America to support its allies.
7) Winning the hearts and minds of the Vietnamese is a tough task. Most Vietnamese simply want to be left alone, and most do not identify with Saigon. And many are either too attracted to the VC or too afraid to volunteer much information about the VC in their midst.

This, then, is a partial analysis of how —and why —the Central Intelligence Agency concluded in 1966 that the war in Vietnam that became such ahorrific debacle —could not be won.

— Thomas Fensch

This document contains classified information affecting the national security of the United States within the meaning of the espionage laws, US Code Title 18, Sections 793, 794, and 798. The law prohibits its transmission or the revelation of its contents in any manner to an unauthorized person, as well as its use in any manner prejudicial to the safety or interest of the United States or for the benefit of any foreign government to the detriment of the United States.

It is to be seen only by US personnel especially indoctrinated and authorized to receive ☐ information; its security must be maintained in accordance with ☐ REGULATIONS.

No action is to be taken on any ☐ which may be contained herein, regardless of the advantages to be gained, unless such action is first approved by the Director of Central Intelligence.

An Analysis of the Vietnamese Communists' Strengths, Capabilities, and Will to Persist in Their Present Strategy in Vietnam.

26 AUGUST 1966

This memorandum has been produced by the Directorate of Intelligence of the Central Intelligence Agency. It was jointly prepared by the Office of Current Intelligence, the Office of Research and Reports, the Office of National Estimates, and the Special Assistant for Vietnamese Affairs in the Office of the Director of Central Intelligence.

CONTENTS

Page

SUMMARY DISCUSSION 1

I. Introduction 1
II. The Vietnamese Communists' Investment in the Struggle 1
III. Vietnamese Communist Capabilities for Persisting in Their Present Strategy 4
IV. The Vietnamese Communists' Probable Estimate of the Current State of the Struggle 6
V. Probable Communist Near-Term Military and Political Strategy 14
VI. Key Trends and Factors 17
VII. The Day of Decision 17
VIII. Alternate Communist Strategic Options 18

PRINCIPAL FINDINGS 19

ANNEX I

THE ECONOMIC, MILITARY AND LOGISTIC RESOURCES AND CAPABILITIES OF THE VIETNAMESE COMMUNISTS

I. North Vietnam I-1

    A. Manpower I-1
    B. Effects of the Rolling Thunder Program I-6
    C. The State of Civilian Morale I-12

II. The Significance of Laos and Cambodia I-16

    A. Laos I-17
    B. Cambodia I-22

Appendix A. Recuperability of the Transportation System in North Vietnam I-25

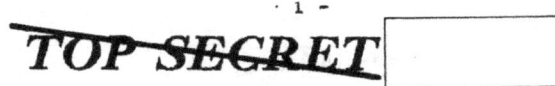

~~TOP SECRET~~

Page

Tables

I-1. Estimated Manpower Available for Military Service in North Vietnam, 1 January 1966 . . . . I-1

I-2. Civilian Labor Force of North Vietnam with Sex Breakdown, 1 January 1966 <u>following page</u> I-3

I-3. Selected Recuperation Times on Repair Work in Military Region IV <u>following page</u> I-33

I-4. North Vietnam: Transport Performance, 1964-1965, and First Half 1966. . . . . I-35

Illustrations

Figure I-1. Military and Economic Damage Resulting from Air Attacks Against North Vietnam, March 1965 - June 1966 and Projected July 1966 - June 1967 (chart) <u>following page</u> . I-6

Figure I-2. Supplies Trucked from North Vietnam into the Laotian Panhandle During the 1965 and 1966 Dry Seasons (chart) <u>following page</u> I-17

Figure I-3. Laos Panhandle Area: Communist Roadnet Development (map) <u>following page</u> I-19

Figure I-4. Laos Panhandle: Road Capacities and Development (map) <u>following page</u> I-19

Figure I-5. Schedule of Road Construction in Laos, August 1965 - April 1966 (chart) <u>following page</u> . . . I-21

Figure I-6. Northeast Cambodia: Road Improvements and Communist Activity, 1965-66 (map) <u>following page</u> I-22

	Page
Figure I-7. North Vietnam: Destruction of Bridges Versus Repair, 1 November 1965 - 1 June 1966 (chart) <u>following page</u>	I-29
Figure I-8. North Vietnam: Status of Highway Bridges, 1 November 1965 - 1 June 1966 (chart) <u>following page</u>	I-29

ANNEX II

THE EFFECTS OF SOVIET AND CHINESE INVOLVEMENT IN THE WAR ON THE VIETNAMESE COMMUNISTS

I.	Introduction	II-1
II.	The Significance of Economic and Military Aid	II-1
	A. General Level of Aid	II-1
	B. Economic Aid	II-2
	C. Military Aid	II-4
	D. Bloc Aid as a Critical Factor in Continuing the War	II-6
III.	The Rationale for Chinese Support	II-8
IV.	Vietnamese View of Soviet Support	II-9

Tables

II-1.	Communist Economic Aid Extended to North Vietnam, 1955-64 <u>following page</u>	II-3
II-2.	Estimated Soviet and Chinese Deliveries of Military Equipment to North Vietnam, 1953 - June 1966 <u>following page</u>	II-4

ANNEX III

THE COMMUNIST ORGANIZATION AND CAPABILITY FOR POLITICAL SUBVERSION IN SOUTH VIETNAM

		Page
I.	Communist Concepts of Political Subversion	III-1
II.	The Apparatus for Subversion	III-1
	A. Party Organization and Role	III-2
	B. Party Numerical Strength	III-5
	C. Numerical Strength of the Party Youth Group	III-8
	D. Numerical and Other Limitations on Party Effectiveness	III-9
	E. The National Liberation Front	III-10
	F. Numerical Strength of the Front	III-12
III.	Numerical Strength of the Communist Political Apparatus in Urban Areas	III-14
	A. General Position	III-14
	B. Numerical Strength in Saigon and Environs	III-15
IV.	Strength of the Political Apparatus in Rural Areas: A Sample	III-17
V.	The Communist Propaganda Apparatus and Its Influence	III-18
	A. Propaganda Apparatus	III-19
	B. Effectiveness of the Propaganda	III-20
VI.	The Overall Effectiveness of the Political Subversive Apparatus	III-22
	A. With the Rural Vietnamese	III-22
	B. In the Cities: Saigon in Particular	III-24

	Page

Illustrations

Figure III-1. Communist Command Structure in South Vietnam and Organization of the Viet Cong Logistics System (chart) <u>following page</u> .. III-3

Figure III-2. South Vietnam: Population and Area Control (chart) <u>following page</u> III-24

ANNEX IV

THE GROUND WAR IN SOUTH VIETNAM

I. The Build-Up of Forces	IV-1
II. Casualties	IV-2
Appendix A. The Ground War in South Vietnam	IV-5

Tables

IV-1. South Vietnam: Actual and Projected Growth of Total US/Third Nation Forces, December 1964 - June 1967 <u>following page</u> IV-5

IV-2. South Vietnam: Comparative Actual and Projected Regular Allied Troop Strength, December 1964 - June 1967 <u>following page</u> IV-5

IV-3. Total South Vietnamese Armed Strength, December 1964 - June 1967 <u>following page</u> IV-5

IV-4. Major South Vietnamese Ground Force Deployments by Corps Area, Mid-1966 .... IV-6

IV-5. South Vietnam: Estimated NVA/VC Forces, December 1964 - Mid-1967 .... IV-7

		Page
IV-6.	South Vietnam: Estimated Strength, Composition and Deployment of NVA/VC Main Force Elements by Corps Area, Mid-1966	IV-8
IV-7.	South Vietnam: Actual and Projected Deployment of US/Third Nation Forces, by Function, July 1965 - June 1967 <u>following page</u>	IV-10
IV-8.	South Vietnam: Actual and Projected Deployment of US/Third Nation Maneuver Battalions, by Service and Corps Area, February 1965 - June 1967 <u>following page</u>	IV-10
IV-9.	South Vietnam: Actual and Projected Deployment of ARVN Maneuver Battalions, by Corps Area, February 1965 - June 1967 <u>following page</u> . . .	IV-11
IV-10.	South Vietnam: Ratio of Allied Maneuver Battalion Strength to Estimated NVA/VC Main Force Troop Strength, July 1965 - June 1967 <u>following page</u> . .	IV-12
IV-11.	South Vietnam: Ratio of Allied Maneuver Battalion Strength to Estimated NVA/VC Main Force Troop Strength, by Corps Area, Mid-1966	IV-13
IV-12.	South Vietnam: Projected Critical Troop Ratios: Allied Maneuver Battalion Strength to Estimated NVA and VC Main Force Strengths	IV-14
IV-13.	South Vietnam: Absolute Indicators of Communist Performance in Battle	IV-18
IV-14.	Relative Indicators of Communist Motivations in Battle, Expressed in Terms of the Scale of Combat, 1964-66	IV-18
IV-15.	South Vietnam: Estimate of Communist Losses, 1965 - June 1967	IV-22
IV-16.	Selected Wounded to Killed Ratios	IV-23

Illustrations

		Page
Figure IV-1.	South Vietnam: Major Allied Deployments of Regular Troops, by Corps, Mid-1966 (chart) following page	IV-5
Figure IV-2.	South Vietnam: Actual and Projected Growth in US/GVN/Third Nation Forces and Communist Forces, December 1964 - June 1967 (chart) following page	IV-8
Figure IV-3.	South Vietnam: Approximate Composition of Actual and Projected Growth in Regular Allied Forces (US, TN, and RVNAF), December 1964 - June 1967 (chart) following page	IV-8
Figure IV-4.	South Vietnam: Approximate and Projected Growth in Communist Forces, December 1964 - June 1967 (chart) following page . .	IV-8
Figure IV-5.	Composition of US Maneuver Battalion and Artillery Battalion Strength to Total US Army and USMC Troop Strength, July 1965 - June 1967 (chart) following page . .	IV-10
Figure IV-6.	Approximate Composition of ARVN Maneuver Battalion Strength to Total ARVN Troop Strength, 1964 - June 1967 (chart) following page	IV-11
Figure IV-7.	South Vietnam: Troop Disposition, by Corps of Allied Maneuver Battalions and Estimated VC/NVA Main Forces (MF), June 1966 (chart) following page	IV-11
Figure IV-8.	Comparative, Actual, and Projected Allied and US/Third Nation Maneuver Battalion Strength to VC/NVA Main Force Strength, July 1965 - June 1966 and Projected for December 1966 and June 1967 (chart) following page	IV-14

~~TOP SECRET~~

	Page

Figure IV- 9. Approximate Communist KIA, by Inflicting Force, 1965 - May 1966 (chart), <u>following page</u> IV-16

Figure IV-10. Relationship of Communist and US/Third Nation KIA to Build-Up of US/Third Nation Maneuver Battalion Strength, July 1965 - May 1966 (chart) <u>following page</u> IV-16

Figure IV-11. Composition of Reported VC/NVA KIA, by Inflicting Force, July 1965 - May 1966 (chart) <u>following page</u> IV-16

Figure IV-12. Approximate Distribution of Reported VC/NVA KIA, by Corps Area, July 1965 - May 1966 (chart) <u>following page</u> IV-16

Figure IV-13. Relationship of Communist and GVN KIA, to Build-Up of GVN Maneuver Battalions, July 1965 - May 1966 (chart) <u>following page</u> IV-17

ANNEX V

THE RESOURCES AND LOGISTIC CAPABILITIES OF THE COMMUNISTS IN SOUTH VIETNAM

I. The Viet Cong Economy and Its Manpower V-1

    A. The Viet Cong Economy V-1
    B. The Economic Impact of Increased Military Pressure V-2
    C. The Manpower Situation V-4

II. Communist Logistic Operations in South Vietnam . . .   V-5

  Appendix A. The Communist Logistics System in South Vietnam V-8

~~TOP SECRET~~

Page

Illustrations

Figure V-1. South Vietnam: Communist Logistic Support, June 1966 (map) following page V-11

Figure V-2. South Vietnam: Daily VC/NVA Logistic Requirements, as of Mid-Year 1966, by Class and Source of Supply (chart) following page V-13

Figure V-3. South Vietnam: Disposition of VC/NVA Regular Forces, by Corps Area, Mid-1966 (map) following page V-18

Figure V-4. South Vietnam: Daily VC/NVA Logistic Requirements, as of Mid-Year 1966, by Corps Area (chart) following page V-18

Figure V-5. South Vietnam: Daily Logistic Requirements of VC/NVA Forces at Varying Levels of Combat, June 1966 and Projected June 1967 (chart) following page V-19

ANNEX VI

THE MORALE OF THE COMMUNIST FORCES

A.	The Viet Cong View of Morale	VI-2
B.	Morale of the Cadres	VI-4
C.	Morale of the Soldiers	VI-6
D.	Gauges of Military Morale	VI-13

~~TOP SECRET~~

Page

ANNEX VII

MORALE AMONG THE PEOPLE IN VIET CONG AREAS VII-1

ANNEX VIII

VIETNAMESE COMMUNIST VIEWS ON THE LIKELY LENGTH OF THE WAR

I.	The Anticipated Timing of Victory in 1955 and 1956 . .	VIII-1
II.	Victory Timing in the Period 1956-1959	VIII-2
III.	The Time Frame and Goals in 1959	VIII-3
IV.	The Initial Deferral of Victory Anticipations	VIII-4
V.	The Growth of Communist Optimism in 1964 and Early 1965	VIII-6
VI.	The Communist Reassessment in Mid-1965	VIII-8

ANNEX IX

THE COMMUNIST VIEW AND APPLICATION OF LESSONS LEARNED IN FIGHTING THE FRENCH

I.	The Three Phased War	IX-1
II.	Tactical Military Lessons	IX-4
III.	Political Lessons	IX-5

ANNEX X

THE EFFECT OF THE INTERNATIONAL POLITICAL CLIMATE ON VIETNAMESE COMMUNIST PLANS AND CAPABILITIES

I.	World Public Opinion	X-1
II.	Domestic Opposition in the United States	X-2
III.	Cambodian Attitudes	X-5
IV.	The Effect of Links with Western Leaders	X-6
V.	The Public Posture of the National Liberation Front (NFLSV)	X-7

~~TOP SECRET~~

Page

ANNEX XI

THE PROBABLE NEAR TERM MILITARY AND POLITICAL
STRATEGY OF THE VIETNAMESE COMMUNISTS

I.	General Concepts	XI-1
II.	Probable Areas of Communist Operations	XI-3
	A. The Highlands	XI-3
	B. Coastal Areas of II Corps	XI-4
	C. I Corps	XI-5
	D. III Corps	XI-6
	E. IV Corps	XI-7
III.	Prospects and Problems	XI-8
IV.	The Near Term Political Strategy of the Vietnamese Communists	XI-8

ANNEX XII

AN HISTORICAL ANALYSIS OF ASIAN COMMUNIST
EMPLOYMENT OF THE POLITICAL TACTIC
OF NEGOTIATIONS

Summary		XII-1
	A. The CCP-KMT Civil War (1937 to 1949)	XII-5
	B. The Korean War (1950 to 1953)	XII-13
	C. Vietnam (1953 to 1954)	XII-27
	D. Implications for Vietnam Today	XII-49

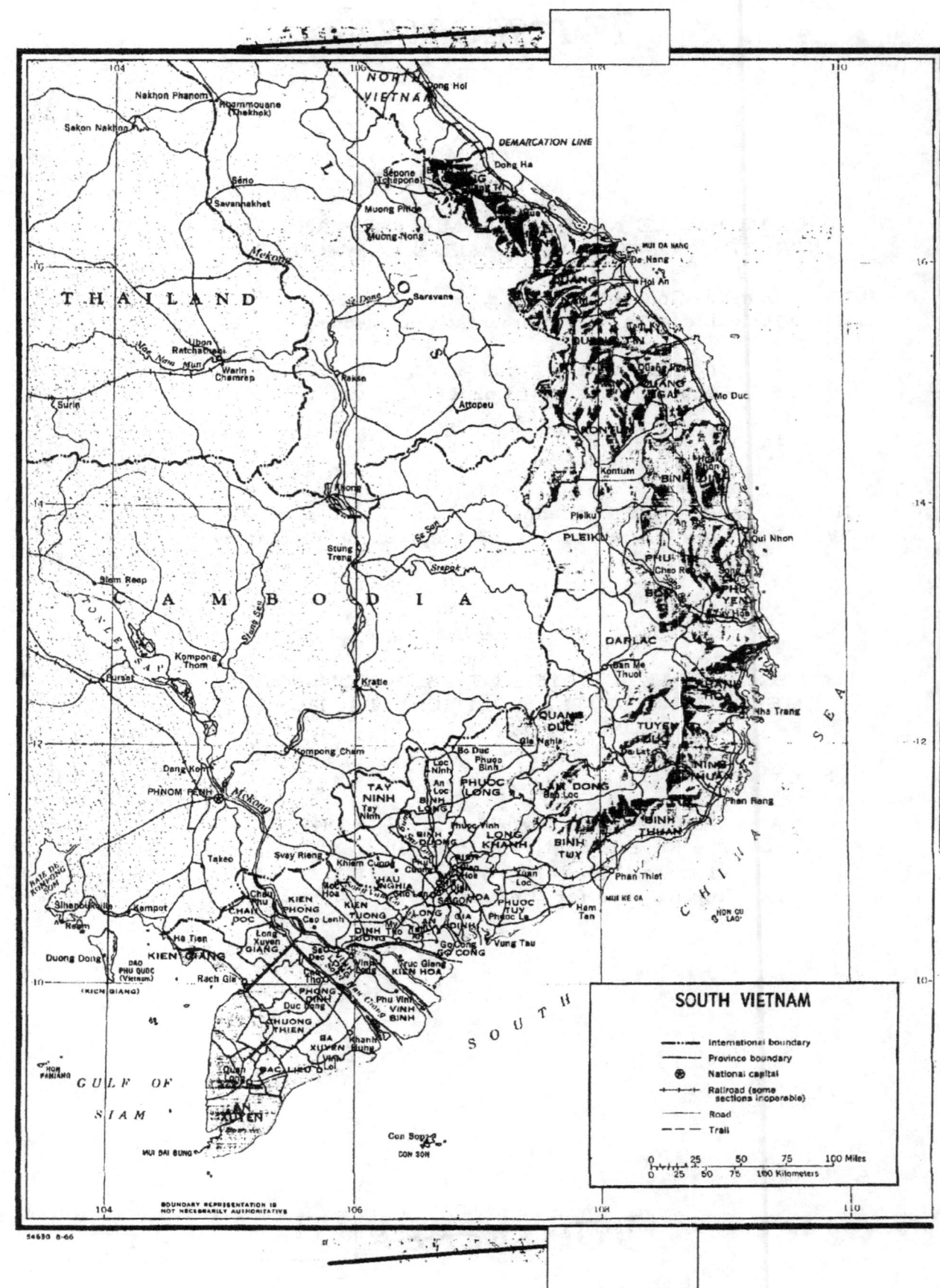

SUMMARY DISCUSSION

I. Introduction

1. For thirty-six years the Vietnamese Communist Party has struggled unrelentingly to acquire political control of Vietnam. During this period the Vietnamese Communists have often altered their strategy but never their objective, which remains today what it was when the Party was founded in 1930. Since 1959 their strategy has focused on a "War of National Liberation"--a blend of military and political action in South Vietnam designed to erode non-Communist political authority, to create an aura of Communist invincibility, and, eventually, destroy the South Vietnamese and U.S. will to resist.

2. The Lao Dong (i.e., Vietnamese Communist) Party now controls only the government of North Vietnam (the DRV), but it is national in scope, even though, for cover purposes, its members in the South operate under the name of the "People's Revolutionary Party." It instigated the present insurgency and has controlled it from its inception. In every significant respect the Communist movement throughout Vietnam is a single political entity whose strengths, capabilities and strategic intentions cannot be properly assessed unless it is analyzed as such.*

II. The Vietnamese Communists' Investment in the Struggle

3. During the early years of insurgency, the Vietnamese Communists fought at negligible cost to the DRV itself. The Viet Cong's political apparatus and its military forces were almost entirely composed of ethnic southerners. Even cadre and technicians infiltrated from North Vietnam were primarily Southerners who had gone north in the post-1954 regroupment. The insurgents

---

*Additional details on Vietnamese Communist organization are given in Annex III.

lived off the land and obtained a large proportion of their supplies, including weapons and ammunition, from pre-1954 caches or capture from GVN forces. While the war ravaged the South, North Vietnam's own territory and economy were untouched. All of this, of course, has changed since 1961, and particularly since 1964. Hanoi's continued expansion of the insurgent effort has altered the complexion of the struggle and the ground rules under which it is waged.

4. This has required a drastic increase in the Communist investment. On a population base of around 18 million, North Vietnam now is supporting a military establishment of at least 400,000 men. By mid-1966 Hanoi was maintaining a force of at least 38,000 North Vietnamese troops to fight in the South. We estimate that this figure will rise to 60,000 by the end of 1966 and to 75,000 by mid-1967. Furthermore, to sustain its commitment in the struggle, North Vietnam has undergone partial mobilization and has had to divert at least 350,000 laborers to military or war-related tasks. North Vietnam's economy has been dislocated, its transportation system disrupted and the personal lives of its citizens adversely affected. To facilitate the dispatch of troops to South Vietnam and the external supplies they now require, Hanoi has had to develop and maintain an elaborate road and trail network through Laos in the face of continued interdiction and harassment.*

5. In South Vietnam, the Communists have developed an insurgent structure which includes an armed force estimated to be around 232,000 in addition to the 38,000 North Vietnamese troops already mentioned. This figure includes Viet Cong Main and Local Force troops, political cadre and combat support elements, and Southern Communist irregulars. Recently acquired documentary evidence, now being studied in detail,

---

*See Annex I for further details on North Vietnamese resources and capabilities.

suggests that our holdings on the numerical strength of these irregulars (now carried at around 110,000) may require drastic upward revision.* To direct the execution of their insurgent campaign, the Communists have developed a party apparatus in the South estimated to number around 100,000 members, supported by a somewhat smaller youth auxiliary.** The Communists have also probably enrolled around 700,000 people in some component of their front organization, the "National Front for the Liberation of South Vietnam." This total apparatus must be controlled, funded and supplied, although most of its requirements may be met from resources within South Vietnam.

6. Casualties the Communists have incurred and are incurring in ever increasing numbers represent another major element of human cost. We estimate that total Communist losses in South Vietnam alone--killed in action, captured, seriously wounded and deserted--ranged from 80,000 to 90,000 during 1965, counting both North and South Vietnamese.*** We estimate that during 1966 these losses may range from 105,000 to 120,000. We further estimate that the Communists may incur an additional 65,000 to 75,000 losses during the first six months of 1967, if current rates of combat are maintained and presently projected troop strengths are achieved.

---

*Details on Communist military forces in South Vietnam are given in Annex IV.

**Around 25,000 party members and somewhere between 15,000 to 20,000 members of the youth auxiliary are thought to be serving in the Communist armed forces. They would be included in the military strength totals already cited. If our estimate of the number of Communist irregulars proves to require upward revision, our estimate of the size of the party apparatus in the South and of its youth auxiliary will also require compensating adjustments. Details on the Communist organization in South Vietnam are given in Annex III.

***See Annex IV.

III. Vietnamese Communist Capabilities for Persisting in Their Present Strategy

7. **The Northern Base:** North Vietnam's role in the present insurgency is that of a command and control center, a source of manpower and a channel of supplies. The command and control function is something relatively invulnerable to physical pressure or external assault. Present Communist strategy is imposing some strains on North Vietnam's manpower reserves, but the strains are more qualitative than quantitative, and they are not likely to become insurmountable. The major pressures on manpower have resulted from the Hanoi regime's inability to manage manpower effectively, a relative scarcity of technicians and skilled laborers, and an excessive drain on the agricultural labor force. Over the next 12 months North Vietnam should be able to meet the manpower requirements generated by its internal needs, as well as those generated by projected further deployments of troops to the South, but these needs will be met at increasing costs in the economic, educational and social fields.

8. North Vietnam's own industrial plant makes only the most marginal contribution to Vietnamese Communist military strength. With minor exceptions (e.g., a modest small arms ammunition manufacturing capability) the Vietnamese Communists' military hardware is entirely supplied from external sources. Thus Hanoi's ability to provide continued materiel assistance to Communist forces in South Vietnam is largely dependent on North Vietnam's continued receipt of materiel support from China, the Soviet Union and East European Communist countries.* So far, the US aerial pressure program has not appreciably impeded North Vietnam's receipt of materiel support from abroad and its dispatch to South Vietnam. Despite the disruptions inflicted, the North Vietnamese transport and logistic system is now functioning more effectively after almost 18 months of bombing than it did when the

---

*This aspect of Vietnamese Communist capability is discussed in detail in Annex II.

Rolling Thunder program started. Both internal transportation and infiltration traffic in 1966 were carried on at higher levels than in 1965. So long as the US air offensive remains at present levels, it is unlikely to diminish North Vietnam's continued ability to provide materiel support to the war in the South.

9. <u>The Logistic Supply Network</u>: Communist forces in South Vietnam are supplied with manpower and materiel primarily over the Communist-developed and -maintained network of about 650 miles of roads and trails through southern Laos, and to a lesser extent by sea or through Cambodia. Allied harassment and interdiction certainly complicate the Communist supply system. The volume of traffic now moving through Laos, however, is so much below route capacity that it is unlikely that conventional attack can ever reduce the capacity of the Laos trail network below the level required to sustain Communist efforts in South Vietnam. Communist forces use Cambodia with almost complete immunity from allied countermeasures and with minimal interference from the Cambodian government. US and South Vietnamese naval patrols have probably curtailed Communist sea infiltration, but given the extent and nature of South Vietnam's coastline and the amount of small boat traffic in South Vietnamese waters, even this channel can never be completely closed.

10. <u>The Southern Apparatus</u>: The buildup of both VC/NVN and allied forces in South Vietnam and the rising tempo of combat are placing appreciable strains on the Viet Cong's ability to support the war. The distribution of needed supplies, particularly foodstuffs, within South Vietnam has become extremely difficult. This problem has been aggravated by the concentration of VC forces in food-deficient areas.* Furthermore, the manpower squeeze on Viet Cong resources is becoming serious. The Viet Cong have borne the brunt of Communist personnel losses in South Vietnam and have also had to compensate for losses of North Vietnamese personnel. We believe that the Viet Cong capability to recruit and train manpower is adequate to cover losses estimated

---

*See Annex V.

for 1966 but will probably be inadequate to compensate for casualties and losses in 1967. During 1967 the North Vietnamese will have to assume most of the burden of expanding force levels, and an increasing role in replacing losses. These manpower requirements can almost certainly be met from North Vietnamese resources, but they will impose additional strains on North Vietnam's limited supply of skilled personnel and leadership cadre.

11. Apart from military manpower requirements, documentary evidence indicates that the Communist political apparatus in South Vietnam is already stretched thin and is not considered by the Communists themselves as fully adequate to their needs, particularly in urban areas. Cadre and leadership shortages will almost certainly increase in the months ahead. Although these shortages can be ameliorated by additional personnel dispatched from North Vietnam, the injection of an increasing number of northerners into the Southern apparatus will of itself produce some measure of discord within the Communist movement. Although the Viet Cong personnel needs are not likely to prevent the Vietnamese Communists from persisting in their present strategy, they almost certainly represent the weakest link in the Communists' capability chain.

12. <u>Net Capability Assessment</u>: The Communists' present strategy is costly in both human and economic terms and is taxing Communist resources in some areas, particularly within South Vietnam itself. Allied actions are complicating Communist efforts and raising the costs of their execution. However, neither internal resource shortages nor allied actions within present political parameters are likely to render the Vietnamese Communists physically incapable of persisting in their present strategy.

IV. <u>The Vietnamese Communists' Probable Estimate of The Current State of the Struggle</u>

13. The Communists' evaluation of the war and estimate of its future course will involve interlocked judgments on a variety of key factors, some of which are discussed below.

14. **The Communists' "Time Table"**: The Communists almost certainly do not have any fixed or rigid time table for victory. Their consideration of where they stand now, however, must in some measure be influenced by earlier estimates of where they had expected to be in mid-1966. Analysis of available documentary evidence suggests that in the 1959-1960 era, Hanoi's rulers thought it would take at least five years of all-out military and political action to gain control over South Vietnam. Until about 1962, the Communists appear to have been reasonably satisfied with the progress of their insurgent movement and to have felt that things were going more or less as planned. The counterinsurgency efforts of the Diem regime after 1962, however, and the expanded US advisory/support program confronted the Communists with unwelcome obstacles and led them to conclude that the conquest of South Vietnam would take longer than they had originally estimated.*

15. During 1964, as the Communists watched the continuing political disarray in Saigon, and devised tactics to cope with the increased U.S. assistance, Communist documents discussing the war grew progressively more optimistic. Communist optimism apparently reached its apex in the spring of 1965. They still carefully refrained from tying "victory" to a definite calendar date, but the Communists appear to have believed that they were then perhaps within a year or two of achieving a major part of their objectives. They had every reason to be optimistic in the spring of 1965; the GVN's strategic reserve was stretched to the breaking point, and the Communists were scoring tactical military successes with considerable cumulative political impact.

16. The massive infusion of US combat strength which began in mid-1965 probably saved the GVN from defeat and certainly disabused the Communists of any hopes of early victory. Their propaganda began to shift away from the theme of early victory to its present theme of inevitable victory. During 1966, Communist documents and public pronouncements have indicated that the Communists

---

*See Annex VIII.

expect a long war. The Communists must be disappointed in comparing the present situation with that which existed in the spring of 1965. At least indirectly, they have acknowledged that the infusion of US and Allied combat forces has created new problems which must be overcome before victory can be won. Yet Communist realism is presently tinged more with defiance than pessimism; the Communists may be disappointed, but they do not yet seem to be discouraged.

17. <u>The Lessons of the Franco - Viet Minh War</u>: Present Vietnamese Communist strategy is appreciably influenced by the 1946-1954 struggle in which the Communist-controlled Viet Minh forced the French to withdraw from Vietnam. In Communist eyes, probably the most significant feature of this earlier successful campaign was the fact it was won without inflicting a strategic defeat on the French Military Forces.* During their nine-year struggle, the Communists successfully used military pressure as a political abrasive. They worked more on French will than on French strategic capabilities, and eventually succeeded in making the struggle a politically unsaleable commodity in metropolitan France. Communist strategy, in short, succeeded in creating a climate in which the government in Paris lost its will to fight even though the French Expeditionary Corps remained effective and largely intact as a military force. The Communists suffered horrendous casualties and went through periods of severe setback, but their persistence eventually paid off.

18. <u>Soviet and Chinese Support</u>** There is substantial evidence that the political positions of the Soviet Union and Communist China vis-a-vis the Vietnam struggle, and the amount of military assistance they both provide, are major influences on Vietnamese Communist policy. A cessation of bloc war aid would probably make

---

*The battle of Dienbienphu was a major tactical--rather than strategic--reverse for the French. It certainly did not destroy the French Expeditionary Corps as an effective military entity.

**See Annex II.

it impossible for the Vietnamese Communists to sustain their struggle at its present level of intensity. Hanoi recognizes, however, that contemporary international Communist politics make such a cessation highly unlikely. Hanoi views bloc support as valuable in sustaining, and in some ways increasing, the military pressure which the Communists can bring to bear in South Vietnam and also sees it as a factor which at least partially inhibits and offsets the military pressure which allied forces can impose directly on North Vietnam. So long as bloc aid continues at least at its present levels, however, it will probably not be a critical factor in any basic determination the Vietnamese Communists might make on whether to continue the conflict. North Vietnamese assertions that, in the final analysis, they must rely mainly on their own resources to prosecute the revolution appear to reflect a genuine and deeply-held belief. Hanoi apparently believes that there are distinct limits to the amount of political and material support which it can count on from Peking and Moscow. Furthermore, the Vietnamese would not want to receive a degree of external (i.e., Chinese) aid that would jeopardize their control of the war, unless such aid were required to prevent the extinction of the Communist regime in North Vietnam.

19. Despite Peking's willingness to pressure Hanoi, the Chinese probably could not force the Vietnamese Communists to stay in the war if they decided of their own volition to end the fighting. The Vietnamese probably estimate that, in view of the limitations on the Chinese commitment, Peking would do little more than complain if the conflict were terminated short of an insurgent victory. The Chinese, in fact, seem to recognize this, for they have repeatedly left themselves an out by emphasizing that all decisions on the war are "strictly" up to the Vietnamese.

20. On the basis of Moscow's assistance so far, the Vietnamese probably judge that the Soviet commitment in the war is considerably more restrained than that of the Chinese. Hanoi is fully aware that Moscow, like Peking, is anxious to avoid steps which might lead to a direct military confrontation with the U.S. It is also doubtless clear to the Vietnamese that the Soviets

would welcome an early end to the war. On balance, however, it is probable that Soviet backing has the effect of buttressing the Vietnamese Communist will to persist in the conflict. The Vietnamese probably judge that they can continue to count indefinitely on Moscow's assistance along present lines so long as the war continues in its present context. They probably believe, in fact, that the Soviets now are locked into a struggle in view of Moscow's desire to retain leadership of the Communist camp.

21. **The Course of the Military Struggle in the South**: Any objective assessment the Communists make of the course of the military struggle in South Vietnam will acknowledge that although they may not be losing the war at the present time, they are certainly not winning it. They have gone for months without a major tactical success. They are suffering severe and increasing casualties. They no longer enjoy a virtual monopoly of the initiative. Their base areas are no longer virtually sacrosanct; instead they are increasingly subject not only to aerial harassment but also to penetration by allied troops. Their plans are constantly being disrupted by allied spoiling actions, to which Communists must react either by fleeing or by fighting an unplanned engagement. The absolute strength of the forces with which the Communists must contend is steadily increasing. The time-honored guerrilla principle of ensuring numerical superiority at the point of attack has been undercut by the mobility of allied forces who cover ground by helicopter instead of by road. The Communists are far from being defeated, but they are faced with problems greater than any they have had to contend with before in this struggle. Furthermore, for the time being at least, Communist forces have lost the aura of invincibility which in days past (and in the Franco - Viet Minh war) was one of the Communists' most potent political assets.

22. **The Price Being Paid in the North:*** The air strikes against North Vietnam have created problems for

---
*See Annex I

the Communists, but in both military and economic terms, the damage inflicted so far has probably not exceeded what the Communists regard as acceptable levels. In most cases the reconstruction or repair of damaged facilities can be postponed or effectively achieved by cheap and temporary expedients. In both financial and material terms, the cost inflicted on North Vietnam by allied aerial attack is more than covered by the military and economic aid and technical assistance provided by other Communist countries. Although economic growth has stagnated and will probably deteriorate further in the coming year, air attacks conducted under present rules of engagement almost certainly cannot stop North Vietnamese activities essential to the support of the Communist war effort. In short, North Vietnam is taking punishment in its own territory, but a price it can afford and one it probably considers acceptable in light of the political objectives it hopes to achieve.

23. <u>Communist Capabilities For Additional Force Commitment</u>: In absolute numerical terms the Communists cannot hope to match present and projected allied force commitments. However, it is extremely unlikely that they feel any need to do so. An analysis of relative force levels shows that the apparent present free world superiority of six to one over VC/NVA Forces is largely eliminated when one compares the relative ratios of actual maneuver battalions--i.e., tactical combat troops available for commitment to offensive ground operations.* The present ratio of allied to Communist maneuver battalions is nearly one to one. If present estimates of allied and Communist force projections are accurate, by mid-1967 the Communists will have a slight advantage in this critical ratio. The Communists almost certainly feel that if they can maintain a <u>maneuver battalion</u> ratio in this range, they will be able to prolong the struggle indefinitely and wear down U.S. will to persist.

24. <u>The Calculation of International Attitudes</u>:** There is considerable evidence that the Vietnamese

---

*<u>Maneuver</u> battalion ratios are analyzed in detail in Annex IV.

**See Annex X.

Communists believe popular opposition throughout the Western world to U.S. policy in Vietnam can be an important political factor in the ultimate outcome of the struggle. Even though Hanoi appears to be concerned with the Vietnamese Communists' relatively limited ability to spur Western agitation against the allied policy by dint of their own propaganda apparatus, they obviously welcome the widespread belief that the struggle in South Vietnam has its roots in what is essentially a southern civil war and not, as Washington claims, in North Vietnamese aggression. Consideration of world popular opposition to U.S. policy would certainly enter into any eventual Vietnamese Communist decision on whether to revise present strategy but would almost certainly not be a decisive factor.

25. *The Calculation of U.S. Domestic Attitudes*: The Vietnamese Communists pay close attention to evidence of opposition to current U.S. policy arising within the United States itself. Despite some occasional signs of realism about the actual political force of such opposition, by and large the Vietnamese Communists almost certainly overestimate its present strength. Detailed knowledge of the realities of U.S. domestic politics is a fairly scarce commodity in Hanoi. Furthermore, not only do the Communists want to believe that there is strong American domestic opposition to current U.S. policy, but the course and eventual outcome of their previous struggle with the French almost certainly predisposes them to draw invalid parallels to French domestic opposition in the Indochina war and to look for signs of American domestic political pressures capable of forcing policy changes on Washington.

26. The Communists also appear to believe that the U.S. cannot match the continued input of North Vietnamese forces into the struggle (particularly in light of the maneuver battalion comparison outlined above) without going on a virtual wartime footing. They believe this would involve at least partial mobilization and create economic pressures which would drastically increase American opposition to the war, particularly as casualties continue. The Communists may hope that all of these pressures would be sufficiently unpopular within the U.S. to make the war politically unsaleable.

27. <u>Morale in North Vietnam</u>:* The wearing effects of the war are causing some decline of civilian morale in North Vietnam, and there are indications the regime fears there may be a further deterioration. The decline, however, has not had any meaningful impact upon the determination of the regime to continue with the war or the policy options it may elect to achieve its objectives.

28. <u>Communist Morale in South Vietnam</u>:** Morale within Communist military forces and the political apparatus in South Vietnam has declined since mid-1965. It is conceivable that at some future point, the prospect of indefinite struggle if not defeat could break the morale of key elements of the Communist southern apparatus. Although Communist morale is obviously fraying badly in some parts of the insurgent structure, nowhere has it yet deteriorated to the point where the battle performance of Communist units is adversely affected. It has certainly not declined to a point presently sufficient to force any major revision in the basic Communist strategy.

29. <u>Attitudes Among the People in Viet Cong Areas</u>:*** There is a substantial body of evidence that morale and, consequently, support for the Communist cause, is dropping in Viet Cong - controlled areas of South Vietnam. The flow of refugees from such areas has increased drastically, and even if a desire for safety is the main motive for this exodus, the exodus itself attests to popular realization that no Viet Cong region is now immune from attack. Furthermore, there are indications that the refugee flow is caused not only by a quest for safety but also by a desire to escape increasingly onerous Communist levies of taxation, forced labor and

---

*See Annex I.

**The critical subject of morale in Communist Forces is the subject of Annex VI.

***This subject is examined in detail in Annex VII.

conscription. Even though distaste for the Viet Cong is not necessarily positive support for Saigon, this shift in popular attitude could eventually cause the Communists serious problems.

30. <u>The Course of South Vietnamese Political Development</u>: Communist prospects obviously brighten perceptibly during periods of political turmoil within South Vietnam. Conversely, the development of a popularly rooted, viable non-Communist South Vietnamese state is the thing which, over the longer term, the Communists have the greatest reason to fear. Hanoi cannot ignore the fact that although the present Saigon regime is fragile, is far from effective or genuinely popular, and is beset with internal stress, it has nonetheless successfully weathered storms which several of its predecessors were unable to survive. The Communists must also recognize that the events of last spring made painfully manifest how weak they were in urban areas and how limited were their capabilities for capitalizing on political strife among contending non-Communist factions. While the present Saigon government would probably stand no chance of unaided survival in a contest with the Viet Cong, even if all North Vietnamese troops were withdrawn from South Vietnam, there are trends in South Vietnamese political life which are probably a source of disquiet to the Communists. Furthermore, they must recognize that the type of political activity represented by the Rural Development program, even if it is only moderately successful, strikes at the roots of their insurgency's indigenous strength and alters one of the necessary conditions for a successful "war of national liberation" strategy.

V. Probable Communist Near-Term Military and Political Strategy*

31. If they are objective, the Communists must acknowledge that during the past year their insurgent campaign has lost momentum in both the military and political fields. There are signs that the Communists have indeed recognized that developments of the past year have created problems which they must solve,

---
*Discussed in further detail in Annex XI.

along with a situation quite different from that which they faced in fighting the French. Acknowledgment of the existence of these problems does seem to have provoked debates over strategy within the Communist hierarchy, but there is no present sign of any Communist intent to abandon or significantly alter the Communists' present strategy.

32. This strategy in the near term will probably revolve around two major efforts: (1) to keep intact, as far as possible, Main Force units in South Vietnam, and (2) to build up the Main Force strength, both in quantity and in quality, in order to be able to counter allied power when US forces in Vietnam have built up to the level of 400,000 expected by the Communists at the end of 1966. The North Vietnamese leaders probably believe that if they can go into 1967 with an ability to field a Main Force strength of about 125,000, as compared to a US strength of 400,000, they will be able to continue the war. Hanoi probably estimates that a four-to-one absolute military manpower advantage in favor of the US will not be enough for the US to defeat the insurgents; even under these conditions the Communists will be able to match allied forces in maneuver battalions.

33. Analysis of Communist materials indicates that the military strategy of the Communists during the coming months will be largely a continuation of their operational concepts of 1964 and 1965. They will concentrate mainly on opening simultaneous campaigns in the highlands and the area northwest of Saigon, combined with occasional other major actions in the northern coastal provinces. The latter may accelerate as the northeast monsoons begin. Their primary aim will be to stretch the allied forces as thin as possible and inflict as many casualties as possible on allied units. The primary target of the Communists during the coming months will probably be U.S. forces, rather than South Vietnamese. The Communists will continue their attempts to reduce American military mobility and striking power by harassment and by concentration of Communist forces around U.S. base areas to tie down as many Americans as possible in static defense tasks.

34. To keep U.S. and other allied forces from hitting and hurting large Communist units, the insurgents will probably stick primarily to ambushes, hit-and-run strikes, and guerrilla harassment in situations where they believe the odds of success are decidedly in their favor. Should favorable conditions arise, however, they will almost certainly attempt to conduct operations in regimental strength and greater. The Communists will be working in the meantime on efforts at better concealment of the locations of their main force units in order to counter the improved allied intelligence on the tactical disposition of Communist elements. When large-scale battles occur, the Communists may attempt to devolve them into a series of skirmishes in which Communist ambush and hit-and-run tactics can be used more effectively against small-sized elements of the allied attacking force.

35. On the political side, Communist strategy and goals for the remainder of 1966 and early 1967 will have to take account of recent insurgent setbacks. Captured documents indicate that the Communists will give priority to strengthening and improving their political apparatus, notably by trying to improve the quality of political cadres down to the village level, and by continued emphasis on the recruitment of party members and sympathizers in both rural and urban areas. They will probably continue to concentrate their subversive efforts on the South Vietnamese army and civil service. Laboring class elements may also attract increasing attention in the hope that economic discontent with the inflation spiral in South Vietnam can be exploited to the insurgents' advantage.

36. There is an increasing number of reports that the Communists will make serious efforts to disrupt the constitutional assembly election on 11 September. It is doubtful at this time that the Communists themselves have any significant number of followers among the candidates who have filed, though many of the candidates are relative unknowns even to local government officials. Communist propaganda statements have vigorously denounced the coming election as a farce and a trick. The Communists may feel impelled to take an active role through covert campaigning against candidates, or through terrorism and other direct sabotage efforts.

VI. Key Trends and Factors

37. In addition to their own logistic, manpower and morale problems, future Communist strategic decisions will probably be primarily influenced by developments in three areas: the course of South Vietnam's political evolution, the course of the military struggle in South Vietnam, and the attitude of the United States--or, more accurately, their estimate of American will and the US Government's political ability to persevere. The Communists, for example, will be paying particular attention to the outcome of the September elections in Vietnam and their resultant effect on South Vietnamese political stability and strength; Communist success or failure in matching allied maneuver battalion strength and achieving at least some tactical successes; and the outcome and import--or what the Communists believe to be the import--of next November's elections in the United States.

VII. The Day of Decision

38. The timing of any Vietnamese Communist decision on altering basic strategy--and the nature of such a decision--will be greatly affected by a variety of considerations including those outlined in the preceding paragraph. We estimate that none of the pressures upon the Communists which we can now identify is severe enough to force a major change in Communist strategy over the next eight to nine months. The Communists would be even less inclined to alter their strategy if they should find political and military developments during this period running in their favor--for example, serious political deterioration in South Vietnam, a series of major Viet Cong military successes, or what they construe as a significant rise of anti-war sentiment in the United States. If on the other hand pressures on them are maintained, and the course of events gives them no grounds for encouragement, they will probably feel compelled by late spring of 1967 to take stock and consider a change in their basic strategy.

VIII. Alternate Communist Strategic Options

39. Should the Vietnamese Communists decide at this point that continuation of their insurgency along current lines would not be profitable, they would have three basic policy options. They could: (1) convert the struggle into a major war by inviting massive Chinese Communist military intervention; (2) relax Communist pressure and withdraw some North Vietnamese troops, in the hope that the appearance of tranquility would eventually impel the US to disengage the better part of its forces without any formal commitments from the Communists in return; or (3) enter into some form of negotiations.

40. We believe Option (1) is the option the Vietnamese Communists would consider least in their long-term interests. Option (2), despite some advantages, would entail major problems for the Communists. It carries no guarantee that the U.S. would in fact disengage, and puts the Communists in a position of bidding by successive increments to bring this about. It would engender serious morale problems for the Communists during a protracted stand-down without simultaneous U.S. response. It would be hard to explain as anything but acknowledgement of a serious reverse for long-range Communist objectives.

41. In our view, the Vietnamese Communists would be most likely to try some variant of Option (3)-- negotiation. They would hope initially to achieve a reduction of allied offensive pressure, including a suspension of bombing in the North.* They would probably work to keep the talks going in order to prolong such a respite. During the course of the negotiations, they would probably determine whether they would seriously explore the possibilities of an acceptable political solution, or examine the alternative courses still open to them.

---

*Communist behavior in periods of negotiation is examined in Annex XII.

PRINCIPAL FINDINGS

1. So long as the U.S. air offensive remains at present levels, it is unlikely to diminish North Vietnam's continued ability to provide materiel support to the war in the South. North Vietnam is taking punishment on its own territory, but at a price it can afford and one it probably considers acceptable in light of the political objectives it hopes to achieve.

2. The Viet Cong have borne the brunt of Communist personnel losses in South Vietnam and have also had to compensate for losses of North Vietnamese personnel. We believe that the Viet Cong capability to recruit and train manpower is adequate to cover losses estimated for 1966 but will probably be inadequate to compensate for casualties and losses in 1967. During 1967 the North Vietnamese will have to assume most of the burden of expanding force levels, and an increasing role in replacing losses. These manpower requirements can almost certainly be met from North Vietnamese resources, but they will impose additional strains on North Vietnam's limited supply of skilled personnel and leadership cadre.

3. The Communists' present strategy is costly in both human and economic terms and is taxing Communist resources in some areas, particularly within South Vietnam itself. Allied actions are complicating Communist efforts and raising the costs of their execution. However, neither internal resource shortages nor allied actions within present political parameters are likely to render the Vietnamese Communists physically incapable of persisting in their present strategy.

4. In absolute numerical terms the Communists cannot hope to match present and projected Allied force commitments. However, if present estimates of Allied and Communist force projections are accurate, by mid-1967 the Communists will have a slight advantage in maneuver battalions--i.e., tactical combat troops available for commitment to offensive ground operations.

5. Nevertheless, if they are objective, the Communists must acknowledge that during the past year their

insurgent campaign has lost momentum in both the military and political fields. Although they may not be losing the war at the present time, they are certainly not winning it. The Communists are far from being defeated; but they are faced with problems greater than any they have had to contend with before in this struggle. Furthermore, Communist forces have at least temporarily lost the aura of invincibility which was one of their most potent political assets.

6. Morale within Communist military forces and the political apparatus in South Vietnam has declined since mid-1965 but not to a point presently sufficient to force any major revision in basic Communist strategy.

7. The Communists must be disappointed in comparing the present situation with that which existed in the spring of 1965. At least indirectly, they have acknowledged that the infusion of U.S. and Allied combat forces has created new problems which must be overcome before victory can be won. Yet Communist realism is presently tinged more with defiance than pessimism; the Communists may be disappointed, but they do not yet seem to be discouraged.

8. Consideration of world popular opposition to U.S. policy would certainly enter into any eventual Vietnamese Communist decision on whether to revise present strategy but would most certainly not be a decisive factor.

9. The Vietnamese Communists pay close attention to evidence of opposition to current U.S. policy arising within the United States itself. The outcome of their previous struggle with the French almost certainly predisposes them to draw invalid parallels to French domestic opposition in the Indochina war and to look for signs of American domestic political pressures capable of forcing policy changes on Washington.

10. The timing of any Vietnamese Communist decision on altering basic strategy--and the nature of such a decision--will be greatly affected by a variety of considerations, including those outlined in this paper. We estimate that none of the pressures upon the Communists

which we can now identify is severe enough to force a major change in Communist strategy over the next eight to nine months. The Communists would be even less inclined to alter their strategy if they should find political and military developments during this period running in their favor--for example, serious political deterioration in South Vietnam, a series of major Viet Cong military successes, or what they construe as a significant rise of anti-war sentiment in the United States. If on the other hand pressures on them are maintained and the course of events gives them no grounds for encouragement, by late spring of 1967 they will probably feel compelled to take stock and consider a change in their basic strategy.

~~TOP SECRET~~

ANNEX I

THE ECONOMIC, MILITARY AND LOGISTIC RESOURCES
AND CAPABILITIES OF THE VIETNAMESE COMMUNISTS

~~TOP SECRET~~

ANNEX I

THE ECONOMIC, MILITARY AND LOGISTIC RESOURCES AND CAPABILITIES OF THE VIETNAMESE COMMUNISTS

I. North Vietnam

   A. Manpower

      1. The Population Base

The manpower problem in North Vietnam, viewed solely in terms of numbers, is not yet acute, although in a qualitative sense it is becoming more severe. In spite of substantial manpower levies the country still has a wide range of unused opportunities to replace men with women, to withdraw males from sectors where labor is underemployed, and to transfer labor from nonessential or postponable tasks. North Vietnam has not yet had to resort to full mobilization.

The population of North Vietnam as of 1 January 1966 is estimated at between 17.9 and 19.2 million persons. (See Table I-1) North Vietnam's manpower resources for military service consist of 4.1-4.5 million males in the 15-49 age group of which 2.1-2.3 are physically fit for military duty. Over 110,000 physically fit males reach draft age each year.

Table I-1

Estimated Manpower Available for
Military Service in North Vietnam
1 January 1966

Thousand Persons

	Total		Males		Females	
	Low	High	Low	High	Low	High
Total population	17,895	19,210	8,730	9,374	9,165	9,836
Persons age 15-49	8,561	9,182	4,146	4,457	4,415	4,725
Those physically fit for military service	--	--	2,110	2,267	--	--
Persons of draft age (18)	--	--	175	188	--	--
Those physically fit for military service	--	--	107	115	--	--

2. <u>The Manpower Drain</u>

The major drains on manpower resources in North Vietnam have resulted from the build-up of the armed forces, the reallocation of labor to military support activities and the repair or reconstruction of bomb damaged facilities, particularly the lines of communication in North Vietnam and Laos.

We are not able to give precise estimates of the extent to which mobilization has taken place in North Vietnam. It is apparent that mobilization of manpower for military duty or military support activities has not reached a point of exhausting North Vietnam's manpower resources, although it has placed an increasing drain on administrative and management skills. Unless the US greatly stepped up its bombing, North Vietnam could make substantial increases in its armed forces and make additional manpower inputs into military support activities without placing an inordinately severe strain on its manpower resources.

Current estimates of the build-up of NVA forces in the past year indicate that a minimum of 125,000 persons were called for military duty. To this total should be added those numbers of NVA personnel infiltrating into South Vietnam, not as part of the build-up of NVA forces there, but as replacements and fillers for killed or seriously wounded NVA troops. 8,000 infiltrators can be placed in this category for 1965 and 10-30,000 for 1966 according to current estimates of the rates of infiltration and build-up of NVA forces in South Vietnam. On this basis we can estimate that certainly over 150,000 persons have already been called into military service. This total is about 70 percent of the number of physically fit males reaching draft age during 1965 and 1966. Even if the North Vietnamese armed forces should expand by 25 percent--to 500,000 persons--the drain on manpower resources for military service in numerical terms would not approach burdensome proportions.

In addition to the manpower drain for military service, the North Vietnamese have had to reallocate labor to repair or reconstruction activities and to tasks associated with dispersal programs and emergency activities. These programs require the full-time services of 200,000 workers and the part-time utilization of another 100,000. An additional diversion of the labor force results from the obligation of some 150,000 persons to fulfill civil defense obligations on a part-time basis.

Excluding the part-time diversions of labor, the measurable mobilization of manpower to date for military duty or war-associated tasks would seem to involve a minimum of 350,000 persons. This commitment could be at least 450,000 persons if the armed forces were to expand to 500,000 persons. The commitment would be even greater if air strikes against the logistics target system increased and could amount to an additional 40,000-50,000 persons. The additions to the labor force probably need not be greater because of the large amount of work already done in expanding the road system and building by-passes and other temporary crossings. The main thrust of future labor efforts will be in maintenance and repair of this expanded road system. However, the requirement for an additional 40,000-50,000 persons could create additional strains on North Vietnam's limited resources of skilled manpower.

3. Alternative Sources of Manpower

North Vietnam has several alternatives to be used in drawing upon its labor force of over 9.5 million people to replace the manpower mobilized for military and war-related activities. A primary source for the replacement of manpower diverted to mobilization programs is the large number of women in the labor force. Over 1.7 million women are reported by Hanoi to be ready to replace men in the labor force. We have little evidence, however, to support a judgment that the number of females in the labor force has increased significantly since mobilization measures began in April 1965. As late as October 1965 the regime still claimed that women accounted for 60 percent of the agricultural labor force, the same percentage claimed before mobilization. (See Table I-2)

In addition to the possibilities of women replacing men in the labor force, Hanoi has several alternative resources for manpower. The natural annual increment to the total labor force is in the order of 350,000 persons a year. We also estimate that from 300,000-350,000 males could be released from trade and services enterprises, institutions and educational establishments without disrupting essential economic activity. Finally there are

Table I-2

Civilian Labor Force of North Vietnam with Sex Breakdown a/
1 January 1966

Thousand Persons

	Total	Male	Female
Total	9,522	4,482	5,040
Production and Distribution	8,700	N.A.	N.A.
Agriculture	7,000	2,800	4,200
Industry	806	494	312
State-owned	(206)	(146)	(60)
Handicrafts	(600)	(348)	(252)
Construction	200	138	62
Transport and Communications	328	N.A.	N.A.
State-owned	(106)	N.A.	N.A.
Non-State	(222)	N.A.	N.A.
Trade	282	171	111
State-owned	(75)	(51)	(24)
Non-State	(207)	(120)	(87)
Other	84	N.A.	N.A.
Services	822	N.A.	N.A.
Administration	74	70	4
Banking	8	7	1
Consumer Services	402	233	169
Culture, education, science	187	130	57
Medicine and social services	83	49	34
Civil Defense	1	N.A.	N.A.
Other	67	N.A.	N.A.

a. Employment data refer to full-time labor force in various branches. Unless otherwise indicated, figures on total work force in various branches are taken from North Vietnamese official data for 1963. Increases in employment in these branches that may have occurred during 1964 are assumed to be counterbalanced in 1965 by diversion of workers from their normal occupations to the regular armed forces, and to employment in construction and transportation.

substantial numbers--35,000-65,000--of draft-age male students at the college and high school level that would be available if full mobilization were undertaken.

4. Pressures on Manpower

Mobilization in North Vietnam has not dried up the pool of excess labor. Although the manpower situation is tight the regime for the most part still avoids coercive programs in channeling workers into essential jobs. The withdrawal of manpower from production has not resulted in many of the austerity measures which would be associated with full mobilization. Rationing of food has been within moderate limits, agricultural taxes have not increased nor have food and cloth imports increased significantly. School enrollments in 1966, of the 14-21 age group, are reported by the regime to be double the level of last year. With the exception of some disruption to normal routine and some minor deprivations, there are few indications that the population has been asked to make extreme sacrifices in support of the war effort.

The major pressures on manpower result from the regime's inability to manage manpower effectively, a relative scarcity of skilled manpower, and an excessive drain on the agricultural labor force.

The management problems reflect the difficulties associated with a rapid transfer of masses of low-level workers to essential wartime tasks. The transfers effected to date were disorderly and poorly planned and resulted in uneven and unproductive allocations of the labor force. The drain of manpower from agriculture was, for example, an important factor in the disappointing fifth-month harvest. At the same time the regime found that the allocation of workers to construction work camps was apparently so excessive or irrational that some of these workers could be returned to the agricultural labor force or to other production tasks.

Skilled manpower resources in North Vietnam total about 300,000 workers or only 3 percent of the civilian labor force. This total is inadequate to meet all the requirements of mobilization and normal economic activity. The strain on these resources has been reduced somewhat by the presence of an estimated 25,000-45,000 men in Chinese Communist engineer units engaged in railroad and airfield construction work in the northern part of North Vietnam. Despite this Chinese technical assistance the supply of skilled manpower remains tight. Water conservancy which is vital to agriculture is one area where the shortage of skilled manpower seems to be particularly acute. In the spring of 1966 the regime noted that it had become difficult to man water conservancy brigades because of the loss of cadres to wartime tasks.

5. Prospects

If the commitment of manpower to regular military forces over the next twelve months does not exceed currently estimated levels, North Vietnam should be able to meet its manpower requirements but at an increasing cost to other economic, educational and social programs.

Although in terms of numbers the North Vietnamese have adquate manpower to replace losses and to build-up forces in South Vietnam, there are factors that may reduce their enthusiasm for sustaining this drain. The manpower being sent to South Vietnam is in qualitative terms probably the best the country can muster. Its loss over the long term is not one to be borne lightly by any power. Moreover, even though North Vietnam probably can meet its basic manpower commitment in South Vietnam, there is considerable drain on manpower within North Vietnam and the prospects are good that this drain will increase as the air war requires greater reconstruction efforts and as a lagging agriculture requires additional inputs of manpower. Finally an increasing scarcity of skilled manpower and qualified leaders--both military and economic--should make the drain of North Vietnam's manpower an increasingly difficult burden.

If the manpower drain does become acute, it will probably be in the area of agricultural manpower. In February 1966 the regime felt that the agricultural labor force could remain stable at about 7 million persons, that annual withdrawals would be almost exactly balanced by the normal annual addition to the work force. By April 1966 the regime had apparently concluded that this balance was too low and that a reallocation of labor back into agriculture was necessary. We do not know if this reallocation has been made. However, the disappointing fifth-month harvest makes it likely that the regime will be compelled to provide more agricultural manpower in order to achieve a successful 10th month harvest. If the regime is unsuccessful in this effort, strong pressures will develop in early 1967 for an even greater commitment of manpower to agriculture. This probably could not be accomplished without disrupting the operations of other sectors of the economy, particularly if the reallocation of manpower to agriculture involves large numbers of skilled workers.

B. Effects of the Rolling Thunder Program

1. Economic and Military Target System

Damage caused by air strikes against economic and military facilities and equipment in North Vietnam through June 1966 amounted to $86 million of which $52 million were sustained by the economy and $34 million by the military.* (See Figure I-1)

If the bombing of North Vietnam persists during the 12-months to mid-1967 along the same scale and character (exclusive of the strikes against petroleum storage) as during the first five months of 1966** an additional $38 million of damage to the economy may be expected. The cost of replacing the destroyed bulk petroleum facilities will total an additional $4 million. The total cumulative measurable damage to the economy of North Vietnam by mid-1967 will then total $94 million.

Damage inflicted to military facilities and equipment during the first five months of bombing during 1966 (February through June) amounted to only $7 million and was exceedingly low when compared with 1965. The bulk of this loss consisted of the destruction of aircraft and

---

*These dollar costs assigned to bomb damage are values indicating a general measure of the effectiveness of the bombing program. They are not intended to indicate immediate outlays which have to be undertaken by the Hanoi regime.

**There was a pause in the bombing of North Vietnam from 24 December 1965 through 30 January 1966.

Figure I-1

MILITARY AND ECONOMIC DAMAGE
RESULTING FROM AIR ATTACKS AGAINST NORTH VIETNAM
March 1965 - June 1966 and Projected July 1966 - June 1967

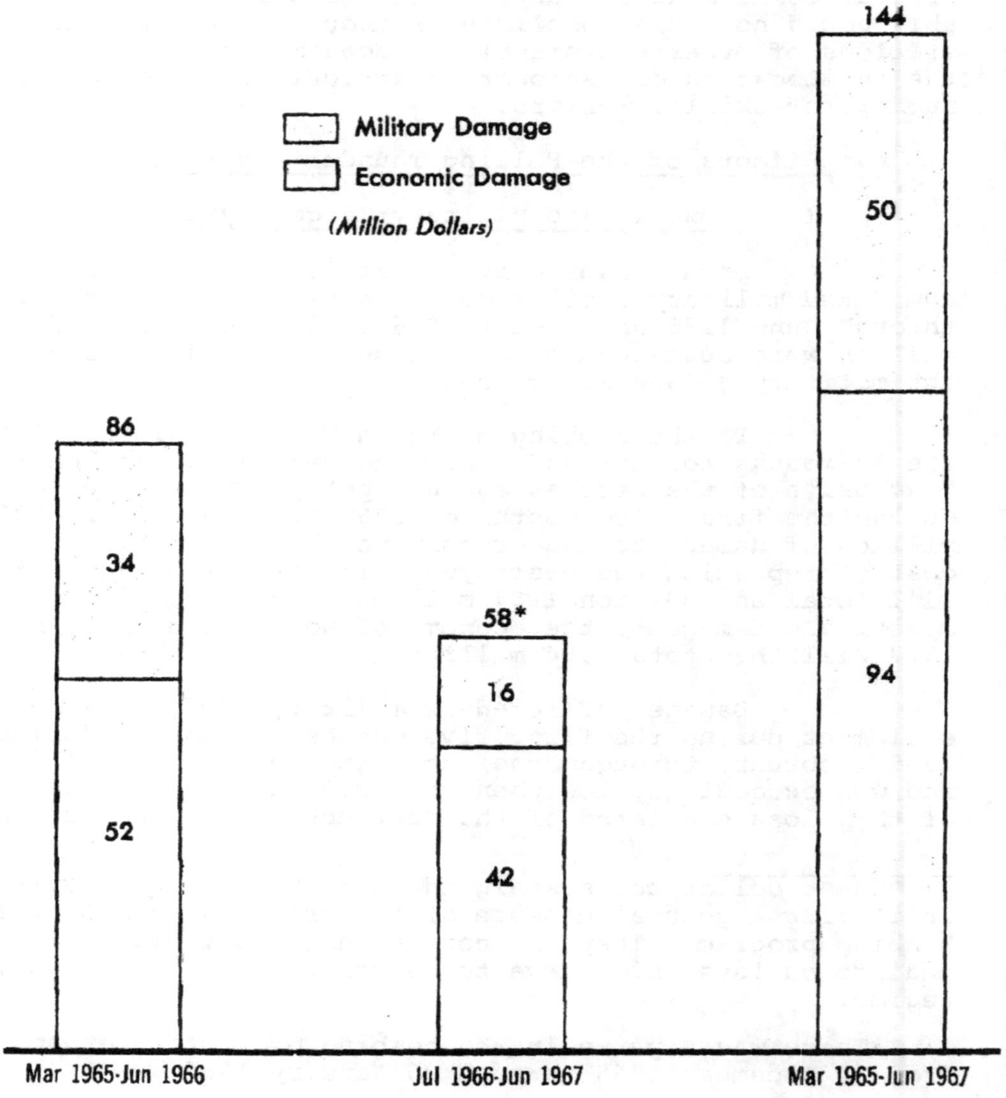

- Military Damage
- Economic Damage

(Million Dollars)

Mar 1965-Jun 1966	Jul 1966-Jun 1967	Mar 1965-Jun 1967
86 (34 / 52)	58* (16 / 42)	144 (50 / 94)

*Projection based on scale and character of air strikes during first five months of 1966

54642 8-66 CIA

naval craft. No important military barracks and supply depots were attacked because of their location in sanctuary areas. The average monthly damage to military facilities and equipment amounted to about $1.3 million. On the assumption that the air war will continue against military targets at about this scale during the forthcoming twelve months, the total loss sustained by military targets will amount to only $16 million. The total cumulative damage to military facilities and equipment as of mid-1967 will then be about $50 million.

Using the same assumptions, we estimate that the cumulative economic and military damage as a consequence of the Rolling Thunder program will total $144 million by mid-1967. In addition, there are and will be other losses and indirect costs to the economy and the military establishment to which values cannot be assigned.

Losses at this level will not present a significant drain on North Vietnam's resources. Much of the cost represents damages to facilities such as military barracks which are not in active use, or to facilities such as bridges which do not require permanent repair. The North Vietnamese have chosen so far not to repair the damaged petroleum storage facilities. The only known reconstruction of the damaged electric power stations has been Uong Bi station and this presumably has been done by or with the help of Russian technicians.

The damage sustained by air attacks against North Vietnam is in large measure a bill that can be passed to the USSR and Communist China. The increasing aid commitments of these countries far overshadow the small dollar value of the damage caused by air attack. These commitments imply an obligation on the part of the USSR and Communist China to underwrite the economic restoration of the country on favorable terms and explain in large measure Hanoi's attitude toward the loss of its modern economic facilities.

2. Effects of the Air Attacks at Present Levels

   a. Economic

The bulk petroleum storage facilities in North Vietnam represent the first important military/economic target system attacked in depth by the Rolling Thunder program apart from the sporadic strikes against transportation in the northern part of the country. The neutralization of the petroleum storage system will present Hanoi and its allies with an immediate problem in improvising an adequate flow of petroleum products. Hanoi has already gone to considerable lengths to reduce the vulnerability of its bulk petroleum storage centers by dispersal and other passive defense measures, including burying tanks, so that an emergency plan for an alternative system of supply undoubtedly exists. To the extent that off-loading and improvised storage cannot be fully realized at Haiphong, the logical alternative system would be based on China's Fort Bayard and port facilities and its connecting rail links.

The immediate impact in North Vietnam will be felt, therefore, in the need to convert to a new system of supply and distribution. This conversion will necessitate costly measures and create significant problems in adapting to a new situation. If a petroleum shortage develops its burden will fall on less essential or nonessential and civilian uses, which may comprise as much as one-third of normal consumption.

We estimate, nevertheless, that the supply of petroleum for the essential military and economic functions will continue, and that the flow of supplies to the insurgent forces in South Vietnam can be sustained if not increased.

Even before the attacks on the bulk petroleum storage facilities the bombings were causing increasing disruption of economic activity. After adjustments have been made to operate a makeshift supply and distribution system for petroleum the continuation of attacks on transportation will cause further disruption. Hanoi will have to reallocate capital and additional labor for repair and construction within the transport sector at the expense of industry and agriculture.

The cumulative debilitating effects of the bombing had already slowed down growth in industry and agriculture during 1965. There will probably be no growth in industry and agriculture during 1966 and the first 6 months of 1967, and some plans for economic development including new industrial construction projects will probably have to be abandoned. The stagnation of industrial growth

I-8

will have no overriding effect on the waging of a war which, for other than manpower, is essentially sustained by material inputs from outside North Vietnam. North Vietnam's modern industrial economy makes almost no direct or significant contribution to the war effort. The stagnation of agricultural growth may, however, create problems particularly if the 10th month harvest is poor. Even so the primarily agrarian nature of this subsistence economy means that there will be no sustained or critical hardship among the bulk of the population as a consequence of the effect of the air war at its present levels.

b. Military

Air attacks on military targets in North Vietnam to mid-1967 if maintained at the scale and of the same nature as that of the first part of 1966 will not impair the military capability of North Vietnam. The military targets being attacked in the present air war are not those that would have a highly disruptive effect on the military establishment or significantly impair its training, and defense capabilities or its capability to support the insurgency in South Vietnam.

3. Effects of an Expanded Air Offensive

The effectiveness of air attacks in creating burdensome pressures and strains on North Vietnam would be greatly enhanced by an expanded bombing program that included intensive 24-hour interdiction against the road and rail connections to Communist China and neutralization of the many significant military/economic targets such as the remaining petroleum storage facilities and the Haiphong cement plant.

Such a program could cause an overloading of the main transport connections to China and create severe internal distribution problems.* Although expanded air attacks would not stop activities essential to support of the war, they could cause a drastic decline in the level and efficiency with which the economic and military sectors function.

---
*See Appendix A for a more detailed discussion of the transportation problems resulting from this postulated attack.

4. The Logistics Target System

The Rolling Thunder attack against lines of communication, bridges and transportation equipment targets has resulted in losses to North Vietnam of over $30 million or over three-fourths of the estimated direct damage inflicted on all economic targets. Forty six bridges or 20 percent of the bridges on the rail lines subjected to air attacks have been damaged or destroyed, and 212 highway bridges have been destroyed or damaged. In spite of the continued and increasing armed reconnaissance attacks on the five major railroad lines, on only two--Hanoi to Vinh and Hanoi to Lao Cai--has through rail service been effectively interdicted for most of the time since the bombings began. The Hanoi - Dong Dang line has been interdicted for through service several times but for a total of only a few months. The Hanoi-Haiphong line has been interdicted for a total of only a few weeks. The Hanoi - Thai Nguyen line has been able to maintain through traffic almost constantly.

Losses of transporation equipment, particularly motor trucks, have increased sharply in recent months. According to pilot reports over 2,000 trucks have been damaged or destroyed. These pilot reports undoubtedly overstate actual results but even without adjustment, reports indicating this level of destruction would amount to only two-thirds of the trucks known to have been imported by North Vietnam in 1965.

The North Vietnamese responded to these attacks with a crash construction effort to implement a pre-strike planning program designed to keep lines of communication open to develop more sophisticated methods of concealment for roads, bridges and ferries, and to complete an impressive proliferation of bridge bypasses and alternate routes. By the end of 1965 an estimated 70-100,000 workers had been added to the labor force of construction work-camps engaged in rail and road repairs.

The success of these countermeasures is seen in statistics on the number of bridges destroyed or damaged and the repair measures adopted by North Vietnam to keep traffic moving. Of the total of 258 bridges damaged--46 rail or rail/highway bridges and 212 highway bridges--North Vietnam

I-10

has found it necessary to repair only 67 bridges--22 rail
or rail/highway and 45 highway bridges. The major emphasis
has been to construct temporary crossings or by-passes, over
173 of these having been constructed to replace damaged highway bridges. The savings resulting from these expedients
are impressive. North Vietnam has had to expend only $3
million on temporary repairs compared to a cost of over
$12 million if all the damaged or destroyed bridges were
permanently repaired or reconstructed.

Although the air strikes have patently made it
more difficult and costly to maintain traffic movement, the
countermeasures adopted have proved extremely effective.
Overall transport performance has been maintained at pre-
bombing levels. The known movement of supplies into Laos
and South Vietnam during the 1965-66 dry season was double
that of the previous year.

After an initial shaky response to Allied bombings, the North Vietnamese were able to consolidate their
position and are now able to maintain and improve their transportation system even though the bombings have increased.
The ease with which they converted to a wartime construction
base during 1965 indicates that further increases in air
attacks would undoubtedly be countered by an expansion of
existing capabilities to keep open all important routes to
South Vietnam.

The level of interdiction carried on through
June 1966 has been insufficient to create any major strains
in the North Vietnamese transport system. If interdiction
continues at current levels through mid-1967, the North Vietnamese should have no difficulty in maintaining current levels
of traffic, including imports and exports by land.

Meaningful pressures on North Vietnamese transport capabilities would require an air attack program that
denies the country its ability to maintain seaborne imports
and exports, increases import requirements, and concentrates
transport on the land connections to Communist China. Such
an air attack program would have to include measures to
close North Vietnam's major seaports, the neutralization
of remaining petroleum storage facilities and vital economic
targets such as the Haiphong cement plant, and a highly intensified program of armed reconnaissance against surface

transport and lines of communication linking North Vietnam and Communist China.

The two rail connections to China are currently used at only about one-third of their normal capacity. If measures against the major seaports could stop as much as 50 percent of normal import trade, these rail lines would be forced to operate at approximately full capacity under interdicted conditions. If more seaborne traffic had to be diverted to overland movement and additional import requirements were generated, by neutralization of the cement plant for example, the rail traffic requirement would increase even beyond the uninterdicted capacity of the rail lines.

Sustained interdiction of the lines would force the Communists to allocate considerable amounts of manpower and materials to maintain the railroad lines and alternate highway routes. Virtually all daylight traffic would stop and night traffic would be disrupted thus slowing down movement and making the logistic resupply of Communist forces considerably less reliable than at present.

Some economic requirements would have to go unsatisfied and many of the Bloc aid projects and domestic construction programs would have to be postponed. Modern industrial production would be slowed down and there would be increasing though not critical problems in food and distribution problems.

There would, of course, be adequate transport capacity to support the military establishment and to continue the present level of aggression in South Vietnam and Laos. But the support of these activities would be a much more costly and difficult burden. The population of North Vietnam would also be more keenly aware of the deprivations and costs associated with the war.

C. The State of Civilian Morale

1. General Review

The initial response of North Vietnam's civilian population to the US/GVN air attacks was characterized by a high degree of patriotic enthusiasm. The air attacks in large measure have been a strong force for unifying the population in its resistance to the "US aggressors." As the

TOP SECRET

air attacks have continued and intensified, there has been a waning of popular enthusiasm. This has not, however, reached the point that it has any meaningful impact upon the determination of the regime to continue with the war or the policy options it may elect to achieve its objectives.

Almost every segment of the civilian population of North Vietnam has been forced to make some sacrifice in its standard of living as the result of the bombing. However, civilians living in the southern part of the country-- about 15 percent of the population--have suffered far greater hardships in the form of personal and property losses, shortages of consumer goods, and sharp declines in income resulting from interruption of normal economic activity. Letters from residents of the southern part of the country to relatives in Thailand cite personal hardships and anxieties resulting from air strikes more frequently than in the past and more often than letters from residents of other parts of the country.

Data released by the Ministry of Labor in the spring of 1966 on the excessive rates of absenteeism among construction workers in the southern provinces may reflect the poor state of morale there. Absenteeism due to illness among construction workers largely engaged in repair work on the transportation system in the southern part of the country averaged 16.3 days per worker in 1965 or 5 percent of total working days scheduled. indicate that morale and discipline problems resulting from shortages of food continue to hamper operations at both civilian work camps and at military units in the southern provinces.

Elsewhere, the hardships caused by evacuation from urban centers, splitting of families, reductions in quality of consumer goods and services, increases in work hours largely without additional compensation, and losses of income resulting from transfers from normal jobs to lower paying defense-related tasks are less severe but apparently have depressed civilian morale to some extent. There is little explicit evidence available on the morale of civilians living outside of target areas. A March 1966 Hanoi press report stated that a decline in the health and morale of workers at the country's second largest machinery plant--the Tran Hung Dao Machinery and Tool Plant in Hanoi, which produces items for military as well as civilian use--

I-13

TOP SECRET

had occurred due to the increase in regular working time and in outside duties.

Nevertheless, recent public discussion of the need to tighten control over both party members and the general population implies that the regime fears there may be some deterioration of public morale. An article in the March 1966 issue of the party journal Hoc Tap, detailed weaknesses in the party's techniques for disciplining erring members, and in April 1966, Ho Chi Minh called for "harsh disciplinary measures" against a number of party members and cadres in party cells who failed to carry out party policies correctly. Less than two weeks later the chairman of the Supreme Peoples Organ of Control in the government called for a revision of the sections of the legal code dealing with counterrevolutionary activities, protection of state property, and the rights and duties of citizens "in order to satisfy the demands of wartime."

This recent emphasis upon breakdowns of discipline implies that patriotic appeals alone are no longer sufficient to maintain civilian enthusiasm for the war. The original strength of appeals to the patriots was evident from the response of over 3 million youths (ages 16-30) and 1.7 million women, or about 50 percent of the working age population, to give active support for the war effort by performing various essential economic and paramilitary tasks under the "three readies"* and "three responsibilities"** movements. Intercepted letters indicate that the participants in the movements were highly motivated to contribute to the war effort.

The continuation of bombing appears, however, to be gradually intensifying economic and political problems to the point that the patriotic fervor with which the population initially greeted the air strikes is being diminished.

---

*The "three readies" for youth are: (1) ready to fight; (2) ready to join the army; (3) ready to go wherever the country requires them.

**The "three responsibilities" for women are: (1) responsibility to produce and do other tasks to free the men to fight; (2) responsibility to take over family affairs and to encourage their husbands and sons to serve in combat; (3) responsibility to serve in battle if necessary.

Discussions of civilian mobilization in North Vietnamese publications during 1966 indicate that the regime is encountering difficulties in effectively employing those already mobilized. These difficulties are largely blamed on the lower level cadres in both the government and the party, who are said to discriminate against young people in general and women in particular in the assessment of responsibilities. The morale-depressing effects of prejudice and discrimination in the mobilization effort is compounded by the sheer inability of North Vietnam's cadre force to manage the task. Managerial inefficiencies have proliferated since air strikes began in February 1965, and have prevented an orderly reallocation of the labor force. Cadres have been criticized in the North Vietnamese press for mobilizing construction workers and starting projects without plan.

In an effort to stimulate patriotic fervor the regime's propaganda makes clear the direct connection between North Vietnamese support for the war in the South and the bombing of North Vietnam. Intercepted letters and reports indicate that civilians in North Vietnam do in fact see the bombing as a direct consequence of the support furnished by North Vietnam to the Viet Cong. They, moreover, take great pride in their country's achievements in downing American aircraft and often mention the well publicized achievements of Communist forces in South Vietnam.

Despite the regime's propaganda on the success of the "liberation forces" in the south, the population in North Vietnam is probably increasingly aware that the war is not going well and that heavy casualties are being suffered by North Vietnamese troops who have been sent south. North Vietnamese soldiers who have been captured or who have defected in South Vietnam reveal that some indication of the hardships, sickness, and injuries suffered by infiltrated troops is provided the people at home through letters and by eyewitness reports from wounded veterans who have returned home. If these casualties mount and the morale of the North Vietnamese troops in South Vietnam drops seriously, there is likely to be a comparable drop in the morale of the civilian population. Knowledge of military reverses in the field rather than the effect of bombing at home was a major factor in

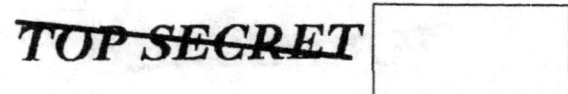

the decline of popular morale in Japan and Germany in World War II.

2. Prospects

Civilian morale is likely to continue to decline in North Vietnam over the next 12 months because of the probability of further declines in civilian living standards. Agricultural difficulties--resulting at least in part from the mobilization effort--have already affected the current harvest, intensifying the already tight food situation in North Vietnam. Pham Hung, a member of the party politburo and director of the Financial and Trade Bureau of the Premier's Office stated in May 1966 that prices of food on the free market have already started to rise because of setbacks in the spring harvest and that "some...comrades...doubt it will be possible to stabilize the situation in the forthcoming period." In addition to the pressure on food supplies, other strains on civilian living standards will probably increase. Despite the possibility of a further decline in civilian morale during the next year, such an eventuality is not likely in the foreseeable future to deprive the leadership of freedom to pursue the conflict in whatever manner it chooses.

II. The Significance of Laos and Cambodia

The ability of the Communists to launch and to sustain the insurgency movement in North Vietnam has been greatly facilitated by the essentially free access they have had to those areas in Laos and Cambodia which border South Vietnam. Laos has developed as the major route for the infiltration of men and supplies into South Vietnam. Cambodia, which has been used to a limited extent as a source of supplies and has served principally as a safe-haven for Communist forces, is becoming increasingly important as an integral part of the logistics system. The unique value to the Communists of both countries lies in their neutral status. The logistic resupply activities in Laos are hindered only by aerial interdiction and such ground activities as have been conducted to date. Both of these measures have had only a limited effectiveness. Cambodia, on the other hand, provides the Communists an almost complete immunity from US/GVN and allied military reaction. The opportunities to apply political or economic pressures to induce a Cambodia reaction against Communist use of its territory are also extremely limited.

A. Laos

1. Supply Requirements and Road Capacity

The Communists have been able to use three routes to supply their forces in South Vietnam--the sea route from North Vietnam (or China), the Laotian land route, and the Cambodian route.* Although the use of any particular route has varied over time, the overwelming share of supplies needed to meet the external logistic requirements of the Communist forces in South Vietnam are being moved by truck from North Vietnam through the Laotian Panhandle.

The increasing use of the Laotian supply route is shown graphically in Figure I-2 which compares the movement of supplies by truck into the southern panhandle during the 1965 and 1966 dry season. During the 1965 dry season trucks carried an average of some 34 short tons of supplies a day into the infiltration corridor of Laos for a total resupply of over 6,000 tons. During the 1966 dry season, however, the daily movement of supplies into Southern Laos was about 84 tons or almost 17,000 tons during the season of which 15,100 were delivered to the infiltration corridor. In both years the flow of supplies was also supplemented by a small--2 tons a day--movement around the DMZ. Figure I-2 also shows the dramatic increase in the through movement of supplies to the borders of South Vietnam. Although the Communists had to increase the flow of supplies for their forces in the Panhandle they were at the same time able to increase the flow of supplies by truck to South Vietnam from at least 900 tons in 1965 to 7,350 tons thus far in 1966.

a. The Logistic Requirement

The estimated VC/NVA military strength in South Vietnam in mid-1966 was between 260,000 and 280,000 which includes an estimated 118,000 regular troops. These troops require approximately 150 tons of supplies daily

---
*The reference here is to supplies moved into South Vietnam from any point in Cambodia, and is not intended to refer to supplies that move on the Laotian route and merely cross northeast Cambodia before entering South Vietnam.

I-17

Figure I-2

SUPPLIES TRUCKED FROM NORTH VIETNAM INTO THE LAOTIAN PANHANDLE DURING THE 1965 AND 1966 DRY SEASONS

1965
Average Daily Receipts in Panhandle ? tons

1966
Average Daily Receipts in Panhandle 84 tons**

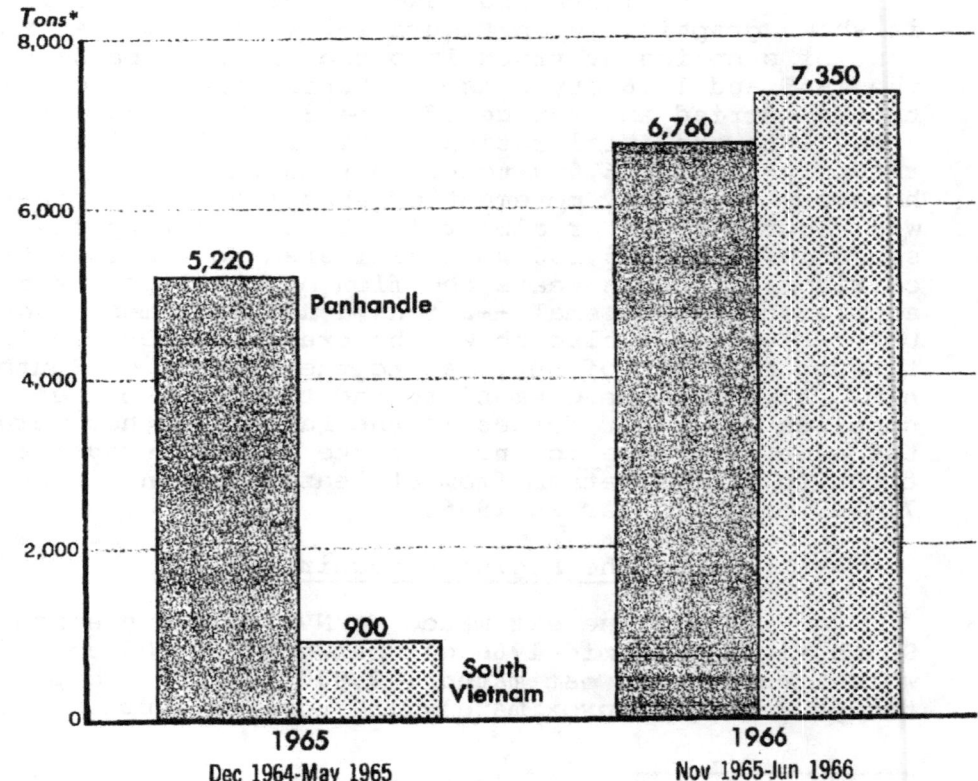

* Short tons
**Deliveries into the Laotian infiltration corridor shown here reflect 20% less in transit due to pilferage, spoilage, and aerial interdiction. In addition to these deliveries, both Laos and South Vietnam received some supplies from Cambodia.

54644 8-66 CIA

at present levels of combat. Only a small part of this daily requirement--some 20 tons of Class II (weapons), Class IV (quartermaster, engineer, and medical) and Class V (ammunition) supplies--must be obtained from out of country. We have noted in recent months, however, that because of internal distribution problems within South Vietnam the Communist forces stationed in the food-deficit central highlands are obtaining rice supplies from Cambodia. The present estimates of the probable build-up of Communist forces and rates of combat by mid-1967 would, of course, increase these requirements substantially. The total daily requirement by mid-1967 could be in the order of 210 tons a day. The external requirement would then be 35 tons a day at present levels of combat or some 55 tons a day if the level of combat should double. These external supply requirements are small and their fulfillment requires the use of only a small percentage of the capacity of the supply routes through Laos.

      b. Logistic Capacity

The capability to move supplies overland through North Vietnam and Laos to South Vietnam is restricted by the capacity of the roads in Laos. The current uninterdicted capacity of the infiltration network in the Laotian Panhandle for truck movement to points within a few miles of South Vietnam is about 400 tons a day in the dry season and 100 tons a day in the rainy season. Come rain or come shine this capacity ranges from 5-20 times the current external logistic requirement of the Communist forces in South Vietnam and from 2-7 times the probable external requirements under current estimates of the probable build-up of Communist forces by mid-1967.

The prospects are dim that conventional air interdiction can reduce the capacity of this network to a level that would represent an effective ceiling on the volume of supplies that can be moved through Laos. During the 30-day bombing pause from December 1965-January 1966 some 8,000 sorties dropped 16,000 tons of ordnance on the main supply routes in the Panhandle. In spite of this attack the level of truck traffic moving south during the same period--29 trucks per day--was twice the level of truck traffic in the same period one year earlier. Similarly, a photographic analysis of 26 route segments interdicted during 1965 in MR IV in North Vietnam showed that route capacity was reduced on only nine segments. On only two of these segments was capacity reduced more than 25 percent.

In view of these assessments and the fact that the level of traffic moving on these routes is a small volume of military traffic using, on the average, only slightly over 20 percent of road capacity, the Laotian supply network must be regarded as relatively invulnerable to conventional air interdiction.

2. Maintenance and Improvement of the Route Through Laos

The difficulty in interdicting the supply network through Laos is compounded by the intensive efforts which the North Vietnamese have expended in camouflaging roads, in effecting rapid repairs, in resorting to night travel, and other innovations to keep traffic moving, and at the same time to improve and expand the original network. As shown in the map (Figure I-3) the infiltration network through Laos now consists of some 650 miles of roads compared with about 150 miles at the end of the 1964 dry season.

a. Road Construction

At the end of 1964 the truckable road network in Laos extended only as far south as Muong Nong. By the end of 1965 the network had advanced another 100 miles farther south. During the 1966 dry season a more intensive effort was put forth. The southward route was extended another 60 miles to the tri-border area and more than 100 miles of new roads were built in Laos and Cambodia to connect the infiltration network with the Cambodian road system. In addition, 130 miles of new alternate roads, including the alternates to Mu Gia Pass, were built in the northern part of the country. The details of the 1965-66 construction are shown in Figure I-4. The net effect of the expansion in 1966 has been to provide an alternate route for every road that existed prior to the end of 1964. Furthermore the main north-south network has improved to the extent that some through truck traffic

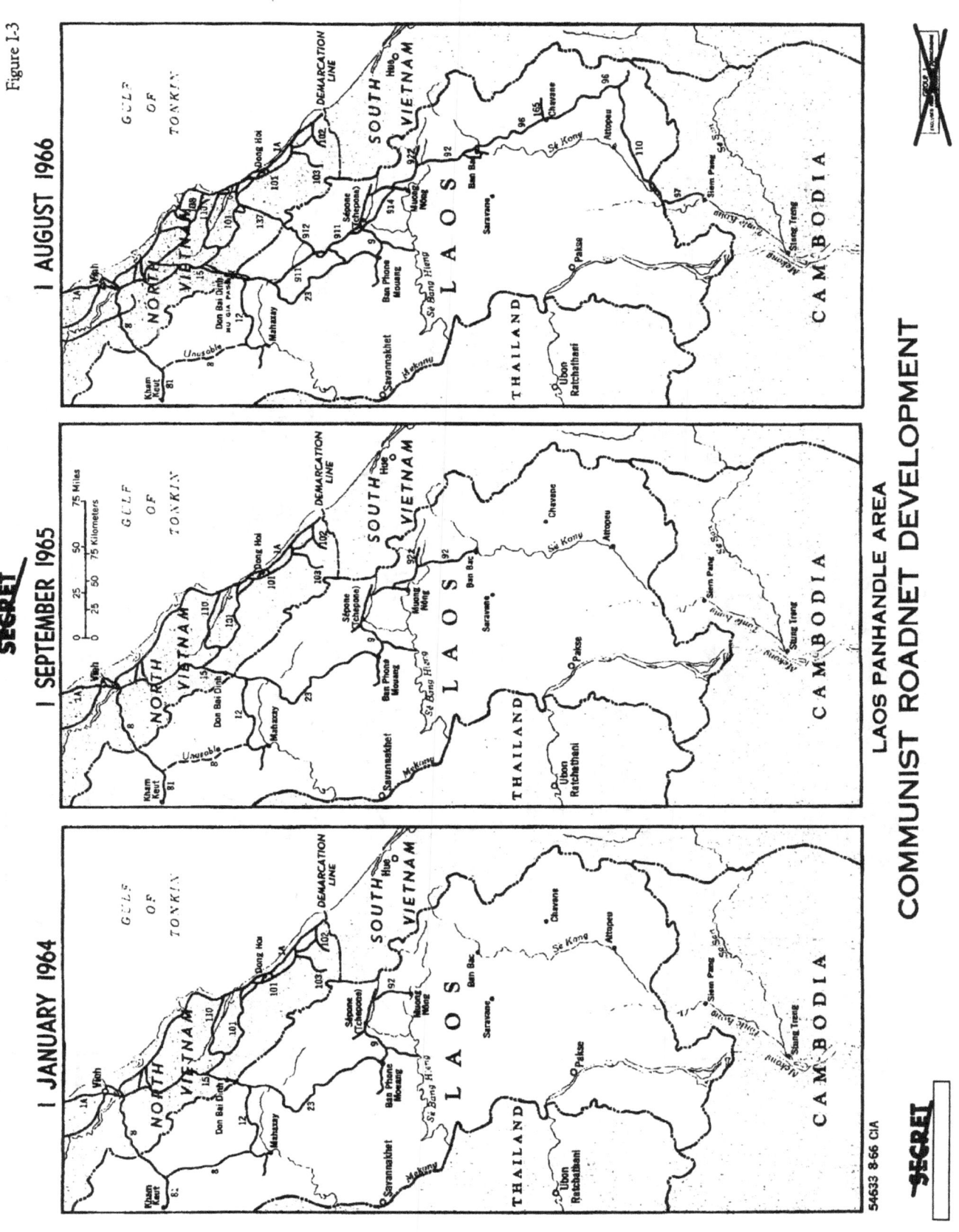

Figure I-3

LAOS PANHANDLE AREA
COMMUNIST ROADNET DEVELOPMENT

Figure I-4

LAOS PANHANDLE
ROAD CAPACITIES AND DEVELOPMENT

— Communist roadnet mid-1965
— Communist roadnet developed since mid-1965 (Laos only, except for 137 and 97)
— Other road

Communist controlled area

Road capacity in tons per day
Dry season 600/125 Rainy season

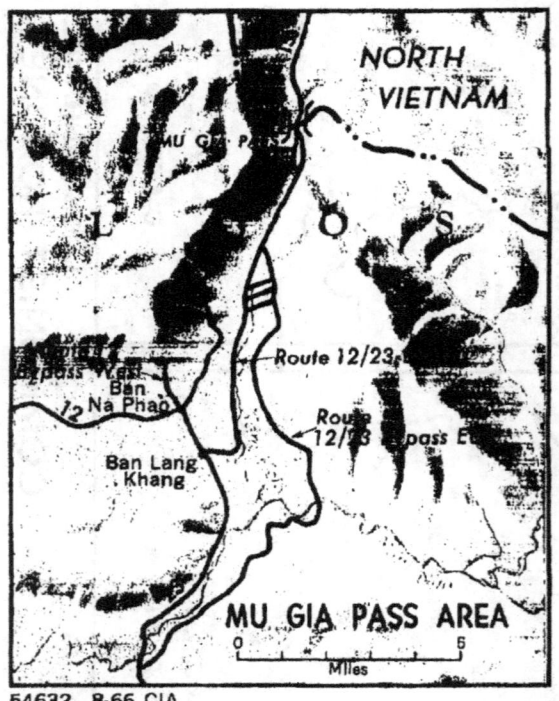

MU GIA PASS AREA

54632 8-66 CIA

apparently is moving for the first time during any rainy season.

 b. <u>Labor Utilization</u>

  In earlier years the supply movement through Laos was essentially jungle trails. In 1961, for example, some 2,000 men were required to operate the trail movement through Laos. The construction of an improved road system and the need to maintain it under conditions of air interdiction required substantial inputs of manpower.

  The labor force engaged in building and maintaining roads in the Laos Panhandle has an estimated total strength of 20-25,000 laborers, comprised of Communist engineering troops supported by locally conscripted labor. The Panhandle is sparsely populated so that a large part of this labor force has been brought in from other parts of Laos or from countries adjacent to the Laos border including North Vietnam. We are unable to determine the number of North Vietnamese in this labor force. Available reports indicate that North Vietnamese labor does work on routes 23, 911 and 92 if not others.

  The labor force on roads in Laos is organized into workcamps similar to those in North Vietnam. They are located along the entire road system and probably dispersed as follows:

Location	No. of Camps	Estimated Strength
Mu Gia Pass/Rte 23 (Including a rock quarry)	1	4,500
Route 911/912 (including a rock quarry)	3	9,000
Route 914/92	1	3,000
Route 96	1	3,000
Route 110	1	3,000
	Total	22,500

These workcamp organizations are responsible for designated segments of roads. The total strength of a workcamp will vary with the volume of work under way and the availability of local labor. Figure I-5 illustrates the rate at which these laborers have been able to complete road construction projects. The rapid expansion of the road net in 1965-1966 and increases in traffic have made a larger maintenance force necessary. Given the remarkable increase in the mileage of new motorable roads constructed in the past year, it is believed that the present labor force can maintain the road net and can expand the network even if the level of air strikes increases during 1966-67.

Some construction equipment is being used for road building in Laos and has contributed to the rapid completion of new roads. Aerial photography has shown unidentified pieces of construction equipment, probably bulldozers and roadgraders, at key routes under construction. It is believed that the inventory of construction equipment in the Laos Panhandle could be increased during 1966-67 if the level of interdiction by air strikes were increased.

c. Repair Activities

Workcamps in Laos have been as efficient in the repair of bomb-damaged roads and bridges as their counterparts in North Vietnam. They have been able to build a new timber bridge at Ban Nape on route 8 within the 3-day interval of comparative aerial photography. Photography also reveals the clearing of landslides caused by bombings on route 92 within 3 days and repairs to interdicted portions of route 110 within 3-4 hours. Moreover, the repairs have been carried out while the road system was in a stage of considerable expansion.

3. Vulnerability of the Laotian Route

The Communists in the Panhandle are better able to counteract the bombings now than they were a year ago. They apparently have the ability and resources to increase and improve countermeasures to air attack. Experience in Laos and in North Vietnam shows that conventional air interdiction is unlikely to create any significant or sustained reduction in the road capacity of the infiltration network in Laos, as long as the Communist forces require such a small volume of logistic support from North Vietnam.

SECRET

SCHEDULE OF ROAD CONSTRUCTION IN LAOS
August 1965 - April 1966

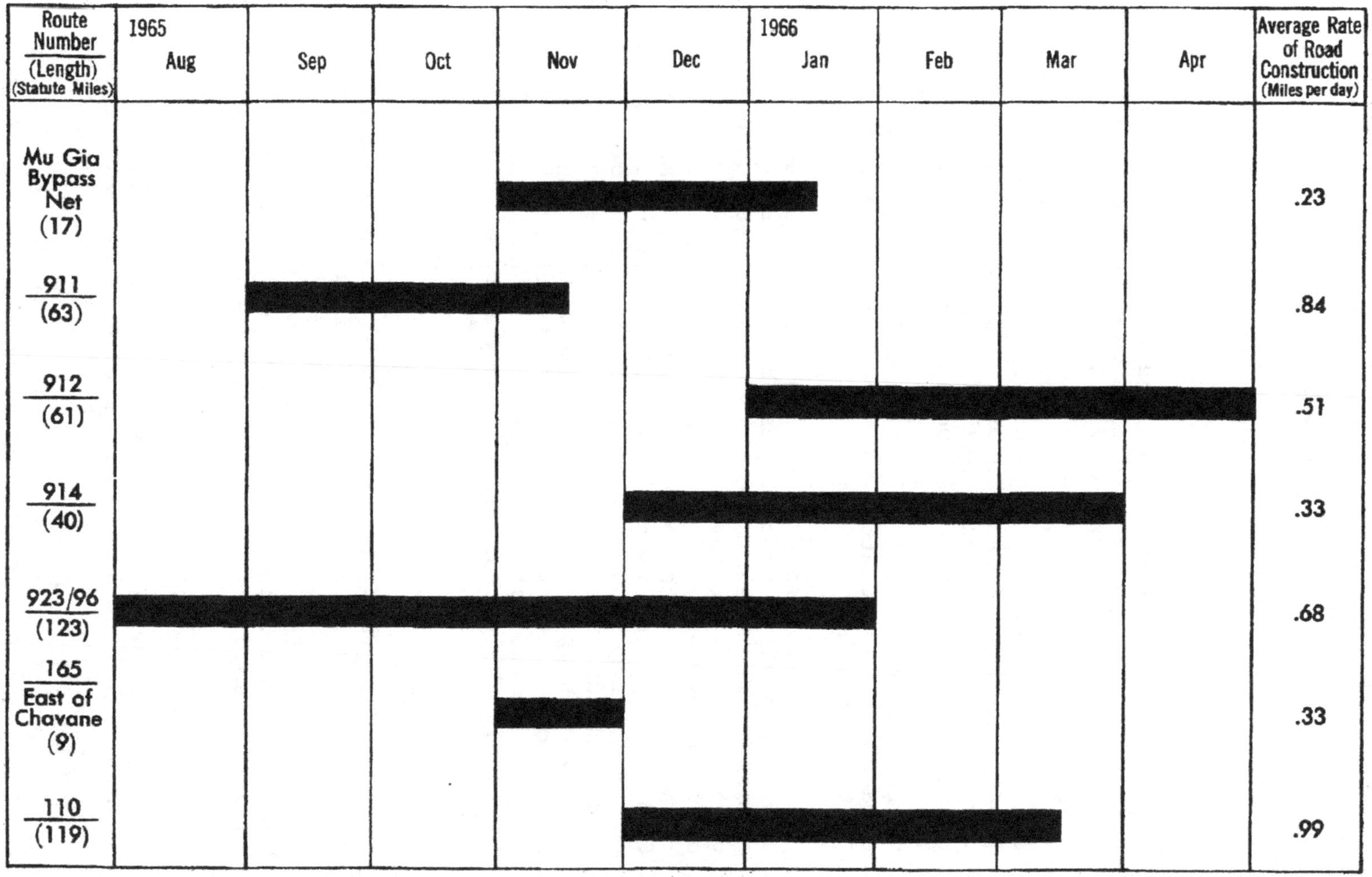

Figure I-5

Route Number (Length) (Statute Miles)	1965 Aug	Sep	Oct	Nov	Dec	1966 Jan	Feb	Mar	Apr	Average Rate of Road Construction (Miles per day)
Mu Gia Bypass Net (17)				■	■	■				.23
911 (63)		■	■	■						.84
912 (61)						■	■	■	■	.51
914 (40)					■	■	■	■		.33
923/96 (123)	■	■	■	■	■	■	■			.68
165 East of Chavane (9)				■						.33
110 (119)				■	■	■	■	■		.99

54645 8-66 CIA

SECRET

The enormity of the task assigned to air interdiction is apparent in this example. We assume that the nature of the VC/NVA external logistic requirements remains essentially unchanged and that air interdiction has produced a sustained 25 percent reduction in the capacity of the supply network. Even under these assumptions conventional air interdiction could not effectively reduce resupply capabilities through Laos until the VC/NVA force structure reached a level of at least six times the build-up estimated by mid-1967 at current levels of combat, or until the mid-1967 force engaged in combat at a rate some ten times greater than that being waged in South Vietnam.

The most promising means of effectively reducing Communist resupply capabilities are by denying them access to supplies in South Vietnam, forcing them to engage in a greater level of combat and at the same time denying them access to the Cambodian and sea infiltration routes. During the past dry season we estimate that the Communist forces in the food-deficit central highlands may have been receiving as much as 15 tons of rice daily from Cambodia. If this source were denied and the rice had to be supplied from North Vietnam through Laos the logistic problem would become more difficult. It would not be critical at this time, but as the VC/NVA build-up continues the excess of route capacity over supply requirements would be reduced significantly.

B. Cambodia

For years the Viet Cong have used Cambodia as a sanctuary and as a minor source of supplies. With the expansion of Communist activities and the introduction of NVA units into the conflict, even greater use is being made of Cambodia as a sanctuary area and as a source of supplies.

1. Sanctuary

The Viet Cong and, more recently, North Vietnamese forces use Cambodian territory in many areas along the 600-mile border for sanctuary and bivouac purposes. Important Viet Cong and North Vietnamese Army military facilities, such as rest camps, training areas, hospitals, workshops, and storage depots, now operate in Cambodia. Photography shows at least two Communist base areas in northeast Cambodia. (See the map, Figure I-6)

Figure 1-6

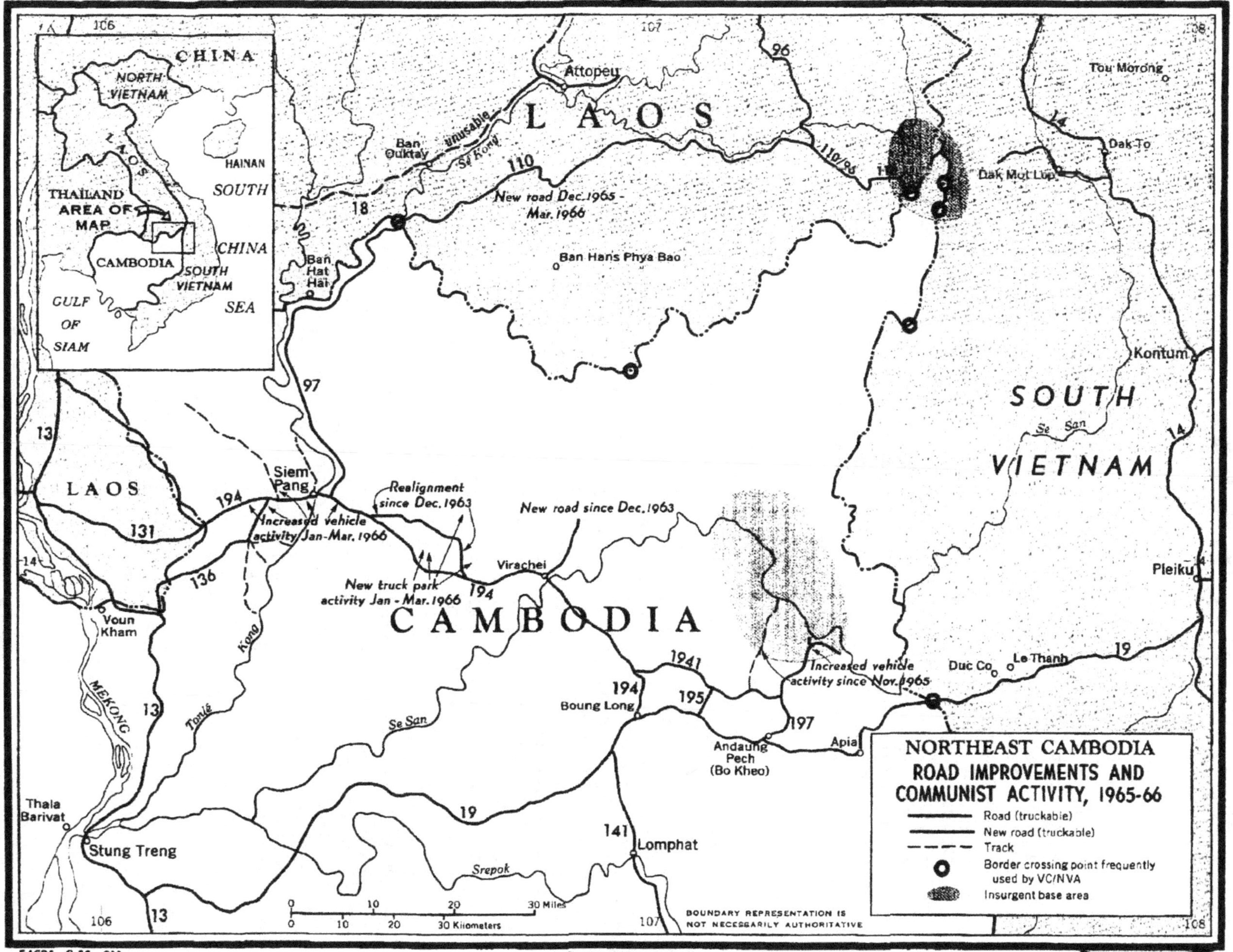

NORTHEAST CAMBODIA
ROAD IMPROVEMENTS AND
COMMUNIST ACTIVITY, 1965-66

A recently captured Viet Cong document reveals in the clearest terms to date how the Communists have been using Cambodian territory for sanctuary with the complicity of at least local Cambodian officials. The document is a report of an early April 1966 Viet Cong meeting dealing with problems associated with the use of Cambodian territory. It makes clear the importance which the Viet Cong attaches to its Cambodian sanctuary and suggests that Cambodia will loom even larger in Communist planning as the war intensifies in South Vietnam. The document indicates that the principal use of Cambodian territory, at least in the Tay Ninh - Svay Rieng area, is to harbor rest and recovery camps for Viet Cong wounded.

2. Cambodia as a Source of Supplies

Most of the supplies procured by the Communists in Cambodia have been purchased in the open market in small amounts and moved clandestinely across the border by primitive transport. In the past year, however, the volume of supplies moved to the Communists has definitely increased. Recent reporting, including captured documents, indicate that the VC are acquiring in Cambodia substantial quantities of cloth, pharmaceuticals, surgical supplies, salt, fish, gasoline, communications equipment, and office supplies. Sihanouk has also made so called "humanitarian" gifts of medicine and food to the Viet Cong. We estimate that at least 5,000 tons of rice and probably as much as 10,000 tons have been sold to the Communists. A frequently reported figure of 20,000 tons appears to be possible. During late 1965 and early 1966 Cambodian traders reportedly moved substantial amounts of rice northward on the Mekong River to Cambodian towns of Kratie and Stung Treng. The rice was then moved onward by small water craft or by truck to the South Vietnamese and Laotian borders. For the first time we have reliable reports that truck convoys carrying rice also crossed the border four or five miles into Vietnamese territory after nightfall. The Viet Cong control the border on four routes that enter Tay Ninh and Binh Long Provinces. The purchase of rice in Cambodia probably is a logistic expedient to supply VC/NVA units operating in rice deficit areas, instead of attempting to move the rice from surplus areas within South Vietnam.

The use of Cambodia as a transfer area or as a source of arms and ammunition is difficult to assess.

Almost certainly, the Communists have established arms caches on Cambodian territory for support of the VC and NVA forces. Cambodian troops may occasionally have provided arms to the VC, but such incidents have not been widespread and apparently have not involved collusion or foreknowledge on the part of the Cambodian government.

Arms shipments probably have also moved south from Laos through northeastern Cambodia into South Vietnam. Developments in the fair-weather road network during the past dry season strongly suggest that the route was intended to support such traffic during the dry season (See the map). This traffic could have moved with permission of the local Cambodian authorities but without the knowledge of the officials in Phnom Penh.

Even without the cooperation of the Cambodian government the Communists could make greater use of Cambodian territory. They could expand the current type of small-scale infiltration by sending more people to purchase supplies in the open market and by making more use of legitimate import houses and the Communist apparatus in Phnom Penh. Instead of moving these supplies across the border by clandestine means, they can hire trucks to move supplies to the border in the same manner that some shipments of food have already been made.

Cambodia, accordingly, must be regarded as a definite asset to the Communist forces both as a sanctuary and as a major route for obtaining food and other supplies.

APPENDIX A

RECUPERABILITY OF THE TRANSPORTATION SYSTEM IN NORTH VIETNAM

"In the task of ensuring communications, we scored many good achievements and gained much good experience in 1965. In the years to come, to develop past successes we must increase reserve projects, means of production, tools and equipment, and rationally organize the manpower necessary to repair and restore bridges and roads rapidly so as to ensure continuous transport."

> Nguyen Con, Chairman, State Planning Committee, to the National Assembly of North Vietnam - 27 April 1966

I. Effects of the Rolling Thunder Program

A. Overall

As of mid-year 1966 direct losses caused by air strikes against the transportation system in North Vietnam amounted to over $30 million or over three-fourths of the estimated cost of replacement of all economic facilities damaged by the Rolling Thunder program. The air attacks have accounted for the damage or destruction of 46 rail and rail/highway bridges and 212 highway bridges. Losses of transport equipment were as follows*:

	Destroyed	Damaged
Vessels	1,700	2,800
Vehicles	800	950
Railroad Freight Cars	570	825
Locomotives	8	6

---

*These figures are basically those obtained from pilot reports but adjusted downward on the basis of photography and analysis of bomb damage assessments of individual strikes in an effort to eliminate both exaggeration and duplication.

TOP SECRET

In addition to these losses, damage and disruption to the transport system has resulted from interdiction strikes against road systems and from attacks on railroad yards at Vinh, Yen Bai, Thai Nguyen, and Nam Dinh. Both the amount of time and cost of repairing the damage resulting from these strikes has been negligible.

The air strikes to date have concentrated primarily on transportation targets in the southern part of North Vietnam. The most significant strikes, however, have been against transport routes in the northern and central parts of North Vietnam. The interdiction program has produced relatively uneven results in attaining its objective of halting rail traffic.

Only one rail line--Hanoi to Thai Nguyen--has been open for through traffic almost continuously since the air strikes began. The Hanoi to Vinh line has been effectively interdicted for through rail service for most of the period. Through rail service on the Hanoi - Lao Cai line, which carried an estimated 30 percent of total rail traffic in 1964, has been halted during most of the period since mid-July 1965. Interdiction of this line disrupted the export of apatite and stopped the movement of Chinese transit traffic to and from Yunnan Province.

The important Hanoi - Dong Dang and Hanoi-Haiphong lines which carry the bulk of North Vietnam's imports have been subjected to the least amount of bombing. They are also the two lines transiting territory which provides more alternatives for bypasses and other expedients to maintain traffic movement. The Hanoi - Dong Dang line has been interdicted for through service for a total of only a few months. The Hanoi-Haiphong has been interdicted for a total of only a few weeks. Successful interdiction of the Hanoi - Dong Dang line would have particularly important and measurable effects. When the line came under heavy attack in late 1965 the import of Chinese coal was shifted from rail to sea transport. The coal movement was shifted back to rail transportation in March 1966 but was noted to be again moving by sea in May when the rail line was again interdicted for through traffic.

B. Damage to Bridges

The status of the bridges damaged or destroyed by air attack is shown in the following tabulation:

	Rail and Rail/Highway Bridges	Highway Bridges	Total
Damaged or Destroyed	46	212	258
Repaired	22	45	67
To Be Repaired	24	167	191

The North Vietnamese have found it necessary to repair slightly over 25 percent of the bridges damaged or destroyed. Rather than effect costly and probably short lived repairs they have chosen to concentrate on the construction of alternate bypasses such as fords, ferries and temporary bridges. A total of 173 alternate crossings have been confirmed by aerial photography. These alternate crossings have been used particularly to sustain highway transport. The net effect is that North Vietnam now has more highway crossings than it had before the start of the bombings.

The use of temporary expedients to ensure continuous transport is particularly attractive to the North Vietnamese not only because the expedients are generally less vulnerable to air attack but also because they can be implemented at far less cost. The permanent repair or reconstruction of the bridges attacked to date would cost North Vietnam an estimated $12.2 million. The cost of temporary repairs and other expedients to maintain traffic, however, has been only $2.9 million.

II. Countermeasures to Air Attack

A. Repair of Bridges

As indicated above, one of the major responses of the North Vietnamese to the air attack on their transportation has been to use temporary expedients to keep traffic moving. The following survey of the damage or destruction of bridges on the principal rail lines illustrates this point in detail.

Hanoi to Vinh

This line is approximately 170 nautical miles (nm) in length and includes 26 major bridges (over 90 feet in length) and 48 minor bridges (less than 90 feet long). Eleven of the 26 major bridges have been damaged by air strikes. Seven of these have an operational bypass bridge or one under construction. Four have no bridge bypass, but in all cases there is evidence of some means of crossing such as foot bridges, pontoon bridges, or ferry crossing.

Although 15 bridges have not been damaged, three of them have bypass bridges already under construction; a reflection of North Vietnam's widespread pre-strike planning.

Vinh to Xom Khe

On this stretch of line, which is approximately 52 nm long, 6 major and 4 minor bridges have been damaged or destroyed. Fifty percent have evidence of bypass efforts in addition to attempts at repair of the original bridge.

The North Vietnamese have demonstrated considerable ingenuity and expertise in keeping traffic moving on this line and there is little or no indication that these capabilities have diminished appreciably.

Hanoi to Dong Dang

The line from Hanoi to the Chinese border is approximately 86 nautical miles in length. There are 25 bridges 50 feet and over in length. Ten of these bridges may be considered as major structures.

Photographic coverage is available on seven bridges, of which all but two have railroad bypasses either operable or under construction. At least three major bridges on this line have been damaged by U. S. air strikes. Repairs to these bridges are being carried out with modern equipment; the new substructures are massive and the repairs appear to be of a permanent nature. The nature of these repairs and the installation of dual gauge track in certain locations give every indication that the North Vietnamese hope to keep this line open under all conditions.

Hanoi to Haiphong

This line, the most important for the movement of imported economic goods, is approximately 52 miles in length. Two bridges have been damaged by air attack.

Bypass activity includes a new temporary bridge which is assumed to be operational, as well as an existing ferry crossing in the immediate vicinity. Repairs to the damaged original bridges are in evidence, though lack of photography precludes a determination of the pace of repair.

Hanoi to Lao Cai

The line from Hanoi to the Chinese border is approximately 156 nautical miles in length and has 45 major and 29 minor bridges. Photographic coverage shows the damage or destruction of 4 major and 9 minor bridges above Yen Bai and in rough terrain along the Red River. The Viet Tri bridge, located south of Yen Bai, was destroyed late in June of this year. The rugged nature of the terrain and the constrictive nature of the road bed has forced the North Vietnamese to repair the damaged structures rather than resort to bypasses. Only two bypasses are discernible in available photography.

Highway Bridges

Damage or destruction of a highway bridge in North Vietnam does not present the complications associated with such an act in more industrialized countries. This is borne out by a graphic review of the status of damaged highway bridges since November 1965.

Figure I-7 shows the cumulative totals of bridges of all types which have been destroyed or damaged plotted against the total number of bridges in need of repair at any given time. The difference between the two lines is the total number of bridges repaired. During the bombing pause from 24 December 1965 to 30 January 1966 the number of bridges repaired is seen to be appreciable. The difference since that period generally remains the same. The costs to repair or reconstruct the damaged bridges is shown in two categories--the cost of permanent repair and cost of temporary repairs that were made to keep traffic moving around all damaged structures. The decreasing trend shown for the cost of temporary repairs reflects the increased use of alternate methods of bypassing a given vulnerable crossing. This is more clearly shown in Figure I-8.

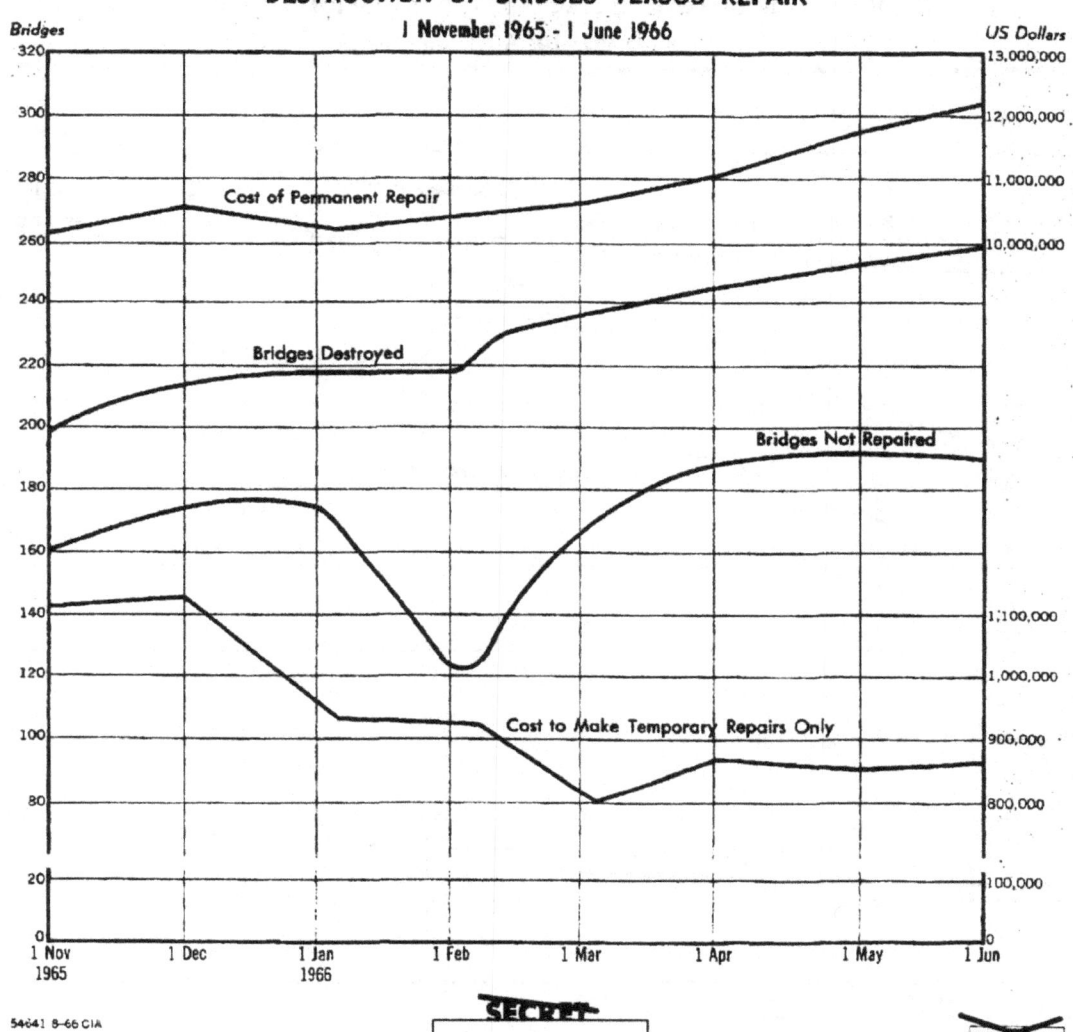

Figure I-7

NORTH VIETNAM
DESTRUCTION OF BRIDGES VERSUS REPAIR
1 November 1965 - 1 June 1966

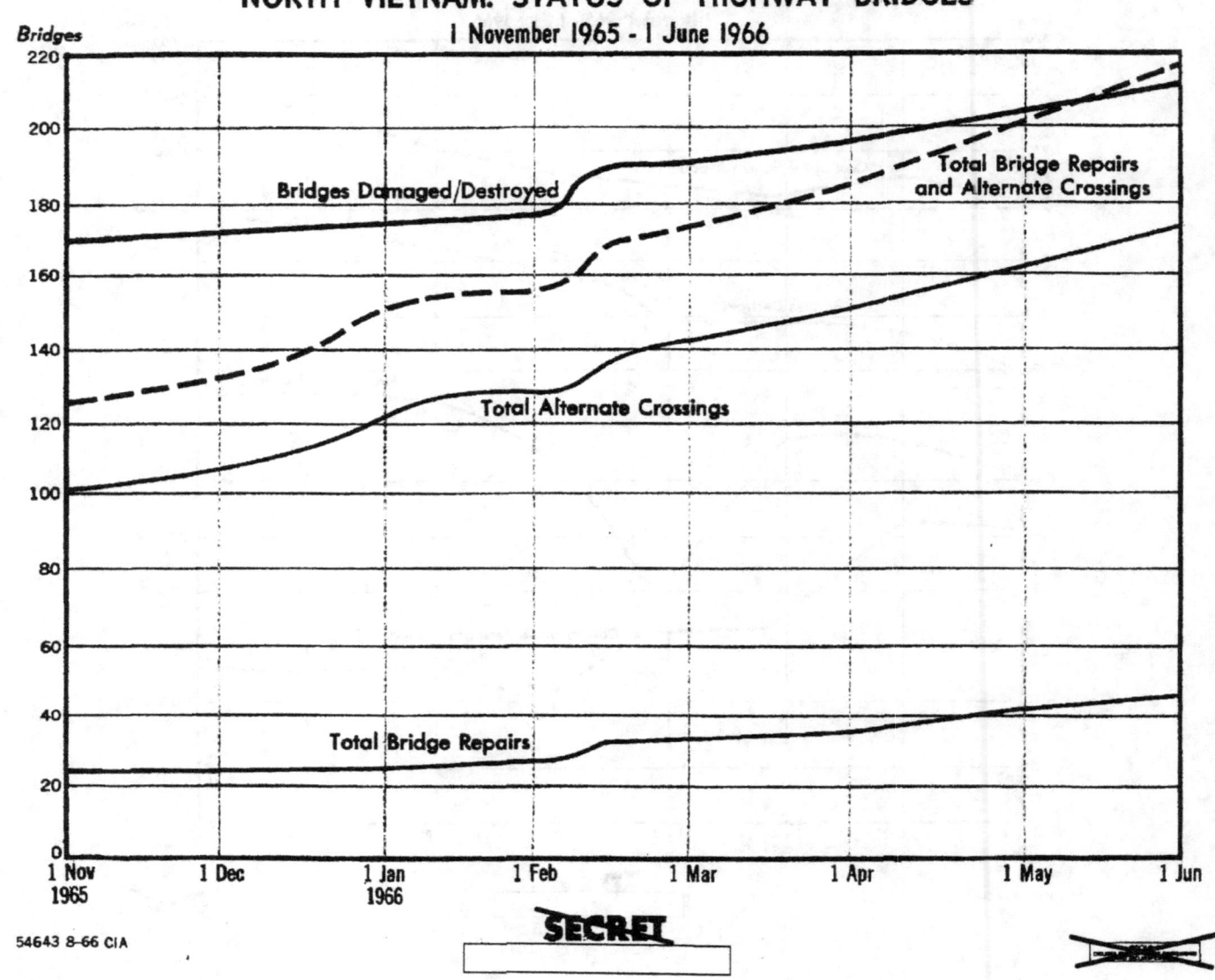

Figure I-8 presents the status of the highway bridges only. The total of highway bridges damaged or destroyed is plotted against the total of bridges actually repaired, the number of alternate crossings, and the number of crossings to which no repairs have been made and no alternate means of transportation have been provided. To further clarify repairs and alternate crossings this is divided into total bridge repairs and total alternate crossings.

The total of bridges repaired (45) is around one-fourth of the total number (173) of new alternate crossings. The total of these two categories now exceeds the total of 212 highway bridges which were damaged or destroyed. As of 1 June, fords accounted for 65 percent of all alternate crossings with bypass bridges, ferries, foot bridges and pontoon bridges ranking in descending order. The largest number of bridges destroyed have been at crossings which have shallow streams, at least during the dry season. The longer and more important bridges are at locations requiring other than crossings by fords. At these more important crossings, more than one type of temporary crossing is usually in evidence.

In sum, the North Vietnamese are presently in a better position to keep their lines of highway transportation open, by having developed a high degree of skill in repairing damaged structures and in building more alternate crossings in order to increase the options available for the routing of highway traffic.

B. Improvement of Rail Lines

As the air strikes extended into the northern part of North Vietnam, the Hanoi regime undertook more permanent measures to ensure the operation of the vital Hanoi - Dong Dang line, and the connecting lines to Haiphong and Thai Nguyen.

Construction is under way to provide greater flexibility and limit the effectiveness of attempts to interdict these lines. A third rail is being laid along the Hanoi - Dong Dang line at least between the Chinese border and Kep, and possibly all the way to Hanoi. When this work is completed, probably within the next few months to Kep, both standard-gauge and meter-gauge rolling stock can be used on the line. As noted above several rail bypasses to bridges and at least one bypass around the city of Lang Son have been constructed or are currently under construction. In addition, a standard-gauge rail line is under construction between Kep and the iron and steel complex at Thai Nguyen. Completion of the Kep - Thai Nguyen line, probably by the end of 1966, will provide the North Vietnamese with an alternate rail supply route in case of interdiction of the Hanoi - Dong Dang line between Kep and the Hanoi area, and will also permit the use of standard-gauge equipment for the movement of coke and coal from China to Thai Nguyen. If the line is interdicted between Kep and Dong Dang, the North Vietnamese can use rail shuttle service between bombed bridges in addition to shifting much of the volume of supplies to sea transportation.

Rail shuttle service also has been noted on the Hanoi-Haiphong line when the Hai Duong bridge is interdicted. Both a highway bypass bridge and a railroad bypass bridge have been constructed to circumvent the Hai Duong bridge in case of interdiction. Both of these bridges have spans that can be detached during the day and floated into place for use at night. Large barges with rails across them are being used as bridge spans for the rail bypass bridge. In addition, there are several waterways connecting Haiphong with Hanoi and other major cities which have a total capacity in excess of the capacity of the railroad.

C. New Road Construction and Improvement

The North Vietnamese have mounted a major effort to keep the road system functioning, particularly the vital links in Military Region IV (MR IV) which carry supplies to the Communist forces in Laos and South Vietnam. Since the beginning of the allied bombing over 200 miles of roads have been constructed and over 300 miles have been improved. At the present time about 60 miles of new roads are under construction.

The emphasis on new road construction is to provide a new inland route south from Thanh Hoa to Dong Hoi in MR IV. This new route, to be completed by the fall of 1966, will provide an alternate to the heavily interdicted coastal route. The new route follows terrain which avoids stream crossings and possible chokepoints. The development of this new route and the improvement of existing routes are providing the Vietnamese with an increased flexibility and capacity for the movement of supplies southward which is becoming increasingly difficult to overcome by bombing methods.

D. Use of Labor, Materials and Equipment

By the end of 1965, the North Vietnamese had developed its workcamp organization into a viable system with an estimated 70-100,000 workers. The air strikes which started in February 1965 concentrated first upon Military Region IV which has its headquarters at Vinh. The initial North Vietnamese response to the air attacks seemed confused and disorganized. This state of affairs apparently lasted for only a relatively short period because the level of traffic flow at that time was only slightly diminished. Before the year was out the level of traffic in MR IV had reached new highs.

The labor force of construction workcamps in MR IV in early 1965 totaled about 5,000 men of varying degrees of roadbuilding experience. Workcamps from northeast and northwest North Vietnam were transferred to the Vinh area during April and May. Common laborers and youth from Hanoi and Haiphong also were sent south to Vinh in June-July and as many as 60,000 youth may have been added to the workcamp force. The original workers who had some skill became the nucleus for teaching the inexperienced labor on the job. In addition, a small share of the labor force was sent to local training classes and to Communist China to learn the operation, maintenance and repair of construction equipment.

These workcamps implemented the contingency plans set up in Hanoi by stationing units at chokepoints, shifting labor to heavily bombed areas, procuring building materials and setting up motor pools for construction equipment.

As a result of this pre-strike planning the North Vietnamese are now better able to counteract the air strikes than they were a year ago. They have the ability and resources to increase and improve the countermeasures still further. The chokepoints are less critical now because alternate routes and crossings have been constructed. Moreover, the labor force has gained a great deal of experience in making quick repairs, using camouflage and carrying out other innovations to deceive the enemy.

The major share of repair work is carried out by simple repair methods and with basic building materials, primarily timber and rock products that are at present in adequate supply. There are an estimated 6 rock quarries in MR IV near key routes such as 1A, 15 and 7 that supply rock products for repair and roadbuilding projects. Bamboo, the universal building material of southeast Asia, is used extensively in construction of temporary highway bridges. Two saw mills in western Nghe An Province provide large dimension timber for repairs to railroad bridges. The North Vietnamese recently have also purchased large dimension timber from Cambodia, which indicates a possible shortage of larger sizes. Although the North Vietnamese use all salvageable components at a damaged bridge, shortages of timber in 1966-67 might necessitate shipment of steel bridge girders from the north, particularly from the assembly area at the Thai Nguyen Iron and Steel Combine or Communist China.

The inventory of construction equipment used by the workcamps has increased since the start of the bombings and continued negotiations by the North Vietnamese with other Communist countries undoubtedly will provide additional units during 1966-67. The estimated inventory of construction equipment in use for road construction and bridge repair in MR IV consists of the following:

Type	January 1965	June 1966
Bulldozers	30	65
Mobile Cranes	25	35
Scrapers	5	20
Road Graders	20	30

Although the USSR and other Communist countries have supplied many dump trucks to North Vietnam for aid projects, it is not known how many have been earmarked for use in construction work in MR IV.

The experience gained by North Vietnamese in expanding the road network and in building alternate as well as additional stream crossings has given them greater expertise and speed in the repair of bomb-damaged structures and roads. As more labor and equipment is made available to the workcamps, even greater speed will be achieved in completing repairs. A selective listing of the speed with which these measures are completed is shown in Table I-3. The listing reflects activity in MR IV and cannot be considered representative of the more extensive repair work that has been observed on the rail bridges farther north.

~~TOP SECRET~~

Table I-3

North Vietnam
Selected Recuperation Times on Repair Work in Military Region IV

Location	Time
Bridge and Ferry on Route 1A (unlocated)	10.5 hours (for small vehicles)
Same work site	30.5 hours (for large vehicles)
Cau Giat Bridge (1915N/10540E)	2 days (for 8-ton vehicles)
Route 15, km 262-266	29 hours
Dia Loi Ferry (1816N/10540E)	21 hours
Route 15 at Dia Loi Build ford and fill craters in road	7 days
Loc Yen Bridge (1810N/10542E)	24 hours
Khe Thoi Ford (unlocated)	30 hours
Muong Sen Ferry (1924N/10408E)	48 hours
Khe Quyen Bridge (unlocated)	48 hours
Hanoi-Vinh Rail line at Dien Chau Repair track at km 300	12 hours
Hiem Bridge (unlocated) Repaired 3 damaged spans	30 hours
Route 15 segment	8 hours

~~TOP SECRET~~

E. Possible Innovations in 1966-67

The main effort by the North Vietnamese in 1966-67 will be to further improve the lines of communications within the Rolling Thunder target zone and additional pre-strike preparations in the Hanoi-Haiphong sanctuary area in anticipation of air strikes against communications in this zone. Additional alternate routes and stream crossings will probably be completed and greater effort made to camouflage them. The Chinese engineer units northeast of Hanoi will continue to maintain the Dong Dang rail line, thereby allowing greater Vietnamese flexibility in allocating resources to maintain lines of communications in other areas. More innovations can be expected in bridge repair methods to speed up restoration, particularly construction of more pontoon bridges, ferries, and fords.

If the rate of air strikes against the logistics targets system were doubled the North Vietnamese would probably be able to cope with the additional damage by increasing the labor force working on lines of communications by 40,000-50,000 persons. The additions to the labor force need not be greater because of the large amount of work already done in expanding the road system and building bypasses and other temporary crossings. The main thrust of future labor efforts will be in maintenance and repair of this expanded road system. The North Vietnamese have made an impressive demonstration of their proficiency in the speedy repair of interdicted roads.

III. Effect of Air Attacks on Traffic Movements

A. Through June 1966

Interdiction of the transportation network at the levels carried out through mid-1966 has not succeeded in reducing the traffic carried by the North Vietnamese transportation system. Unless there is a substantial increase in the level of interdiction, the North Vietnamese should have no serious difficulty in maintaining both the volume of imports and exports carried by land transport in 1965 and in sustaining the total transport performance of all modes of transportation. The estimated volume of imports and exports moved by rail on the Hanoi - Dong Dang line in 1965 was about 30 percent greater than that carried in 1964. This increase created no additional problems for the rail system because of the loss of Chinese transit traffic during the last half of the year. Total transport performance in 1965 by all modes of transportation in terms of tons carried increased by about 5 percent above the 1964 level. Total tons carried during the first half of 1966 are estimated to have continued to increase slightly. (See Table I-4). The slight decreases in railroad performance were more than compensated by increases in highway, inland water, and coastal water performance. Total performance in terms of ton-miles, however, is estimated to have decreased slightly in 1965 and in the first half of 1966.

Table I-4

NORTH VIETNAM

Transport Performance, 1964-1965, and First Half 1966

	1964	1965	Jan - June 1966
Total Performance:			
Million tons carried	20.6	21.7	11.0
Million ton-miles	1,200	1,160	550
International Trade by Rail:			
Imports (thousand tons carried)	180	350	N. A.
Exports (thousand tons carried)	220	170	N. A.

The most serious problem for the North Vietnamese in maintaining the 1965 level of transport performance during July 1966 - June 1967, assuming the current level of air attacks and choice of targets, is the possibility of more frequent interdiction of the Hanoi - Dong Dang and Hanoi-Haiphong rail lines.

More frequent interdiction of these lines would disrupt the normal flow of through traffic from China but we estimate that the interdiction would not reduce the capacity of the lines below the levels needed to handle the normal volume of military and civilian supplies imported over the rail connections to China.

B. **Intensive Interdiction of Transportation**

A significant escalation of the air attacks against North Vietnam could have more meaningful results. To illustrate this we assume an escalated program of air attacks that results in the continued interdiction of all major rail, highway, and combination rail/highway bridges, including bypass bridges, throughout North Vietnam. Port facilities at Haiphong, Cam Pha, and Hon Gai, the major railroad repair shop at Gia Lam, and all major railroad yards are also assumed to be subjected to effective and repeated air attacks. Significant military and economic targets such as the remaining petroleum storage facilities and the Haiphong cement plant are also taken under attack.

The postulated attack would present North Vietnam with an immediate and severe problem in maintaining normal traffic movements, particularly the vital import traffic.

Sustained interdiction of the lines of communication would force the Communists to allocate considerable amounts of manpower and materials to maintain the railroad lines and alternate routes. Intensive armed reconnaissance would stop all daylight traffic and disrupt night traffic, thus slowing down movement and making the logistic resupply of Communist forces considerably less reliable than at present.

In order to maintain imports normally carried by ocean-going ships the North Vietnamese would have several alternatives. These include the diversion of seaborne trade to South China ports and using land transport routes or coastal shipping to move cargoes to and from North Vietnam; the use of small watercraft to load and unload ocean-going

I-36

ships while they are anchored outside North Vietnam ports; and the use of other minor ports in North Vietnam.

If only one-half of the normal traffic through Haiphong could be handled by lighters and other craft once the port is closed and watercraft are subject to 24-hour armed reconnaissance, the other half would probably move through China by rail to North Vietnam. In this case 800 tons* per day of general cargo imports and up to 400 or 500 tons per day of petroleum imports would be transferred to rail transport. Railroad connections to Communist China are currently operating at only about one-third capacity. This added traffic would compel North Vietnam and China to divert some overland traffic via Yunnan Province and the Hanoi - Lao Cai line. Both lines would then be forced to attempt to operate at full capacity under interdicted conditions. If production in the cement plant were also halted at the same time, an additional import requirement for cement, probably as high as 1,700 tons a day would be generated. This additional tonnage would raise traffic far beyond the uninterdicted capacity of the Hanoi - Dong Dang rail line, the principal import route. The overburdening of the rail lines would become more acute if even less traffic could be handled by lightering and/or coastwise movement.

The North Vietnamese would probably be forced to make greater use of highway and inland water traffic. Although it is extremely difficult to interdict these systems, their greater use would increase the opportunities for harassment of actual traffic movement. The roads from China are estimated to have a limited capacity in the rainy season of about 1,000 tons EWPD. In the area north of Hanoi the height of the rainy season occurs during July through September. A sustained high level of interdiction during this period would be more effective in reducing the gap between transport capabilities and the volume of traffic to be moved.

The intensified attacks would have little impact in halting either essential imports or the flow of petroleum

---
*Short tons are used throughout this Appendix.

necessary to sustain the logistic pipeline to South Vietnam. The amount of petroleum needed to sustain this system is small. North Vietnamese forces and civilian activities in MR IV, which includes the four southern provinces of the country, were consuming petroleum at the rate of 1,500 tons per month at the end of 1965. With the higher level of transport activity observed during the 1966 dry season, the average level of consumption in MR IV probably amounted to about 2,000 tons per month. The delivery of this petroleum as well as other supplies (including food) to MR IV probably requires an additional 500 tons of fuel per month.

The movement of supplies to and through Laos requires the consumption of only a small share of the petroleum moved into MR IV. At the end of 1965, it appeared that only about 400 tons of the 1,500 tons per month shipped to MR IV were used in the Laotian Panhandle. At present, this amount probably has increased to 500-600 tons. Trucks used to carry supplies destined for South Vietnam are estimated to consume about one-fourth of the fuel moved into the Panhandle.

The restrictions of rail traffic and the consequent additional requirements on truck and inland water transportation would seriously affect the availability of transportation for all nonessential economic needs. This lack of transport availability in conjunction with the disruption of imports through the ports would soon cause modern industry to grind to a halt unless substantial stockpiles of raw materials had been accumulated at the plants. Even if some of the plants had stockpiles sufficient to continue operating, internal distribution or export of their products would be seriously handicapped by insufficient transportation. Modern industry, however, represents only a small portion of North Vietnam's economic output.

If modern industry were forced to a standstill by escalated air attacks, demands for internal distribution for the industrial sector would be eliminated. The loss of demand for petroleum for the industrial sector would permit the allocation of most of the available petroleum to the transportation of military supplies, food, and other civilian essentials such as civil defense items and medicines. This transport capacity would be supplemented by the use of primitive transport.

The immediate and direct effect of the increased interdiction of the transport system on the availability of food would not be serious. Existing food storage facilities in the countryside are so decentralized that they require little transportation by modern means. The distribution of food to the cities, mainly Hanoi, Haiphong, and Nam Dinh, however, would be more difficult.

The long-range effect on the production and distribution of food, however, could cause some serious problems. The intensified air attacks on the level assumed in this report probably would aggravate manpower shortages and further disrupt that part of the irrigation system dependent on petroleum and electric power and could cause the decrease in food production. Decreased food production in conjunction with a decrease in transport capability could aggravate the problem of supplying a sufficient amount of food to the larger cities. The transport problem probably still would not be critical, however, because only 4 percent of the population lives in the three largest cities and only 7 percent lives in all cities of more than 10,000 persons.

ANNEX II

THE EFFECTS OF SOVIET AND CHINESE INVOLVEMENT
IN THE WAR ON THE VIETNAMESE COMMUNISTS

ANNEX II

THE EFFECTS OF SOVIET AND CHINESE INVOLVEMENT
IN THE WAR ON THE VIETNAMESE COMMUNISTS

I. Introduction

There is substantial evidence that the political positions of the Soviet Union and Communist China on the war, and the amount of their material assistance to the war effort, are highly significant influences on Vietnamese Communist policy. The importance of Soviet and Chinese support and assistance has been readily admitted by the Vietnamese. In his April 1965 speech setting forth the situation and tasks facing the Vietnamese after the US began bombing the North, Premier Pham Van Dong said simply that the "more" the Vietnamese are "supported and assisted in all fields by the socialist camp, the more they will be able to struggle vigorously and resolutely" against the enemy in Vietnam. In April of 1966, Dong re-emphasized the significance of bloc backing in a declaration that the "victories" of the Vietnamese people are not only the results of their own efforts, but are also the "result of the infinitely valuable sympathy, support and assistance by the fraternal socialist countries."

The Vietnamese view bloc support as valuable in sustaining and, in some ways, increasing the military pressure the Communists can bring to bear in South Vietnam. They also see it as a protective umbrella which partially inhibits direct allied military pressure on the DRV and helps to negate the effects of the bombing of the North. Firm Soviet and Chinese backing also helps complete the ideological equation in the conflict so important to the Communists, i.e., this is a "war of liberation" and it is the duty of all Communists to support and encourage such wars.

II. The Significance of Economic and Military Aid

A. General Level of Aid

In an apparent response to the allied air offensive, military and economic assistance provided by the

II-1

USSR and Communist China increased sharply in 1965. Although the total amounts of aid extended during 1965 are not known, reasonably firm evidence enables us to estimate that military aid amounting to about $250 million and economic aid of about $100 million was probably delivered in 1965. The Communist allies have undoubtedly undertaken commitments to provide additional assistance but we are unable to make any meaningful estimates of the total value of these commitments. There is reliable evidence that the USSR in 1965 did commit itself to extend additional assistance of at least $160 million. We do not know if this extension is for military or economic programs. The weight of available evidence suggests that it is not for weapons but is probably intended as assistance in the rebuilding of bomb damaged facilities or for defense related activities.

The immediate significance of the military and economic aid provided by other Communist countries is that it provides North Vietnam the material means to carry out its aggressive programs. North Vietnam is significant militarily as a logistic base for the transmission of military supplies to South Vietnam, as a source of manpower, and as the center for control of the insurgency. As a primitive economy it has a capability to produce only minor items of military equipment and relies on other Communist countries for all of its heavy military equipment and most of its small arms and ammunition. Material assistance to North Vietnam is also significant as an apparent commitment of other Communist countries to underwrite the material costs of the war and to assist in the reconstruction of North Vietnam's economy. These assurances undoubtedly underlie North Vietnam's apparent willingness to lose its economic facilities to air attack and to persist in its pursuit of the war in South Vietnam. This attitude is undoubtedly strengthened by the knowledge that even more assistance will be forthcoming in 1966. Preliminary data on shipping to North Vietnam show that imports continue to rise above 1965 levels. At the same time exports are continuing to decline so that the growing import surplus can only be financed by additional assistance from Communist countries.

B. Economic Aid

Known economic credits and grants extended by Communist countries through 1962 amounted to more than $956 million. (See Table II-1). About 40 percent of the total was in the form of grants. By the end of 1964 from $550-800 million or 60-80 percent of the extension had been drawn. The USSR accounted for $370 million (40 percent) of total extensions and Communist China provided $457 million (48 percent). The remaining $130 million was supplied by the European Communist countries and token amounts were provided by Albania, North Korea, and Mongolia.

After an apparent hiatus of two years the Soviet program for economic assistance to North Vietnam was revived in February 1965 when Premier Kosygin visited Hanoi. As the war expanded substantial new extensions of economic aid were made in mid-1965. The only public statements about the value and composition of the aid has come from Hungary which is reported to have granted a modest $5.5 million for trucks, telecommunications equipment, medical supplies, and machine tools. Rumania is also reported by intelligence sources to have extended a credit of $4.4 million.

In December 1965 and January 1966 new aid agreements were signed with all Communist countries, suggesting that the mid-1965 agreements were small. Since then other Communist countries have promised increased assistance for North Vietnam. In May 1966, Moscow reported an agreement to provide technical assistance; additional Chinese aid for agriculture was announced in July. All the Warsaw Pact members also pledged increased economic aid to North Vietnam in July 1966.

We estimate that deliveries of economic aid in 1965 were in the order of $100 million or from 20-40 percent above the average annual level in 1955-1964. In June 1966 Soviet specialists were reported in North Vietnam to determine equipment needs for constructing new enterprises and rebuilding those destroyed by US air attacks.

All of these developments foreshadow a substantially increased aid in 1966 and 1967, a trend already confirmed by our intelligence on the volume and composition of North Vietnamese imports.

Table II - 1

Communist Economic Aid Extended to North Vietnam a/
1955-64

Million US $

	1955	1956	1957	1958	1959	1960	1961	1962	1963-64	1955-64
Communist China	200	b/	b/	b/	100	b/	157	b/	b/	457
USSR	100	8	12	21	25	200	4	N.A.	b/	369
Eastern Europe	50	8	7	b/	2	Negl.	62	b/	b/	130
Total	350	16	19	21	128	200	223	N.A.	b/	956

a. This is the minimum of economic aid extended by the Soviet Bloc and Communist China. In addition, insignificant amounts of aid have been extended by Albania, Mongolia, and North Korea. Because of rounding, components may not add to the totals shown.
b. No extensions are known to exist, although some may have taken place.

C. **Military Aid**

Military aid to North Vietnam which had previously been on a relatively small scale reached at least $250 million in 1965.* About three-fourths of this aid, by value, was provided by the USSR as the supplier of North Vietnam's modern air defenses, particularly its SAM system and jet interceptors. The approximately $50 million provided by Communist China was limited principally to conventional arms.

1. **Soviet Military Aid**

By the end of 1965 Soviet military aid to North Vietnam approached $450 million. The sequence and value of Soviet arms aid to North Vietnam was as follows (in million US $):**

1953-63	222
1964	53
1965	<u>167</u>
Total	442

Military aid extended after August 1964 and in early 1965 probably was completely delivered by the end of 1965. Major deliveries included equipment for about 20 surface-to-air missile firing battalions, 8 IL-28 light jet bombers, 11 MIG-21 jet fighters, 25 MIG-15/16 jet fighters, over 1,000 AA guns ranging from 37-100 mm., and hundreds of vehicles. (See Table II-2).

The USSR has also provided military technicians to instruct the North Vietnamese in the operation of the SAM system. In addition the North Vietnamese have received pilot training in Soviet jet fighters both in North Vietnam and the USSR. We estimate that the number of military technicians may have been as high as 1,500 in mid-1965, but diminished when the North Vietnamese began to

---

*The value of military aid is expressed in Soviet foreign trade prices.
**Values, reported in rubles, have been converted to dollars at the official exchange rate: 1 ruble = US $1.11.

Table II-2

Estimated Soviet and Chinese Deliveries of Military Equipment to North Vietnam
1953 - June 1966

Million US $

Equipment	USSR Quantity	USSR Value	Communist China Quantity	Communist China Value	Total Quantity	Total Value
SAM Firing Battalion	24	127.0	-	-	24	127.0
Aircraft	163	55.4	44	5.7	207	61.1
IL-28 light jet bomber	8	2.8	-	-	-	-
MIG-21 jet fighter	25	20.0	-	-	-	-
MIG-15/17 jet fighter	35	4.5	44	5.7	-	-
MI-6 helicopter	6	12.0	-	-	-	-
Other	89	16.1	-	-	-	-
Naval Craft	20	8.2	34	21.6	54	29.8
SO-1 subchaser	4	4.0	-	-	-	-
P-4 motor torpedo boat	12	3.0	-	-	-	-
Small minesweeper	4	1.2	-	-	-	-
Swatow-class PGM	-	-	30	18.0	-	-
Shanghai-class PTF	-	-	4	3.6	-	-
Artillery (mostly AA guns)	2,800	68.0	200	4.3	3,000	72.3
Armor (tanks, A.P.C.'s, S.P. guns)	150	5.4	-	-	150	5.4
Radar	48	5.0	126	7.5	174	12.5
Trucks and Vehicles	1,500	7.5	1,500	7.5	3,000	15.0
Small Arms and Infantry Weapons	Large Quantities	50.0	Large Quantities	50.0	Large Quantities	100.0
Ammunition	Large Quantities	50.0	Large Quantities	30.0	Large Quantities	80.0
Total		376.5		126.6		503.1

TOP SECRET

assume operational control of the SAM system. The cost of this technical assistance was probably less than $10 million.

Following North Vietnam's active confrontation with the US in the Tonkin Gulf incidents of August 1964, the Soviets extended Hanoi the reported $53 million grant listed above for antiaircraft and including $17 million for surface-to-air missile systems and missile and flight training for North Vietnamese crews. Shortly after Kosygin's visit to Hanoi in February 1965, another $167 million was reportedly granted for aircraft and additional antiaircraft and SAM equipment.

An indication of continued military aid in 1966 is contained in reports on the "Gratuitous Aid and Technical Assistance Agreement" signed in Moscow in December 1965. Reportedly, the USSR agreed to provide large quantities of 130-mm antiaircraft guns, other ground equipment, and possibly 60 additional MIG-21 jet fighters. Although not enough is known on types and quantities of equipment to permit an estimate of the value of the arms portion of the agreement, the cost of the antiaircraft guns and jet fighters alone will exceed $80 million.

2. Chinese Military Aid

There is little information on Chinese military aid to North Vietnam, but we estimate that total aid by the end of 1965 was on the order of $125 million of which about $50 million was delivered in 1965. Although the North Vietnamese armed forces are structured basically on Chinese rather than Soviet lines, until 1960-61 they were equipped largely with weapons from the USSR. From 1960 to the Gulf of Tonkin incidents in August 1964 Chinese arms aid to Hanoi probably increased to a point where it equalled--if it did not exceed--Soviet arms aid. Following the Gulf of Tonkin incidents, the Chinese continued to provide some weapons, including 44 MIG-15/17 jet fighters and 4 Shanghai-class fast patrol boats, but fell far behind the USSR as the major arms supplier. The major Chinese contribution to Hanoi's war effort has been as a provider of military construction units and materials and, possibly, operational antiaircraft elements.

Some elements of Chinese military units are positioned in Northeast and Northwest near the main railroad lines leading to Yunnan and Kwangsi. Elements of two railway engineer divisions of the Peoples Liberation Army (PLA) and an antiaircraft division are known to be in these areas. Although little is known regarding the size of this force, it is estimated that from 25,000 to 45,000 Chinese may be involved.

Aside from these operational units, Chinese military technicians in North Vietnam may exceed 1,000. Unconfirmed reports state that 200 North Vietnamese pilots and ground crews trained in China in 1961-64. Although little is known on the numbers of Chinese technicians advising North Vietnam in the period 1961-64, they are believed not to have been so large as to move the cost of this military technical assistance above the $10 million spent by the USSR.

3. Other Communist Military Aid

Military aid supplied to North Vietnam by the Communist countries of Eastern Europe before 1965 was negligible. The major items of military and emergency reconstruction aid extended or delivered by these countries since then may be summarized as follows:

Donor Country	Nature of Aid
Czechoslovakia	Small Arms, Ammunition
East Germany	10 Field Hospitals
Hungary	Medicines, Hospital
Poland	Barges, Trucks, Hsopital
Rumania	Vehicles, Trucks

East European aid primarily is of a quasimilitary, defense support nature (even the Czechoslovakian small arms were mainly sporting rifles for training purposes). This aid has gained impetus in 1966 and may be expected to increase substantially in the future.

D. Bloc Aid as a Critical Factor in Continuing the War

Although Soviet and Chinese military and economic aid has been small in terms of their capabilities, it is absolutely vital to North Vietnam's ability to adequately defend its territory and to support the insurgency in South Vietnam. A cessation of bloc military aid would, in fact, almost certainly make it impossible for the Vietnamese to sustain the war in South Vietnam at its present level of intensity.

North Vietnam has no productive capability to produce heavy military equipment or the new family of weapons with which the VC Main Forces are being equipped. The NVA and VC Main Forces are totally dependent on outside sources for the 7.62 family of weapons and the heavier weapons being introduced into South Vietnam. If these sources were denied, the VC/NVA forces would be deprived of their major offensive capabilities, and once stockpiles were exhausted these forces would be compelled to revert to a much lower level of military activity.

Since the available evidence points not only to a continuation, but to a probable increase in bloc aid during the last half of 1966, it does not appear likely that the Vietnamese Communists will be faced with devising any substitutes for it or of altering their policy to take account of its cessation during the foreseeable future. Moreover, so long as Soviet and Chinese support continues at least at its present levels, it does not appear that the Vietnamese Communists would view it as a critical factor in any basic determination they might make on whether to continue the fighting. Vietnamese Communist assertions that, in the final analysis, they must rely mainly on their own resources to prosecute the revolution appear to reflect a genuine and deeply held belief. The theme of "self-reliance" has been a persistent one in Vietnamese Communist statements, and has not at all been abandoned or dampened down in the face of the increasing allied military pressure on the Viet Cong and on the DRV.

In March of 1966, for example, DRV party spokesman Truong Chinh declared that the "strategic line" of the revolution was still to rely "mainly on our own forces" while fighting a protracted war. In April, Ho Chi Minh told a Cairo newsman that the Vietnamese people, while "highly appreciating" the assistance of the socialist countries would "basically depend on their own forces." In May, another North Vietnamese politburo spokesman, Pham Hung, reiterated that, even while employing assistance from the bloc, "our dictum is to rely principally on our own strength."

III. The Rationale For Chinese Support

There appear to be several important considerations in the Vietnamese view which tend to reinforce their "do it yourself" attitude. They apparently believe, for one thing, that there are distinct limits to the amount of political and materiel support which can be counted upon from Peking and Moscow. Vietnamese documents and statements indicate that they believe Peking is willing to make a considerable contribution of military, economic, and political assistance to keep the fighting going along its present lines--a protracted struggle by proxy, fought if necessary to the last Vietnamese. Hanoi is also well aware that the conflict provides a test case of Mao's theory that "wars of liberation" can be fought without provoking a US nuclear response against either the local Communists or their sponsors. This war, moreover, is taking place in an area close to China and in a region which the Chinese believe to be their rightful sphere of influence.

However, the Vietnamese also appear to believe that there are limits to the price Peking is willing to pay to keep the conflict going. This is implicit, in part, in the DRV's handling and comment on public Chinese pledges of assistance. For example, a 28 December 1965 editorial in the DRV party daily, which dealt with Chinese assistance, was formulated in a manner which made it clear that the latest pledges of Chinese support were not as strong as those earlier issued by Peking, prior to the escalation of the air war against North Vietnam. The editorial also treated the question of Chinese volunteers for Vietnam in a fashion which suggested some doubt in Hanoi over the ultimate willingness of Peking to bring in combat troops should the situation deteriorate to the point where they might be needed. The editorial followed a new aid pact between the Chinese and the North Vietnamese signed in early December. The pact was treated in the press of both countries with caution and without the usual fanfare. The aid, moreover, was in the form of a loan and not a grant. This, in itself, suggested limitations on the Chinese interest in supporting the Vietnamese.

Peking's caution is not, however, entirely a negative factor in Hanoi's view. The Vietnamese themselves wish to prevent the introduction of such massive Chinese assistance as would undercut Vietnamese Communist control

II-8

and direction of the insurgency, unless it was required to prevent the extinction of the Communist regime in the DRV. This was underscored by DRV politburo member, Le Duc Tho, in an article published in the North Vietnamese party journal in February 1966. The "lines, strategy, and methods" of the revolution, wrote Tho, are a "responsibility which our party must assume, as we ourselves and alone can realize most clearly the problems concerning the revolution in our country."

Tho was doubtless addressing both Peking and Moscow in his remarks, but he probably had mainly in mind the persistent Chinese political pressure on Hanoi designed to keep the Vietnamese steadfast in the war and block any possible move toward negotiations. One prime example of this occurred in June when the Chinese lashed out at a Soviet-sponsored World Peace Council proposal on negotiations to end the war. Although the proposal closely echoed the DRV's own four points, the Chinese maintained that because it did not insist on the "immediate and total withdrawal of US troops from South Vietnam," it had left out the key element in a Vietnam settlement. Hanoi itself has never insisted on immediate withdrawal as a condition for negotiations and did not make any comment on the proposal by the council. Peking, however, was clearly anxious to make it appear that the Asian Communist position on ending the war was tougher than indicated in the Council proposal to which the North Vietnamese had been a party. Peking's quick attack denied Hanoi the opportunity to voice any approval of the proposal lest it indicate an open difference of opinion with the Chinese.

Even given the Chinese willingness to pressure Hanoi, however, it is probable that the pressure would not be sufficient to force the Vietnamese to stay in the war if they decide on their own volition to end the fighting. The Vietnamese Communists probably estimate that, in view of the limitations on the Chinese commitment, Peking would do little more than complain if the conflict were terminated short of an insurgent victory. The Chinese, in fact, seem to recognize this, for they have repeatedly left themselves an out by emphasizing that all decisions on the war are "strictly" up to the Vietnamese.

IV. Vietnamese View of Soviet Support

The Vietnamese Communists probably judge, on the basis of Moscow's assistance so far, that the Soviet commitment in the war is considerably more restrained than that of the Chinese. This can be seen, in part, in North Vietnamese statements dealing with Soviet assistance. Although Hanoi has, in the main, carefully attempted to express equal gratitude for the help of both bloc powers, some remarks implicitly critical of Moscow have occasionally come forth. In mid-1965, for example, at a time when the North Vietnamese signed aid pacts with both Peking and Moscow, DRV spokesmen were much warmer in their description of Chinese assistance than of Soviet. Peking's support was termed at the time the "firmest, the most powerful, and the most effective," while China was hailed as the "most enthusiastic and resolute comrade in arms of all nations fighting against the imperialists."

Hanoi is fully aware that Moscow, like Peking, has also displayed an overriding concern in its actions on the war to avoid steps which might lead to a direct Soviet-US military confrontation. For example, Moscow has throughout the conflict avoided sea delivery to Haiphong of sensitive military shipments. Moreover, important Soviet officials have gone out of their way in private to disavow the significance for Soviet-US relations of the presence of Soviet military-technical personnel in the DRV.

It is doubtless clear to the Vietnamese that the Soviets would like an early end to the war. Evidence suggests that the Soviets did cautiously advise Hanoi to move toward a political settlement of the conflict in early 1965. Following Kosygin's visit to the DRV in February, the Chinese charged that Moscow had sent a formal proposal to Hanoi and Peking suggesting a reconvention of an international conference on Indochina. During the bombing pause early this year, party secretary Shelepin apparently took further soundings on Hanoi's attitude toward possible political alternatives to the conflict. In recent months, in view of the continuing hard-line stand of the Vietnamese, the Russians appear to have avoided applying most of the pressures they could exert on the DRV, probably judging them to be marginal at best. Soviet party chief Brezhnev displayed this cautious attitude during recent talks with De Gaulle. He told the French president that Moscow would be ready to attend a conference only "if and when Hanoi agrees."

Despite the limitations on Soviet assistance and support, it is probable that Soviet backing has, on balance, the effect of buttressing the Vietnamese Communist will to persist in the conflict. The Vietnamese probably judge that they can continue to count indefinitely on Moscow's assistance along present lines so long as the war continues in its present context. They probably believe, in fact, that the Soviets are now locked into the struggle in view of the pretensions Moscow still holds to leadership of the Communist camp, and that it cannot afford to step completely aside.

SECRET

ANNEX III

THE COMMUNIST ORGANIZATION AND CAPABILITY FOR POLITICAL SUBVERSION IN SOUTH VIETNAM

ANNEX III

THE COMMUNIST ORGANIZATION AND CAPABILITY
FOR POLITICAL SUBVERSION IN SOUTH VIETNAM

I. Communist Concepts of Political Subversion

Certain basic principles long stressed by the Vietnamese Communists bear importantly on their efforts at political subversion. Of primary importance is the integration of both military and political forces into an interlocking whole in the conduct of subversion. As their documents put it, the insurgency is a "three-sided attack," comprising "armed struggle, political struggle, and military proselyting." Each participant is expected to "fight both politically and militarily."

The Communists also believe it is necessary to develop and coordinate the insurgency concurrently in the cities and in the rural areas. In general, they seek to secure the rural areas around the cities, towns and strategic installations hamlet by hamlet as a launch point for a final effort in the cities. The Communists hope that a balance of forces will be achieved between government and insurgent military strength which will guarantee the success of the "general uprising" of both the urban and rural populace which the Communists expect will eventually occur. Within the cities, meanwhile, the Communists seek to undermine government strength and purpose, to gain control over the "masses" through subversion and terrorism, and to build in the cities the political and military forces which will assist the "general uprising" and lead to collapse of the government.

II. The Apparatus For Subversion

The apparatus which the Vietnamese Communists are using for political subversion in South Vietnam comprises several major elements: (a) the Communist Party; that is, the southern segment of the North Vietnamese Lao Dong Party, which for tactical purposes maintains a fictional separate identity as the People's Revolutionary Party of South Vietnam; (b) the party's youth auxiliary, the People's Revolutionary Youth Group; and (c) the National Front for the Liberation of South Vietnam and its associated web of regional, functional, and social "Liberation Associations," all covertly controlled by party cadres.

There is also an underground of covert agents and sympathizers utilized by the party to gather information, to help in political agitation, and to procure supplies. Over the years the party has developed extensive and elaborate communications (courier and radio), intelligence nets, and internal security and propaganda systems. These serve to reinforce the cohesion, direction, and unity of effort of the movement throughout South Vietnam, in its political as well as in its military actions.*

    A. Party Organization and Role

The Communist Party provides the organizational core for the subversive apparatus.** A special department of the

---

*The Communist subversive apparatus has been built around several thousand members of Ho Chi Minh's Viet Minh who stayed behind in the South after the division of Vietnam in 1954 to work for a Communist take-over and reunification. They have been reinforced over the years from among the estimated 90,000 members of the Viet Minh movement who went north in 1954. Many of these have returned to the South as needed in political as well as military roles. Many of the original members of this group have spent nearly all their adult years involved in or committed in one way or another to their "struggle," which began in the fight to oust the French.

Their strength in part flows from their dedication, indoctrination, tight organization, discipline, and singleness of purpose.

**Until late 1961, the Communists in South Vietnam made no effort to portray themselves as distinct from Ho Chi Minh's Lao Dong Party. However, to give the revolution a nucleus which would be more southern in identity and orientation, Hanoi directed in late 1961 that the southern Communists assume the mantle of an ostensibly independent party--the People's Revolutionary Party. This party was proclaimed openly in January 1962, and described by implication as the spiritual heir of the Indochinese Communist Party and the "vanguard" for the Liberation Front.

party in Hanoi concerns itself with the problems of the struggle in the South and with the southern party segment.* It acts by and large through the party's Central Office for South Vietnam (COSVN) located in a base area (Zone C) in Tay Ninh Province. COSVN functions in many respects as a headquarters for the People's Revolutionary Party, controlling through covert party channels the National Front for the Liberation of South Vietnam (NFLSV) and acting through party channels as the high command of the Viet Cong forces --the Liberation Army.** (See Figure III-1)

COSVN sends directives down through a traditional pyramidal party structure--a series of regional, provincial, and lower-echelon party committees, each a microcosm of the COSVN organization. The party committees of the provinces (not always identical with government provinces) appear to be the lowest echelon permitted any significant latitude in adjusting policy to local conditions.

The village party committees, and the village or hamlet party chapters and cells they control, provide the essential grass roots. The local party chapters and their component three-man cells provide the party members who lead the local guerrilla units, control the local Liberation

---

*One overt indication of Hanoi's directing role in the insurgency is the fact that the head of this party department is a major general, a vice chief of staff in the North Vietnamese Army. He also heads the government's department in charge of "reunification" affairs.

**COSVN is elaborately organized on the traditional Communist pattern. A small Current Affairs Committee--a standing committee of the principal functionaries--provides continuing direction of all political and military actions and organs. Subsections and departments under COSVN execute policies and provide a central bureaucracy. In directing the Viet Cong military forces, COSVN functions through a Military Affairs Committee, though some major Communist unit headquarters also have direct contacts with Hanoi. The relationship between COSVN political and military channels and between COSVN and Hanoi is not entirely clear. All evidence, however, points to a harmonious command system which appears to give the Communists adequate capability and flexibility for action in South Vietnam.

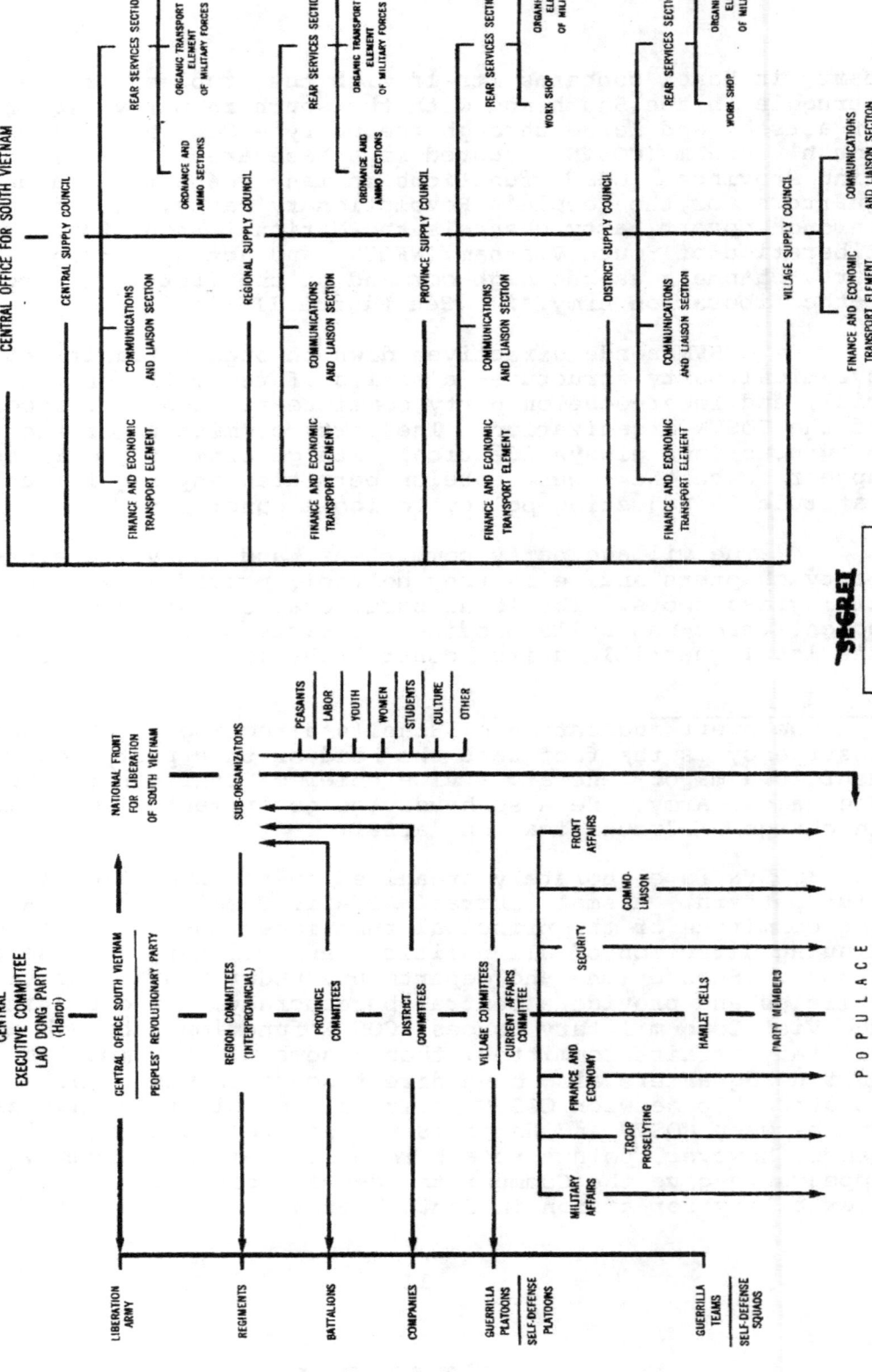

Figure III-1

Front associations, and recruit for the party, the Front or the guerrilla unit.*

If the party has established a local village or hamlet government (a village "Liberation Committee" or a hamlet "Administrative Committee" or "Board"), the party ensures adherence to its directives by planting its members in key positions or by ensuring that the local party secretary monitors village activities. In government-controlled areas and in the cities, it is the party member operating covertly who recruits and agitates and who enlists or buys agents or sympathizers.

In practice, this system has served the Communists well, giving them adequate control and flexibility. It has doubtless been strained, but certainly not critically, by the increasing demands put upon the party cadre as a result of the faster pace of the war. These strains, however, are probably already severe enough to inhibit somewhat the party's capability for expanding and consolidating control over insurgent assets in the rural area.

Within the Viet Cong armed units--regular and irregular--party members occupy most if not all key command and staff posts. Political officers are assigned to every unit. Party chapters and cells within the units seek to develop and maintain political consciousness and steadfastness within the ranks. Documents indicate that party members generally make up about one third the strength of regular units.** Party strength in the ranks of the irregular units appears to be considerably less than in the regular units.

---

*Acting as much as possible through the Front party cadre disseminate propaganda, round up local labor for Viet Cong military units operating in the area, and collect taxes and information--or monitor or control those who do. If the village or hamlet is under firm Viet Cong control, this may be done more or less overtly in the name of the party. If it is not, there may be only a few party members who must attempt all this on a covert basis.

**One document, describing the activities of the party chapters within a military unit formed in October 1965 to handle the processing and training of recruits en route
(continued on next page)

Parallel to the party at all echelons, serving as a reservoir of new members, is the party's youth auxiliary, the People's Revolutionary Youth Group, nominally made up of young men and women 16 to 25. In practice, particularly where the number of local party members is small, Youth Group members perform many of the functions of regular party members.

B. <u>Party Numerical Strength</u>

It is possible to make only a rough estimate of current party numerical strength in South Vietnam since the evidence on the subject, mainly in the form of captured Communist membership lists, is extremely fragmentary. No data of significance, for example, are available for the Mekong delta, long a Communist stronghold, where party membership presumably would be high. The problem is further complicated by the covert nature of party membership, even in some Viet Cong - controlled areas, and by the party's failure--which is attested in captured documents--to develop its organization and strength uniformly in all areas.

Fortunately, a firm figure for party membership in the South at the end of 1961 is available to use as a base for current estimates. It comes from a Communist document produced early in 1963 which stated that the party numbered 35,000 members in the South at the end of 1961. This included members in the Viet Cong armed forces. Since this document contained much other accurate information, it is probable that the membership figure is reliable.

Taking this figure as a foundation, we estimate on the basis of evidence contained in captured documents and

from the delta areas to central Vietnam, provides an illustration of the party make-up of a unit at the main force level. Out of a strength of 490, 202 were party members in 18 party chapters: 168 were Youth Group members. Of 95 men in seven of the 18 party chapters, three were members who had stayed behind in 1954, 41 had been admitted subsequently in the South, 51 were returnees from North Vietnam. No ethnic northerners were indicated, but this would not be unusual for a unit functioning in the southern part of South Vietnam. The proportion of party and Youth Group members is higher than that in a number of other units where figures are available; the higher the main force echelon, however, the greater the party membership.

III-5

prisoner interrogation reports that party membership in the South had approximately doubled by mid-1965 and that it stood at around 75,000. The documents and prisoner interrogations suggest that about 25,000 of the party members operated primarily as members of the insurgent armed forces, the bulk of them in the regular main force units.* The remainder, some 50,000, seem to have been mainly concerned with political action, including subversive operations.**

[*See footnote ** on Page III-4.] Although party members may make up as much as a third of main force strength, their numbers appear from the documents to decline drastically in the irregular units. As a general rule, the lower the echelon, the fewer the party members. A 1965 document captured in Phu Yen Province, for example, indicated that the percentage of party members in the "village guerrillas" in one district was 13%. The percentage among the "hamlet guerrillas" was 3%. On the basis of such information, we believe that party strength in the irregular forces averages less than one party member for every ten guerrillas.

In mid-1965, main force strength was estimated at approximately 55,000. If one third of these were party members, they would number about 18,000. The balance of the 25,000 estimated party members in the military, we believe, were in the irregular units. The total number of party members in the armed forces could be raised somewhat if, in fact, US estimates of irregular strength of the Communist forces are too low. If irregular strength were, for example, around 200,000, it would probably mean that there are an additional 10,000 party members in the South.

**As examples of the material from which this figure was developed, several documents which provide some fairly precise data on party strengths as of mid-1965 in Hoai Nhon District of Binh Dinh Province, and in Cu Chi District of Hau Nghia Province may be cited. Both districts can be regarded as Communist strongholds, the latter of many years standing. The documents indicate that there were approximately 590 party members in Hoai Nhon in mid-1965 working at the village or hamlet level. This was approximately one third of one percent of the population estimated by MACV at that time to be under VC control in the District. In Cu Chi District, there were approximately 900 party members of the same category as in Hoai Nhon in mid-1965. This
(continued on next page)

Captured documents indicate that even before the effects of the US military buildup were felt, party leaders were not satisfied with the party's numerical strength. Since mid-1965 they have put heavy pressure on lower echelons to recruit new members in all areas. If the quotas reflected in many captured documents were applied on a national basis, they could theoretically mean a party membership goal of some 100,000 at the end of 1965, exclusive of party members in Viet Cong regular military units.

was approximately one percent of the population estimated at the time to be under VC control in Cu Chi. If these two cases are averaged out, a figure of about seven-tenths of one percent is obtained. This fits in fairly well with the average of the other samples of party membership available. Seven tenths of one percent of the population believed under VC control in mid-1965 would be about 25,000 party members. To this must be added the party members working throughout the country at echelons above the village level, including district, province, and COSVN cadre. The documents suggest that there are approximately 25,000 such cadre (This is the approximate figure also used by MACV). It would thus appear that there were approximately 50,000 party members working mainly at political tasks in the South in mid-1965.

*One updated document of 1965 specified the quotas to be met during the year by a coastal district in Binh Dinh Province. It called for one member per 100 people in "liberated" areas, one per 150 in "disputed" areas, and one per 250 in government areas. The recruiting of women was to be stressed, to provide 20 to 30 percent of the total. Presumably this document reflected recruitment quotas handed down by the Province Party Committee and would not include the party membership in regular military units.

There are indications that in the last half of 1965, party leaders made a particular effort to speed recruitment in the cities. They directed that party members be sent from the rural areas to the cities to assist in recruiting and other tasks. One analysis indicates that the despatch of 500 to 1,000 party members to Saigon may have been contemplated. Another document from Binh Dinh Province notes a requirement to send about 5% of the party members of one rural district to the district town and to the province capital, for "activities there."

There is insufficient evidence to judge how the recruiting drive has gone. It is highly doubtful, however, that the sort of recruiting goals indicated above have been met, particularly in those rural areas where US military power is felt most. Recent documents include numerous reports of a slow pace in party development. Moreover, party doctrine calls for considerable caution in admitting members; they must be tested, checked, and investigated.

We believe that party membership in the South as of mid-1966 probably still totals no more than 100,000, including both political cadre and those in the armed forces. This would grant an increase of approximately one-third in about one year, which seems quite generous. It is interesting to compare the estimated numerical strength of the party in the South with that of the Communists in North Vietnam. In April of 1966, Ho Chi Minh declared that "presently, in the North, our party has more than 760,000 members." This is approximately double the numerical strength announced by Hanoi in 1960. It is also approximately 6% of the total estimated population of the DRV. Using a figure of 100,000 for party strength in the South at present would mean that roughly 4-6% of the population estimated under Viet Cong control are party members.

C. Numerical Strength of the Party Youth Group

Estimating the numerical strength of the party's youth group is even more difficult than that of the regular party itself. Analysis of the few captured documents bearing on the question, however, indicated rather surprisingly that the party youth in the South are fewer in number than full party members. It appears that the party youth group may be around three-fourths the size of the regular party. On this basis, youth group strength in mid-1965 might have been around 55,000 with about 15,000 to 20,000 of these in regular military and support units. Recruitment to expand the youth group was also stressed in 1965, with indications that in some areas it was to be doubled if possible.

We believe this estimate must be treated cautiously until more evidence is available, since the apparent numerical strength of the Communist youth in South Vietnam stands in sharp contrast with the situation in most Communist-controlled countries. In North Vietnam, for example, there are approximately five party youth for every full-time

III-8

party member. The reasons for the seeming scarcity of party youth in South Vietnam are not readily apparent, although we believe they are probably related primarily to the difficult conditions under which the Communists must operate. They may find it hard to encourage the growth of the party youth apparatus given the covert nature of many party operations and the need to engage available youth in military activities as rapidly as possible.

D. Numerical and Other Limitations on Party Effectiveness

There is no evidence as yet of any weakening in the resolve of the leading political cadres to continue pressing the "struggle." There are indications, however, of limitations on the total capability of the party for effecting further subversion. (Some of these--relating to morale--are discussed at greater length in ANNEX VII of this study.)

The party is stretched thin. The effort to expand testifies to this, as well as to the increasing demands placed upon it both to enable Viet Cong military expansion and to replace casualties. The running of a de facto government in some regions, and particularly the administration of the economy of areas which must provide ever-growing support for a large army, increasingly involves the party cadres in essentially logistic, bureaucratic, and administrative tasks. Local party organs are increasingly being called on to send party and Youth Group members along with the contingents of local guerrillas or conscripts destined for main force units. Party administrative staffs are pared down; documents indicate that even principal sections of the COSVN headquarters have been affected.

---

*The age brackets for party youth in South Vietnam are not entirely clear. It appears, however, that youth from the ages of about 16 to 25 are eligible. In North Vietnam, the age of the party youth was recently raised from 27 to 30 years to enable the regime to facilitate the handling of party-associated individuals in the military. It would thus appear that the buildup of armed forces in the North has disrupted the normal procedures for party youth; the same situation in the South may have a bearing on the apparent smallness of the youth apparatus there.

There are complaints in the documents about the ineptitude and inexperience of the party cadres in several areas. Undoubtedly this reflects the need to reach further down into party ranks and into affiliated organizations for local leading cadres. Party members serving primarily in political capacities are suffering casualties as a result of combat in their areas, the documents report. Moreover, there have been various directives calling for a considerable proportion of the party membership in various rural areas to join the local guerrillas. Presumably this diverts them from political tasks.

These difficulties have probably not yet developed into critical handicaps. But they are factors to which the party leaders must devote increasing attention. The situation has almost certainly placed a limit on the ultimate responsiveness and capability of the party apparatus to react to Communist needs in South Vietnam. At the present time, it is probable that any significant intensification of demands on the party political structure cannot be met as adequately as in the past.

E. The National Liberation Front

Under instructions from Hanoi, the Communists in the South put together the National Front for the Liberation of South Vietnam (NFLSV) at the end of 1960, a year before they announced, again under instructions from Hanoi, the formation of the People's Revolutionary Party.* The NFLSV was to serve as a facade for Communist political and military operations, as a lodestone to attract and organize mass support for the insurgency, and as an infrastructure for the political and economic administration of "liberated" areas (See ANNEX XII for a discussion of the political posture of the Front).

---
*The Communists claim they are only one element in the Front, albeit the "vanguard" element. However, through the selection and manipulation of the membership of the executive committees making up the NFLSV and running its ancillary regional and functional "Liberation Front" associations, the party controls the Front in classic, covert Communist fashion. The headquarters of the central committee of the Front is known to be co-located with COSVN.

On paper at least, the Front structure parallels the party structure down to the hamlet level, through a laddering of committees at every administrative echelon, each of which is dominated by its Communist members. Aligned with the Front are a number of functional "liberation" associations aimed at almost every aspect of life in South Vietnam. The most significant of these are the liberation associations for farmers, for youths, and for women.

While there was apparently some initial enthusiasm for the NFLSV, flowing from memories of the Viet Minh struggle against the French and from local grievances against the Diem government, there is no body of evidence indicating significant popular support of the Front in the areas where government control is relatively effective. In the "liberated" rural areas, however, the evidence indicates that many Front associations are operating entities at the local level.* The importance of the "liberated associations" to the Viet Cong in the rural areas is given considerable stress in captured documents.

It is doubtful that enrollment in one of the Front associations represents in many cases a willing individual commitment to the Viet Cong cause--except, probably, for those recruited covertly in government-held or nearby "disputed" areas. Nonetheless, once enrollment is obtained, it is the Communist intention to get such commitment. In "newly liberated" areas, the Communists see the organization of Front associations as a major step in the consolidation of their control, a wedge further separating the people from the government. This appears to be one of the primary tasks for party cadres in organizing a village or a hamlet after government officials or troops have left.

---

*They serve as instruments through which to garner logistic support and recruits for the insurgent armed forces. They are also useful for the political indoctrination of the populace, for the recruitment of demonstrators or troop proselytors, and for the reshaping of the economic and social patterns of the country as far as the Communists feel it is wise to go at this time. Above all, they are intended to engage and commit the populace in the over-all effort to undermine and destroy the government.

On up the line, the NFLSV apparatus does not appear to be wholly in operation even though Front Committees exist theoretically at every echelon. Instructions on policies affecting Front elements or the component liberation associations appear to pass through party channels. Since the party is the basic control mechanism, the absence of fully operating front committees at higher levels probably has no particular influence on over-all insurgent political capabilities.

F. *Numerical Strength of the Front*

The problems that are encountered in measuring the numerical strength of the Communist party in the South also complicate attempts to assess the numerical size of the NFLSV. In the case of the Front, there is the added problem of defining what constitutes Front "membership." Presumably, some Front members carry something like a membership card, and others should probably be regarded as members primarily because they at least occasionally participate in the activities of some Front association.

The only hard evidence available on the numerical strength of the Front is contained in a few captured Communist documents that list the number of "members" of various Front associations and organs in a few scattered areas outside the delta. We believe that the individuals listed in the documents include both the full, card-carrying NFLSV members, and those whom the Communists consider enrolled in the Front organs even though their participation may be passive and they may not be fully committed to NFLSV or insurgent objectives. Occasionally some of those in the latter category may participate in Front-sponsored activities.

As in the case of the Communist party, we have available a figure for Front strength in an earlier period which is probably reliable. In this instance, a captured document put the strength of the NFLSV in early 1963 at around 60,000.* By mid-1965, our extrapolations from the

---

*The Communists viewed the numerical strength of the Front at the time as inadequate. One document of the period admitted that "we still have a lot of weaknesses in organizing the masses, even though the Liberation bodies exert lots of effect on them."

captured documents listing Front membership indicate that the strength of the NFLSV had grown substantially. It appears that in mid-1965, the Communists probably counted around 500,000 male and female South Vietnamese (presumably over 16) as being enrolled in one or another of the Liberation Associations.* Probably over 80 percent of these were residents of rural areas where the Viet Cong were in firm control or where the government presence was very shaky.

Estimates at the time placed the total rural populace in Viet Cong hands at around 4 million. With acceptance of these estimates and of the standard estimate that about 65 percent of the Vietnamese population consists of persons above age 16, it would appear that the Communists had enrolled about 15 percent or so of the adults under their control in the Front or its affiliated organizations.

A number of documents of the period indicate that the Communists were exhorting their cadres to greater efforts in recruiting Front members in 1965 and were highly critical of the cadres for their failure to use these mass organizations properly "in order to lead the population."**

---

*The following are several examples of regional enrollment available from the documents: In June 1965, the party committee of one coastal district of Binh Dinh Province claimed over 21,000 liberation association members including farmers, youth, and women. This is over 12 percent of the then estimated population of the district. At the time, the district was reported to be largely under Viet Cong control or influence, except for the district town and its environs. The Liberation Women's Association in the Viet Cong province roughly equating to Quang Nam apparently claimed over 17,000 members in mid-1965. This could amount to over 10 percent of the female population in areas under Viet Cong control. The Liberation Farmers' Association in Tay Ninh Province claimed over 6,000 members in 1965. This would be about 4 percent of the total estimated population not under firm government control in mid-1965 or about 23 percent of the population estimated as being under Viet Cong control. By the end of the year, the Association reported 783 new members, an increase of over 11 percent.

**One document complained that "in many places the movement has not been organized yet; some places just have a few cells or core cadres." Cadres in an area comprising
(continued on next page)

Although hard evidence of the actual growth in Front membership during the last 12 months is still sorely lacking, it is highly doubtful that the Communists came anywhere near meeting their recruitment goals, particularly in areas of considerable military activity where there have been indications of growing reluctance on the part of the local populace to provide labor and other support for the Viet Cong. We think it probable, in view of the difficulties the Communists have encountered in enlisting popular support recently, and taking into consideration the past growth rate of the NFLSV, that its strength is still no higher than 700,000 to 750,000 at the present time.

III. **Numerical Strength of the Communist Political Apparatus in Urban Areas**

   A. **General Position**

   In the towns and cities, the Communists must operate covertly. The main targets for recruitment both into the covert ranks of the party and its youth group and into the underground of sympathizers are the lower military and civil ranks of the government, the disgruntled, the poor, the unemployed, manual laborers, students, and intellectuals. Documents suggest that the Communists expect few recruits from the practicing members of certain religious and political factions--the "reactionary" Catholics, the Cao Dai, the Hoa Hao, and the "reactionaries" among the Buddhists.

   Fragmentary documentary evidence is available on the extent of the underground in the cities. Analysis of this limited amount of material suggests that while the underground is pervasive, it still falls far short of Communist hopes--partly in terms of the calibre of those recruited.

---

the bulk of the seven provinces immediately north of Saigon were exhorted to recruit until their Liberation Associations included by the end of last year 65-85 percent (presumably of the population over 16) in liberated villages and hamlets, 35-50 percent in newly liberated villages and hamlets, and 3-10 percent in rural areas "near cities, towns and important installations." While recruiting was not to be indiscriminate--new members were to have a "good class background" and a good "struggle attitude"--the target set was 100,000 new members in the area.

III-14

Available evidence also indicates that the party has long regarded its over-all political apparatus as weak in the urban areas, and that it has steadily exhorted its cadre to greater recruiting efforts.* The added recruiting efforts have partially involved the dispatch of party members and agents from the rural areas to the cities for proselyting activities.**

B. Numerical Strength in Saigon and Environs

In the Viet Cong's Saigon - Cholon - Gia Dinh Special Zone which comprises the Saigon metropolitan area and its surrounding rural sectors, it appears from the documentary evidence that by mid-1965 some 24,000 people were controlled or primarily influenced by the Communists.*** This would have meant that slightly under one percent of the total population of the Saigon metropolitan area was committed in one extent or another to the insurgent cause.

---

*In February 1966, a captured summation of a high-level logistics conference held by COSVN revealed that the Viet Cong considered the element of their apparatus which served to procure supplies in the markets of the government-held cities inadequate. According to the summation, this operation must increase "threefold" during 1966 to meet "requirements in 1967 during the rainy season." The conference reported that "we have almost no cadre operating in the cities; the purchase of goods is mostly done through intermediaries," and it recommended strenuous recruiting efforts.

**Full analysis of the success of this effort must await further evidence, but there is already fragmentary material suggesting that it has been at least partially successful. For example, the party committee for the capital of Binh Duong Province, which borders the heavily populated Saigon - Cholon - Gia Dinh Special Zone to the north, reported at the end of 1965 that it had succeeded during the year in planting in the urban areas 99 new agents who had turned in 150 intelligence reports.

***A document of mid-1965, for example, consisted of a chart compiling the party's personnel assets in this zone, which covers an area of at least 2.5 million inhabitants. Since a marginal notation by the Communist compiler states that "several cadres have not yet reported," it cannot be considered a complete accounting. Nonetheless, it

(continued on next page)

Approximately 6,000 of these supporters were party and party youth, many of them in the Viet Cong armed forces in the rural area of the Zone. In addition to party personnel, the insurgents counted nearly 16,000 members of the Front in the Zone in early 1965.* Almost all of these individuals resided in the rural districts adjacent to Saigon.

---

may have included most of the regularly available political assets controlled by the Party committee of the Zone; it probably did not include a far smaller number reporting directly to COSVN or to Hanoi, nor does it appear to have included the very low level agents or informants used for the gathering of intelligence. As "internal" assets (presumably those living and working, either "legally" or "illegally," in the metropolitan areas) the chart lists:

```
            Party Members ------------------     305
            Youth Group --------------------     133
            "Backbone Agents" --------------     238
            Sympathizers -------------------   1,416
            "Active Agents" ----------------      48
            Liberation Association ---------     343
            Liaison Agents -----------------      22
                                               _____
                 Total                          2,505
```

Analysis of the total document suggests that of the 1,416 "sympathizers," 368 were involved in preparing or disseminating propaganda, 600 were students or teachers, 125 were government employees or were looked to for proselyting among government employees.

In addition to the party and youth members presumably operating in the Saigon metropolitan area, the document suggests that in the more rural areas of the Zone at least an additional 3,300 party and 2,300 Youth Group members were active. Of those operating in the rural areas, however, almost 2,000 were subordinate to the Military Affairs Committee of the Zone, and most of these probably were assigned to the regular military units operating in the Zone as the party's armed terrorist and "armed propaganda" muscle.

*These were broken down into nearly 9,000 liberation farmers, about 1,500 liberation youth, and about 5,500 liberation women.

The evidence is not adequate to make a numerical estimate of Viet Cong assets in the other major cities of South Vietnam. The impression conveyed by the fragmentary material, however, is that the insurgent political strength in the other cities is no stronger proportionally than in the Saigon area and its environs, except possibly in Hue.*

Available evidence clearly indicates that the party has long regarded its over-all political apparatus as weak in the urban areas.

IV. Strength of the Political Apparatus in Rural Areas: A Sample

Several captured documents of the party's district committee in Hoai Nhon, the northern coastal district of Binh Dinh Province, provide some idea of the numerical strength of the insurgent political apparatus which might have been found in a largely Viet Cong area outside the delta in mid-1965. In January 1965, this district had a population of about 170,000. Except for the immediate area of the district town, it was in Viet Cong hands. Prior to 1954, the area had been a Viet Minh stronghold. It is a largely Buddhist region, with a Catholic minority and a history of Catholic-Buddhist friction. As of mid-1965, there were 100,000 refugees in Binh Dinh, 40,000 of them Catholic.

In mid-June 1965, the District Committee reported that exclusive of any troops and cadres responsive to higher headquarters, there were slightly over 20,000 party and

---

*Although no numerical figures on political assets in Hue have been turned up, the success of the Communists in infiltrating and influencing the "struggle movement" there in April and May suggests that the Communists may have obtained a better foothold in this area than in other urban regions. There are indications, for example, that a substantial element of Communist sympathizers exists among the student body at Hue University where a variety of influences, many of them extremist in nature, operate on the students. A number of prominent politicians and teachers in Hue have been active in antigovernment, antimilitary movements in the past two years.

NFLSV members in the district.* This was nearly 13 percent of the total estimated population of the district prior to the large outflow of refugees from the area.**

Another document indicated that the party had called for a big step up in recruitment in the district by the end of the year which would, if achieved, have at least doubled party membership and more than doubled Youth Group membership. Later documents during the year, however, indicated a preoccupation with "enemy" military activities in the district and suggested that development of the party was not meeting requirements.

V. The Communist Propaganda Apparatus and Its Influence

The Communists consider their propaganda operation an extremely important part of the insurgency. They attempt to ensure that it is continuous, ubiquitous, and pervasive. It is the doctrine of the insurgency that every revolutionary, no matter what his job, is also a propaganda agent. According to the captured documents, Communist propaganda seeks to "motivate" all segments of the populace to engage in the "struggle" against the government and eventually to "rise up in a general revolution. It also seeks to widen the

---

*They were composed of:

596	party members (apparently including 136 cadre and men organic to the district party headquarters)
447	Party Youth Group members
4,033	Liberation Farmers Association members
6,143	Liberation Youths
10,869	Liberation Women
22,088	TOTAL

**The NFLSV members amounted to about 18-20% of the population estimated to be over 16 in the Province. Military units under the district committee included a regular unit of 208 men, 12 village guerrilla platoons totalling 338 members, and an additional unspecified number of smaller hamlet guerrilla units--apparently in at least 68 hamlets. Many of those in the military units were probably also members of the party, the Youth Group, or the Liberation Association.

"contradictions between various groups and the Saigon regime," to further "proselyting among the enemy's troops and officials," and to eliminate or reduce the effectiveness of the US presence by creating hatred for the Americans.

A. Propaganda Apparatus

The importance the Communists attach to their propaganda effort can be seen in the elaborate apparatus set up in the South to guide and control it. Beginning at the top with COSVN, the party structure provides for a special propaganda section within its committee structure at each echelon. These sections coordinate, plan, and produce propaganda indoctrination material as well as the curricula for the schools in Viet Cong - controlled areas.*

The propaganda disseminated by radio and through periodicals serves largely to underpin and to provide the general themes for "face-to-face" dissemination of propaganda. The documents suggest that when new policies or tactics are adopted, a "face-to-face" propaganda campaign to explain and justify them is mounted on a highly systematic basis. One directive outlining such a campaign in a district of Bien Hoa Province, for example, scheduled precisely the manner in which a new agricultural policy was to be read and explained to farmers in every hamlet. In addition to the propaganda work of local cadres, roving propaganda teams are assigned and dispatched by higher echelons as part of the campaign to "destroy" government control and presence in a hamlet or village. There are indications that local party cadres are given some latitude

---

*The Communists' "Liberation Radio" produces broadcasts of news, instruction, and entertainment from several mobile sites and from the COSVN base area. There is not enough information to tell the size of the Communist radio audience, but the majority of the residents in Communist-controlled areas probably listen at one time or another.

Under the banner of the Front, the Communists also publish a number of "revolutionary" newspapers; they claim 40 in the "liberated" areas--as well as periodicals and pamphlets for special audiences such as youth and women. Some are prepared clandestinely and are disseminated covertly in government-controlled areas. While much of the material is produced within South Vietnam, a lot of it comes from bloc sources.

in adjusting the propaganda line to take advantage of local conditions and to exploit new developments. The Communists often attempt to follow up on their propaganda by promoting "political struggle" demonstrations in the towns and villages, or by fostering the presentation of petitions or letters of grievance to government authorities.*

B. Effectiveness of the Propaganda

The US military buildup and the increased pace of military action have created significant problems for the Communists, partly because the prospects for early victory could hardly be proclaimed as convincingly following the buildup as in 1964 and early 1965.

The indoctrination line being passed down to the cadres, and thus to the people, shifted after mid-1965 from emphasis on the prospect of early victory to emphasis on the inevitability of victory. Documents suggest this line may not be going over well in those areas most affected by the war.

In their effort to ensure adequate material and manpower support for their armed forces, the Communists have found it necessary to rely increasingly on coercion rather than persuasion even in areas long under their control and to backtrack also on certain propaganda lines regarding social and economic goals. For example, in mid-1965 they found it necessary to dampen down the propaganda directed against the wealthier farmers and landlords since the production of these people and their lands had become so essential to the Communist war effort.

Assessing the effectiveness and appeal of the propaganda lines is difficult, if for no other reason than that it is often impossible to distinguish reaction to propaganda

---

*Directives in 1965 called for the organization in villages and hamlets, particularly those close to government-controlled areas, of "permanent political struggle groups" --with responsible party cadres designated as leaders. The aim, apparently, was to have on tap crowds that could mount demonstrations on short notice. Reports from lower echelons suggest, however, rather spotty success in the organization of these groups.

from reaction to other important influences of the war. It is probable that even the Communists are not certain of the real impact of their propaganda. The documents appear to reflect some dissatisfaction at the top, particularly with respect to the impact of propaganda on the population of areas not under firm Communist control. Assessments by lower echelons are sometimes equivocal, reporting favorable sentiments among the people but implying that these sentiments are not deep and that "armed propaganda" or coercion by force is essential in obtaining their cooperation.

The anti-American line of the Communists undoubtedly has had an impact. The Communists attempt to exploit parochial and nationalist sentiments, and in particular to appeal to those affected personally by the foreign military presence. They have moved peasants to demonstrate against bombings or against displacement from their homes. Through the infiltration of agitators in the northern cities this spring, they succeeded somewhat in adding to the anti-American cast of the "struggle movement" propaganda. However, there is no indication that the Communists have generally managed to evoke the "hatred" of Americans which they have attempted. A refrain seen in Communist documents, in reports to higher authority from lower echelons, is that dislike and hatred and fear of Americans is growing; at the same time, however, concern is expressed that a "fierce" anti-American spirit and an anti-American movement are slow in coming.

It is indisputable that the Communists have appealed successfully to large numbers of individuals and have obtained willing adherents to their cause; moreover, they have succeeded in engaging the aspirations of segments of particular groups--for example, of numbers of montagnards with promises of autonomy. But the lines on broad issues do not appear to have captured the enthusiastic support of any sizable section of the populace outside Communist-held areas.

The net impression of the available evidence is that Communist propaganda has served more effectively as a recruiting device and to neutralize or to assist in controlling broad elements of the populace than as a medium for awakening a sustained political movement.

VI. The Overall Effectiveness of the Political Subversive Apparatus

A. With the Rural Vietnamese

The net impression conveyed by the evidence described in previous sections on Communist political activity throughout the rural areas is that the Communists have achieved the willing cooperation and participation of considerable elements of the populace in the "liberated" areas, but they have not been able to get the willing participation of the large, unaffiliated, locally-oriented mass of the peasantry. The Communists must rely for continuing support even within their controlled areas, on a blend of indoctrination, suasion, agitation, and coercion. In the rural areas they do not now hold, but must, if they are to achieve their ultimate hopes--those surrounding Saigon, for example--the Communists have recruited numbers of adherents. Their documents indicate, however, that they find it necessary to rely primarily on "armed propaganda" and guerrilla warfare to achieve significant influence.

Communist reports indicate an increasing concern over inability to counter effectively the impact of large-scale allied military operations on the populace. In areas where such operations have been mounted, there appears to be increasing popular reluctance to cooperate with, contribute to, or shelter the insurgent armed forces. The documents speak of growing difficulties in recruiting the types of people needed for military and labor-support units, particularly those units which leave their native villages or districts. Coercion must increasingly be applied where propaganda suasion fails.

Lower echelons report that even some insurgent political cadres are fleeing to safe places and staying "politically inactive." Increasing concern is also registered in the documents over the flight of refugees to government-controlled areas, over the government pacification programs, and over government counter-propaganda. Lower echelons report that political organization and proselyting are slow.

It is impossible as yet to judge the extent to which these difficulties are hurting the Communist war effort, or to tell whether they will grow to the point where they will largely block further Communist progress in subverting the rural populace through political action. It seems clear, however, that Communist progress through political action in the rural areas since early 1965 has slowed significantly, at least in these areas affected by allied military operations. (Annex III contains additional discussion of the status of the rural populace under Viet Cong control.)

It is possible to make a rough estimate--on the basis of a data base which is admittedly incomplete--of the total percentage of the populace in South Vietnam which is under the direct control of the Vietnamese Communists. It would appear that at least 3.5 million persons, or about 21 percent of the total population of 16 million (the latest US Government estimate of the total population of South Vietnam), fall into this category.*

Four million other people reside in areas where it is impossible to tell the exact degree of control or influence exercised by either the Viet Cong or the Saigon Government. This group, approximately 25 percent of the population, should probably be regarded as an essentially uncommitted group in that it does not give allegiance by choice either to the government in Saigon or to the Viet Cong. The balance of the population, some 8.6 million, are considered firmly under government control.** This government-controlled segment of the population, which includes 3.2 million urban dwellers and one million refugees, comprises some 54 percent of the total.

Current reporting indicates that about 75 percent of South Vietnam's 66,000 square miles of territory is not

---

*For the purpose here, an area and its inhabitants are considered to be under the direct control of the Communists wherever the Communists are in a position of such unchallenged domination that they have been able to establish at least a semi-overt insurgent governmental apparatus.

**They are, for example, given relatively effective protection by government forces and are relatively responsive to the day to day dictates of government officers who reside and move freely throughout these areas.

effectively or lastingly controlled by either the Communists or the government. Much of this area is wasteland, uninhabited or sparsely settled. The Communists are able to operate at will throughout the area, but probably do not try to exercise exclusive domination except where they have base areas.

The 54 percent of the population which the Saigon government controls probably occupies not more than 12 to 15 percent of the total land area of the country. The portion of the population under direct Viet Cong control is situated on what is probably only about 7 to 10 percent of the total land area. On a day-to-day basis, then, the major populated areas of contention between the allies and the Communists constitute only about one-quarter of the land area of South Vietnam. (See figure III-2)

B. <u>In the Cities: Saigon in Particular</u>

The Communists realize that it is in the cities that the greatest gains need be made if the armed forces and the government are to be riddled from within. Of the cities, Saigon is by far the most important. Analysis of captured documents and other intelligence information relating to Saigon suggests that the Communists may feel that they have succeeded in winning the sympathies of a not inconsiderable segment of the city dwellers. The information suggests further, however, that the Communists do not consider this sympathy--or their influence in the cities generally--as sufficient to ensure effective support for any major overt action on their part. It is certainly clear that they do not believe they have sufficient covert assets within Saigon.

The Communists appear to see their efforts in the cities as proceeding along two mutually supporting paths-- one of organization and preparation for the day when the conditions they seek will arise, and one of terrorism and agitation to help create those conditions. In September 1965, the party's Current Affairs Committee for the capital zone claimed that terrorist attacks had "aroused enthusiasm among the people" and had frightened government personnel. The result according to the document, was that the "people, especially the laborers, clearly sympathize with the Revolution" and "enthusiastically support and cover our activities...". They will be with us, the document claimed, when the general uprising occurs.

SOUTH VIETNAM
POPULATION AND AREA CONTROL

Figure III-2

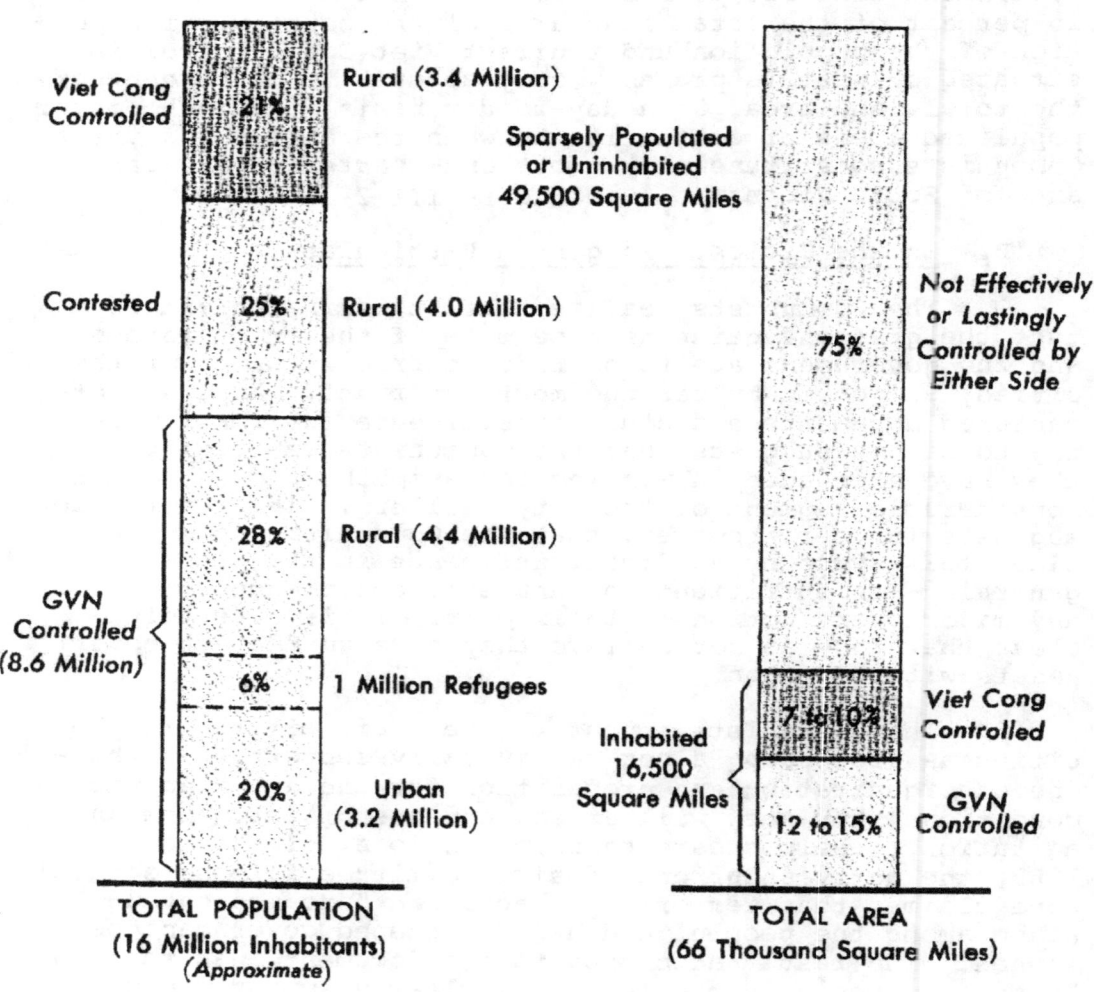

Nevertheless, the document admitted that the Communists were not ready in September 1965 for any major action in Saigon. It recommended that we "draft plans" for seizing control of slums in the capital and for promoting "our political movement through military activities."*

The captured documents also register suspicion of certain groups in the cities, indicating they should be watched, exploited if possible, but not viewed as major sources of support. Such groups include the Buddhists, other political parties--"both the progressive ones and the counterrevolutionary ones"--and the "bourgeois landlords, both progressive and revolutionary."**

On balance, the evidence so far developed indicates that the Buddhist-backed dissidence and the "confrontations" in the cities this spring were not created or controlled by the Communists, but that the Communists did move to exploit them and to manipulate them as much as they could through infiltration. There is evidence, for example, that the leadership of the "struggle" movement in the cities was infiltrated by Communists. There was apparently no overt Communist military move in direct support of the dissidents, however. The Communists probably decided that the time for a major military move was not right, since the over-all conditions were not yet favorable and their own influence and support in the cities was too weak.

---

*A subsequent document, a notebook recording what appeared to constitute the views of the party leaders for the Saigon area at the end of 1965, claimed further progress in gaining popular sympathy, but again admitted weakness in capability. It claimed that the presence of US troops had helped block the disruption of the "antirevolutionary" forces in Saigon, but asserted that agents were still limited, and that their low efficiency was leading to detection and arrest.

**Another directive of the Saigon area's Current Affairs Committee spoke critically of the "intellectual bourgeoisie." It noted that "a progressive faction has been joining the Front and is going to be more inclined toward the Revolution," but "the majority is nonaligned and adopts the attitude of wait-and-see," while "a small faction becomes more and more overtly reactionary by acting as imperialists' lackeys...."

~~TOP SECRET~~

ANNEX IV

THE GROUND WAR IN SOUTH VIETNAM

~~TOP SECRET~~

ANNEX IV

THE GROUND WAR IN SOUTH VIETNAM

I. The Build-Up of Forces

The course of the ground war in South Vietnam is marked by the extent to which, in the conventional military sense, it has become increasingly a confrontation between third country forces. This situation reflects the already heavy commitment of indigenous manpower resources to the war effort. The heavy casualties sustained by local Communist forces (VC) are putting an increasing strain on their ability to mobilize additional military manpower. The GVN has committed substantial manpower resources to pacification programs and internal security and police programs. Over half of the GVN military forces are committed to these counter-insurgency programs. The GVN potential for expansion of its military forces, which would be limited under the best of circumstances, is restrained further by the political unrest in the GVN and the high desertion rate in the ARVN.

Since mid-1965, NVA troops in South Vietnam have increased by nearly 37,000. They now total 38,000 of about 38 percent of the total VC/NVA main force. By the end of 1966, an estimated 60,000 NVA troops will account for nearly half of the VC/NVA main force. By mid-1967 an estimated 75,000 NVA troops will account for 55 percent of main force strength. US/Third Nation* forces at the end of 1964 totaled only 25,000 troops or 9 percent of Allied regular troop strength. In mid-1966 there were 300,000 US/Third Nation troops or 49 percent of total strength. Projected deployments indicate that US/Third Nation forces will account for 470,000 troops or 59 percent of the regular Allied Army strength in South Vietnam by mid-1967.

Regular Free World forces now outnumber the total estimated Communist force by 5 to 1, and hold a 6 to 1 margin

---
*Here and throughout the remainder of the text, South Korean, Australian and New Zealand Forces are referred to as "Third Nation" Forces.

over the VC/NVA main force units. Overwhelming air and artillery support, coupled with considerable troop mobility and naval participation also add significantly to the preponderance of Allied military strength.

There is a sharp distinction between Communist and Allied forces in the number of support troops needed to back up tactical combat troops. Only about one-fifth of the total Allied Army and Marine Corps troops are committed to engaging and destroying the enemy in offensive operations. Thus of a force in June 1966 totaling slightly over 218,000 Army and Marine Corps ground forces only 44,200 represented troops in maneuver battalions. Over 157,000 troops were involved in indirect combat, logistics, construction engineering, security and other support tasks and some 16,400 troops are in artillery battalions. The Communist forces, on the other hand, have to commit only 18,000 troops or a little over 15 percent of their regular forces to combat support, compared to over 80 percent for the Allied forces.

When the relative build up of opposing forces is looked at in this manner the troop strength ratios change dramatically. The troop strength ratio of Allied maneuver battalions becomes nearly 1:1 rather than 6:1. In the II and IV Corps area the ratio is in the favor of the Communists. The projections of estimated Communist main force strength and Allied troop strength in maneuver battalions in mid-1967 indicate a troop strength ratio which gives the over-all strength advantage to the Communists. The advantage is offset, of course, by the air, artillery and naval support of the Allied forces and their highly developed mobility. Nevertheless, the Communist build up, particularly of NVA forces, shows a determination to commit whatever forces are necessary to match the Allied build up and to extend the war as long as possible. Even if the Communists admit that they cannot win a conventional military victory in South Vietnam they may still calculate that a long extended war with increasing US casualties may eventually break down US will and determination to persevere.

II. <u>Casualties</u>

The toll in human lives is, however, presenting an increasingly high cost to the Communist forces. The heavy casualties sustained by VC forces has already stabilized the extent to which they can commit troops and has forced them to rely more heavily on NVA replacements. Total Communist losses--killed in action, captured, seriously wounded and deserters--ranged from an estimated 80,000 - 90,000 during 1965. During 1966 we estimate that these losses may range from 105,000 - 120,000 and from 65,000 - 75,000 for the first six months of 1967 if the current rates of combat are maintained and projected troop strengths are realized. We estimate that some 25,000 - 30,000 of the losses during 1966 will be North Vietnamese; an additional 25,000 - 30,000 North Vietnamese will be lost during the first half of 1967. The bulk of these losses will result from battle deaths and serious wounds. Local Communists will sustain estimated losses of from 80,000 - 90,000 during 1966 and an additional 40,000 - 45,000 during the first half of 1967. About two-thirds of local Communist losses will result from battle deaths and serious wounds. The remainder will be accounted for by captives and deserters.

In terms of the number killed in action on the battlefield, the Allied forces will continue to maintain an advantage. We estimate that about 48,000 Communists will be killed during 1966 and an additional 30,000 during the first six months of 1967 compared to 16,000 Free World soldiers estimated to be killed during 1966 (6,000 US and Third Nation, 10,000 ARVN) and an additional 9,000 that will probably be killed during the first six months of 1967.

Reports on battle fatalities among Communist forces indicate they have increased from slightly under 2,000 a month during the first six months of 1965 to about 3,900 each month during the second half of the year and 4,000 a month during January-May 1966.

On the basis of very limited data we estimate that the number of Communist troops seriously wounded and hence effectively lost has increased from about 1,600 - 2,500 a month in 1965 to from 2,000 - 3,200 a month in 1966. Our estimates indicate that the numbers of Communist personnel captured during 1965 and 1966 do not vary much, ranging from 6,300 in 1965 to an estimated 7,000 in 1966.

The Allied forces have achieved better than a 3 to 1 kill ratio over the enemy. Our data on VC/NVA forces killed in action show a sharp change in the relative shares accounted for by GVN forces and US/Third Nation forces. In the last six months of 1965, US/Third Nation forces accounted for 23 percent of total Communists killed in action. In the first five months of 1966, however, US/Third Nation forces accounted for 56 percent of total Communists killed in action.

The rising casualty rates among Communist forces have had no detectable influence on North Vietnam's desire to continue the war in the South. The enemy continues to buildup his forces in the South, and the Communist forces are performing in battle as well today as they were in 1964 and 1965. The manpower drain on North Vietnam, in numbers alone, has not yet reached a burdensome level. Although the VC units have borne most of the casualties to date and are squeezed for manpower, Hanoi seems willing to increase its commitment. The drain on manpower could, however, become more critical as the casualty rates in the South and the competing demands for more manpower in the North increase. An increase in casualty rates in the South substantially higher than those already estimated through mid-1967 would require an Allied commitment of maneuver battalions substantially greater than that indicated in current deployment programs.

APPENDIX A

THE GROUND WAR IN SOUTH VIETNAM

I. General Troop Strength

　A.　U.S. and Third Nation

　　　1.　Forces - General

　　　　　The U.S. military commitment in South Vietnam, along with that of South Korea, Australia, and New Zealand, has grown from some 25,000 troops at the end of 1964 to approximately 300,000 troops at the end of June 1966. Projected troop strengths indicate that approximately 470,000 U.S./Third Nation forces will be stationed in South Vietnam by mid-1967. (See Table IV-1)

　　　　　In both an absolute and relative sense U.S./Third Nation troop strength in South Vietnam has grown more rapidly since 1964, than has the corresponding buildup in the South Vietnamese regular forces (See Table IV-2). U.S./Third Nation forces represented 9 percent of total Allied regular troop strength in 1964, 41 percent in 1965, and 49 percent in mid-1966. They will account for 59 percent of the planned regular Allied forces in South Vietnam by June 1967.

　　　2.　Deployment

　　　　　U.S./Third Nation ground forces in South Vietnam are predominantly deployed in the I, II, and III Corps areas, with South Vietnamese troops, as of August 1966, maintaining complete military responsibility in the Capital Military Region (Saigon) and IV Corps areas. United States Marines are stationed at Da Nang, Chu Lai and Phu Bai in the I Corps area. Field Force I, with headquarters at Nha Trang (II Corps area), contains the 1st Calvary Division, elements of the 25th Infantry and 101 Airborne Division, ROK forces, and the 5th Special Group. Field Force II, with headquarters at Cu Chi (III Corps area), contains the 1st Infantry Division, elements of the 25th Division, 173 Airborne Brigade, and Australian and New Zealand Units (See Figure IV-1).

　B.　South Vietnam

　　　1.　Forces - General

　　　　　At the end of June 1966, the Republic of South Vietnam had some 700,000 people under arms (See Table IV-3).

Table IV-1

South Vietnam: Actual and Projected Growth
of Total US/Third Nation Forces
December 1964 - June 1967

Thousands

	Dec 1964	Jul 1965	Dec 1965	Jun 1966	Dec 1966	Jun 1967
United States						
Army	15.0	40.0	120.0	160.0	240.0	275.0
Marines	1.0	25.0	40.0	50.0	70.0	70.0
Air Force	7.0	10.0	20.0	40.0	50.0	50.0
Navy and Coast Guard	1.0	5.0	10.0	20.0	25.0	30.0
Subtotal	24.0	80.0	190.0	270.0	385.0	425.0
Third Nation	1.0	5.0	20.0	30.0	45.0	45.0
Total	25.0	85.0	210.0	300.0	430.0	470.0

Table IV-2

South Vietnam: Comparative Actual and Projected Regular Allied Troop Strength
December 1964 - June 1967

(In thousands)*

	1964**	1965	June 1966	December 1966	June 1967
GVN***	250.0	300.0	310.0	320.0	325
U.S. and Third Nation	25.0	210.0	300	430.0	470
Total	275.0	510.0	610.0	750.0	795
U.S. and Third Nation as Percent of Total	9	41	49	57	59

* Rounded to the nearest 5 thousand.
** End of year figures except for June 1966 and June 1967.
*** Excludes some 383 thousand quasi-military/security personnel.

Table IV-3

Total South Vietnamese Armed Strength
December 1964 - June 1967

(In thousands)*

	1964**	1965	1966	1967
South Vietnamese Forces				
Regular Military	250.0	300.0	310.0	325.0
Regional	95.0	130.0	140.0	140.0
CIDG	20.0	30.0	30.0	30.0
Popular	170.0	135.0	140.0	140.0
Armed Combat Youth	45.0	40.0	25.0	25.0
National Police	30.0	50.0	55.0	55.0
Total	610.0	685.0	700.0	715.0

* Rounded to nearest 5 thousand.
** End of year strength with exception of June 1966 and June 1967.

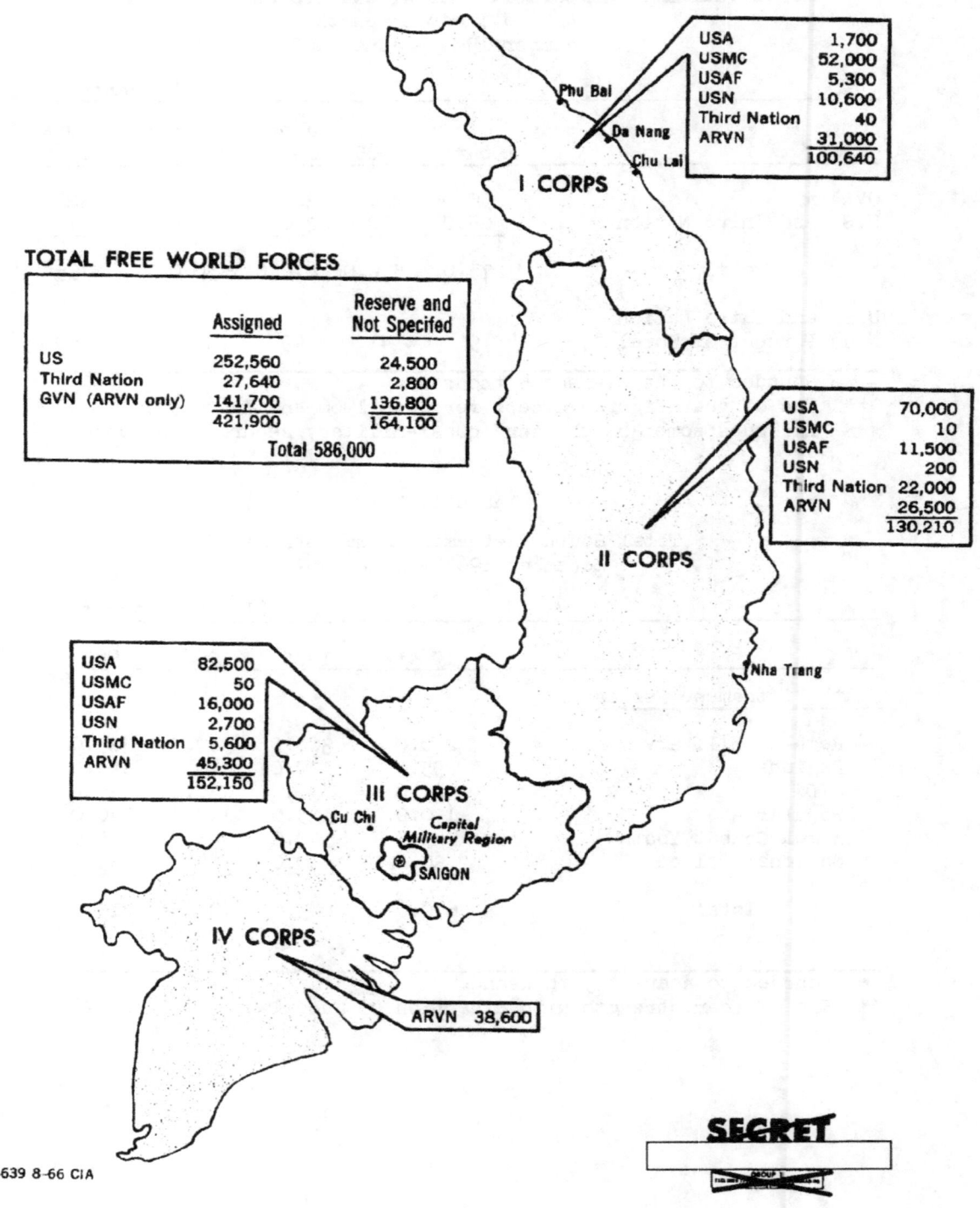

Figure IV-1

SOUTH VIETNAM: MAJOR ALLIED DEPLOYMENTS OF REGULAR TROOPS, BY CORPS, MID-1966

This figure, however, does not accurately reflect the regular South Vietnamese military strength. Only about 45 percent of the total South Vietnamese armed strength is committed to conventional military operations.

The South Vietnamese have responsibility for the bulk of the pacification program and measures to eliminate or neutralize the Viet Cong infrastructure. These programs require the commitment of some 350,000 men in quasi-military, self-defense and national police units. The South Vietnamese regular military force consists of 275,000 army troops, 15,000 air force and 20,000 navy/marine forces.

Since 1964, the regular South Vietnamese military force has increased by some 60,000 men or by about 25 percent. Projected deployments indicate that the regular forces are to be increased by some 10,000-15,000 men, bringing total strength up to 320,000-325,000 men by June 1967.

2. **Major Deployments**

The mid-1966 South Vietnamese Army Order of Battle is presented in Table IV-4 below:

Table IV-4

Major South Vietnamese Ground Force Deployments by Corps Area, Mid-1966

Combat Units	Assigned Strength
I Corps	31,000
II Corps	26,500
III Corps	43,000
IV Corps	38,500
Capital Military Region	2,000
General Reserve	8,500
Support Units and Miscellaneous	128,000
Total	277,500*

*Includes five GVN Marine Battalions with a total strength of 4,000 men. Approximately 21 percent of the combat strength is allocated to I Corps, 18 percent to II Corps, 29 percent to III Corps, 25 percent to IV Corps and 7 percent to reserves and the Capital Military Region.

C. VC/NVA

1. Forces - General

The composition and size of the Communist force in South Vietnam has changed considerably since 1964. The total enemy strength has grown from approximately 127,000 in 1964, to 269,000 by mid-1966, and we estimate that it may reach 310,000 by June 1967. Nearly 37,000 regular North Vietnamese Army troops have joined enemy ranks in South Vietnam since mid-1965. The continued infiltration of North Vietnamese troops has been the primary source of increased Communist troop strength in South Vietnam. The comparative and future estimated growth in enemy forces is illustrated in Table IV-5 below:

Table IV-5

South Vietnam: Estimated NVA/VC Forces,
December 1964 - Mid-1967

(In thousands)

	1964*	1965	1966*	December 1966	June 1967
North Vietnam	---	11.0	38.0	60.0	75.0
VC Main Force	34.0	59.0	63.0	65.0	65.0
Irregulars**	93.0	110.0	110.0	110.0	110.0
Political Cadre, Combat Support	---	57.0	58.0	60.0	60.0
Total Enemy	127.0	237.0	269.0	295.0	310.0

*End of year strengths with exception of June 1966.
**These are the currently accepted irregular figures but, as indicated in the Summary Discussion, these figures are being re-examined and may be subject to upward revision.

2. Deployment

Current North Vietnamese troop strength is primarily centered in II Corps area, and to a much lesser extent in I and III Corps area. No appreciable numbers of NVA troops are known to be in IV Corps. VC main force strength is heavily concentrated in III and IV areas and to a lesser extent in II and I Corps areas. A more detailed deployment is shown in Table IV-6 below:

Table IV-6

South Vietnam: Estimated Strength, Composition and Deployment of NVA/VC Main Force Elements by Corps Area,* Mid-1966

	NVA	VC	Total
I Corps	10,000	8,800	18,800
II Corps	23,500	12,500	36,000
III Corps	4,500	23,300	27,800
IV Corps	Neg	18,400	18,400
Total	38,000	63,000	101,000

*Excludes some 170,000 irregulars, political cadre and combat support forces. Combat support forces are about 15 percent of regular forces strength.

II. Analysis of Troop Strength

A. General

During the past year, Allied strength has grown to the point where regular Free World forces now outnumber the total estimated Communist force by 5 to 1, and hold a 6 to 1 margin over the NVA/VC main force units. (See Figure IV-2). Overwhelming air and artillery support, coupled with extremely high troop mobility also add to the effectiveness of Allied military strength.

Recently both the Allies and Communists have drawn heavily on outside help (Figures IV-3 and IV-4) to build up military forces in the South. In a military sense, the

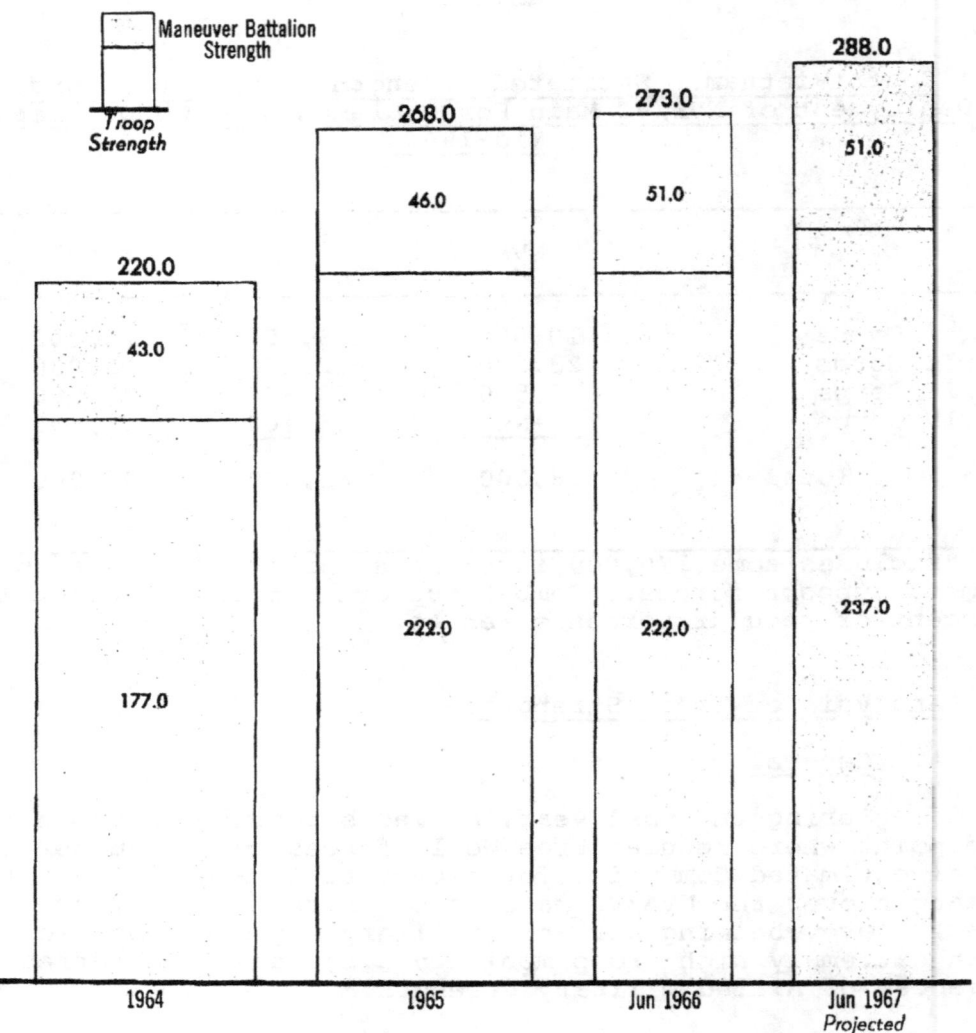

Figure IV-6

APPROXIMATE COMPOSITION OF ARVN MANEUVER BATTALION STRENGTH TO TOTAL ARVN TROOP STRENGTH
1964 - June 1967
(Thousands)

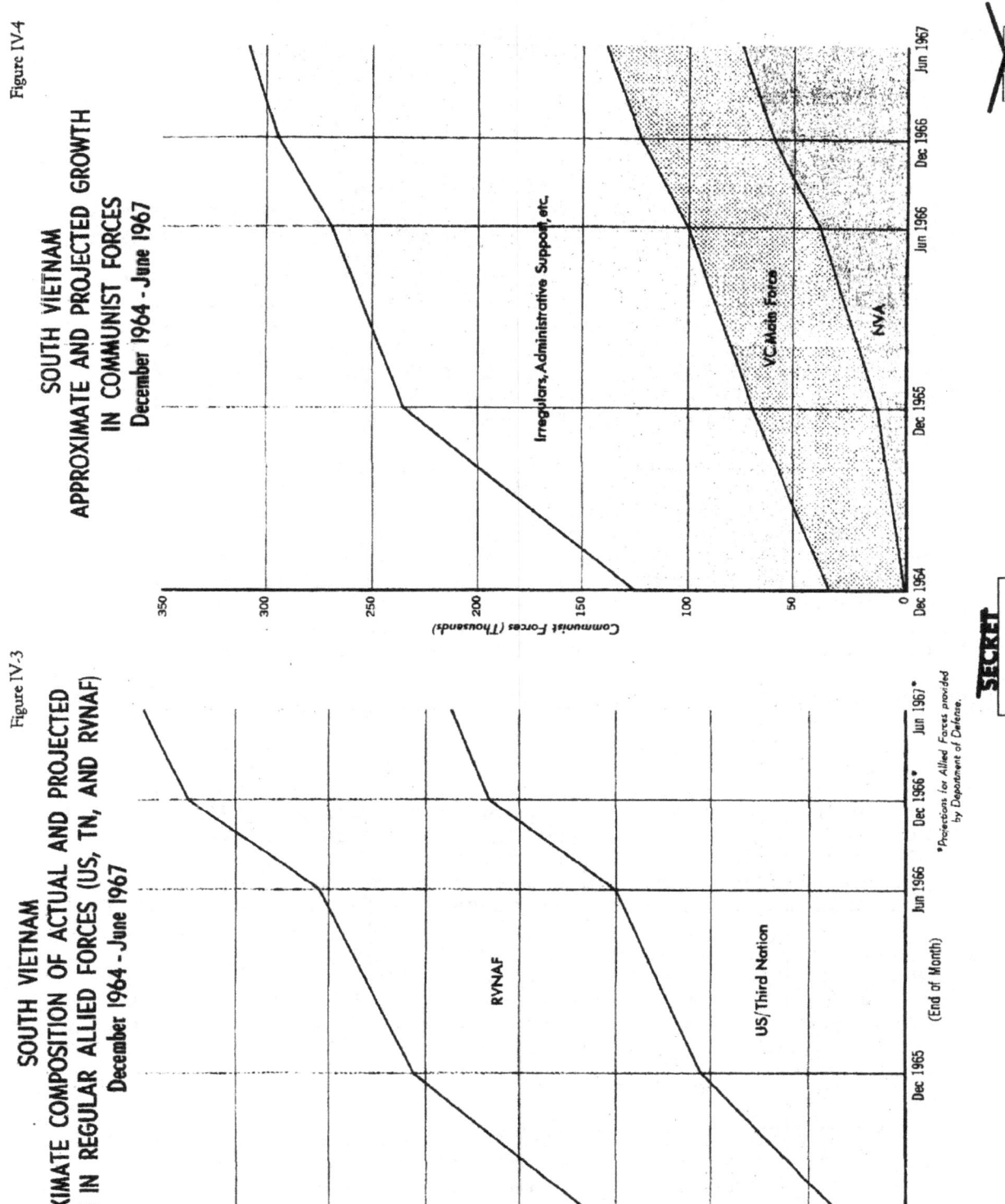

Figure IV-3. SOUTH VIETNAM — APPROXIMATE COMPOSITION OF ACTUAL AND PROJECTED GROWTH IN REGULAR ALLIED FORCES (US, TN, AND RVNAF), December 1964 - June 1967

Figure IV-4. SOUTH VIETNAM — APPROXIMATE AND PROJECTED GROWTH IN COMMUNIST FORCES, December 1964 - June 1967

war in South Vietnam is rapidly developing into a confrontation between the United States and North Vietnam with South Vietnamese forces on both sides playing relatively reduced roles. In spite of rapidly growing Allied troop strength and resulting heavy enemy losses, North Vietnam continues to send regular troops south in increasing numbers. The Vietnamese Communists apparently recognize the impossibility of a classic military solution, but may hope to attain their objectives by unconventional means and apparently intend to extend the war as long as possible in the hope of wearing down US will to see the war through.

An early and successful conclusion to the military struggle rests, therefore, with the ability of Allied forces to hunt down and destroy the enemy on his own ground. It is in this context that the numerical superiority in the ratios of Allied to Communist strength became less impressive. More meaningful relationships and trends in analyzing the present and future course of the ground war depend on the actual number of Allied troops theoretically capable of engaging and destroying the enemy in offensive operations.

B. Critical Troop Ratios

1. Assumptions

Total Allied troop strength in South Vietnam presently stands at some 610,000 men. Current NVA/VC main force strength is estimated to be about 100,000 troops.* At first glance it would appear that Allied regular forces presently enjoy a 6:1 numerical superiority over the NVA/VC main force. In a practical sense, however, this is not the case. Western troops and their South Korean and Vietnamese Allies require considerable numbers of support troops to maintain offensive combat units in the field. Since the scale of combat in South Vietnam at the present time is largely dependent on the level of Allied initiated offensive operations, it seems logical to exclude Allied support

---

*Irregular forces, political cadres and combat support forces are excluded from Communist troop strength in this analysis because of their limited role in conventional warfare.

troops in deriving meaningful ratios of actual Communist/ Allied battlefield strength. The combat strength of the NVA/VC main force is taken at current estimated full strength--about 100,000 men. Allied combat strength is defined to include the number of troops assigned to maneuver battalions--those troops who initiate offensive ground actions and conceptually come into direct contact with the enemy. The critical troop ratio is defined as NVA/VC main force/Allied maneuver battalion strength.

2. Offensive Combat Strength

a. U. S./Third Nation

For purposes of this analysis only ground troops are considered--nearly 60,000 men in the Air Force and Navy are excluded from the analysis. (See Table IV-7). Approximately 20 percent of the total U. S. Army and Marine Corps strength in South Vietnam is committed to maneuver battalions. (See Figure IV-5). An additional 7 percent is assigned to artillery battalions that primarily provide combat support to the maneuver battalions.* The remaining 73 percent of the Army and Marine Corps personnel perform supply, construction, engineering, security, and related support tasks. The percent of maneuver battalion strength to total Third Nation troop strength is considerably higher because these troops are largely supported by US service units. The deployment by Corps area and service of US/Third Nation maneuver battalions is presented in Table IV-8. As of June 1966, 31 percent of US/Third Nation maneuver battalion strength was located in I Corps, 41 percent in II Corps, and 28 percent in III Corps. Projected deployments for June 1967 indicate that some 78,600 US/Third Nation troops in maneuver battalions will be distributed in the following manner: I Corps 23 percent, II Corps 49 percent, and III Corps 28 Percent.

b. South Vietnam

In the analysis of the critical troop ratios only the South Vietnamese Army is given consideration--some

---

*Artillery battalions are excluded from the critical ratio due to the manner in which they are employed in combat.

Table IV-7

South Vietnam: Actual and Projected Deployment of US/Third Nation Forces, by Function
July 1965 – June 1967

(In Thousands)

	1965						1966							Dec 1966	Jun 1967
	Jul	Aug	Sep	Oct	Nov	Dec	Jan	Feb	Mar	Apr	May	Jun			
Combat and Direct Combat Support															
Maneuver Battalions															
USMC	9.0	10.0	12.0	12.0	12.0	12.0	13.0	14.0	15.0	16.0	17.0	17.0	18.0	18.0
USA	6.4	10.4	14.4	16.0	17.6	19.2	24.0	24.0	24.0	26.4	26.4	27.2	39.2	46.4
TN	.8	.8	.8	7.1	7.1	7.1	7.1	7.1	7.1	9.2	10.0	10.0	14.2	14.2
Artillery*															
USMC	2.6	2.6	3.6	3.6	3.6	3.6	4.0	4.6	4.8	4.8	5.4	5.4	5.6	5.6
USA	1.7	1.7	3.7	3.7	6.7	8.7	9.7	9.7	10.2	10.7	10.7	11.0	18.5	21.5
Subtotal	20.5	25.5	34.5	42.4	47.0	50.6	57.8	59.4	61.1	67.1	69.5	70.6	95.5	105.7
Construction, Engineering, Security, Support, etc.**															
USMC	13.9	21.6	20.8	21.2	22.2	22.6	21.6	20.8	28.9	29.0	29.8	31.2	45.4	46.4
USA	31.6	36.0	58.1	73.0	80.2	88.9	89.0	95.3	103.2	111.6	117.1	138.8	190.3	219.1
USAF	11.6	12.7	13.6	15.2	18.3	20.6	25.3	28.7	32.3	33.0	33.9	38.1	50.0	50.0
USN***	4.6	5.3	6.0	8.5	8.8	8.7	9.8	10.5	12.7	13.8	14.8	17.8	24.0	24.0
Subtotal	61.7	75.6	98.5	117.9	129.5	140.8	145.7	155.3	177.1	187.4	195.6	225.9	309.7	339.5
Total	82.2	101.1	133.0	160.3	176.5	191.4	203.5	214.7	238.2	254.5	265.1	296.5	405.2	445.2

* Excludes antiaircraft and missile units, unknown TN artillery included in combat and direct combat support.
** Includes USAF and USN, although recognized that these forces perform indirect combat support roles.
*** Includes Coast Guard.

Table IV-7

South Vietnam: Actual and Projected Deployment of US/Third Nation Forces, by Function
July 1965 - June 1967

(In Thousands)

	1965						1966						Dec 1966	Jun 1967
	Jul	Aug	Sep	Oct	Nov	Dec	Jan	Feb	Mar	Apr	May	Jun		
Combat and Direct Combat Support														
Maneuver Battalions														
USMC	9.0	10.0	12.0	12.0	12.0	12.0	13.0	14.0	15.0	16.0	17.0	17.0	18.0	18.0
USA	6.4	10.4	14.4	16.0	17.6	19.2	24.0	24.0	24.0	26.4	26.4	27.2	39.2	46.4
TN	.8	.8	.8	7.1	7.1	7.1	7.1	7.1	7.1	9.2	10.0	10.0	14.2	14.2
Artillery*														
USMC	2.6	2.6	3.6	3.6	3.6	3.6	4.0	4.6	4.8	4.8	5.4	5.4	5.6	5.6
USA	1.7	1.7	3.7	3.7	6.7	8.7	9.7	9.7	10.2	10.7	10.7	11.0	18.5	21.5
Subtotal	20.5	25.5	34.5	42.4	47.0	50.6	57.8	59.4	61.1	67.1	69.5	70.6	95.5	105.7
Construction, Engineering, Security, Support, etc**														
USMC	13.9	21.6	20.8	21.2	22.2	22.6	21.6	20.8	28.9	29.0	29.8	31.2	45.4	46.4
USA	31.6	36.0	58.1	73.0	80.2	88.9	89.0	95.3	103.2	111.6	117.1	138.8	190.3	219.1
USAF	11.6	12.7	13.6	15.2	18.3	20.6	25.3	28.7	32.3	33.0	33.9	38.1	50.0	50.0
USN***	4.6	5.3	6.0	8.5	8.8	8.7	9.8	10.5	12.7	13.8	14.8	17.8	24.0	24.0
Subtotal	61.7	75.6	98.5	117.9	129.5	140.8	145.7	155.3	177.1	187.4	195.6	225.9	309.7	339.5
Total	82.2	101.1	133.0	160.3	176.5	191.4	203.5	214.7	238.2	254.5	265.1	296.5	405.2	445.2

* Excludes antiaircraft and missile units, unknown TN artillery included in combat and direct combat support.
** Includes USAF and USN, although recognized that these forces perform indirect combat support roles.
*** Includes Coast Guard.

Figure IV-5

COMPOSITION OF US MANEUVER BATTALION AND ARTILLERY BATTALION STRENGTH*
TO TOTAL US ARMY AND USMC TROOP STRENGTH
July 1965 - June 1967
(Thousands)

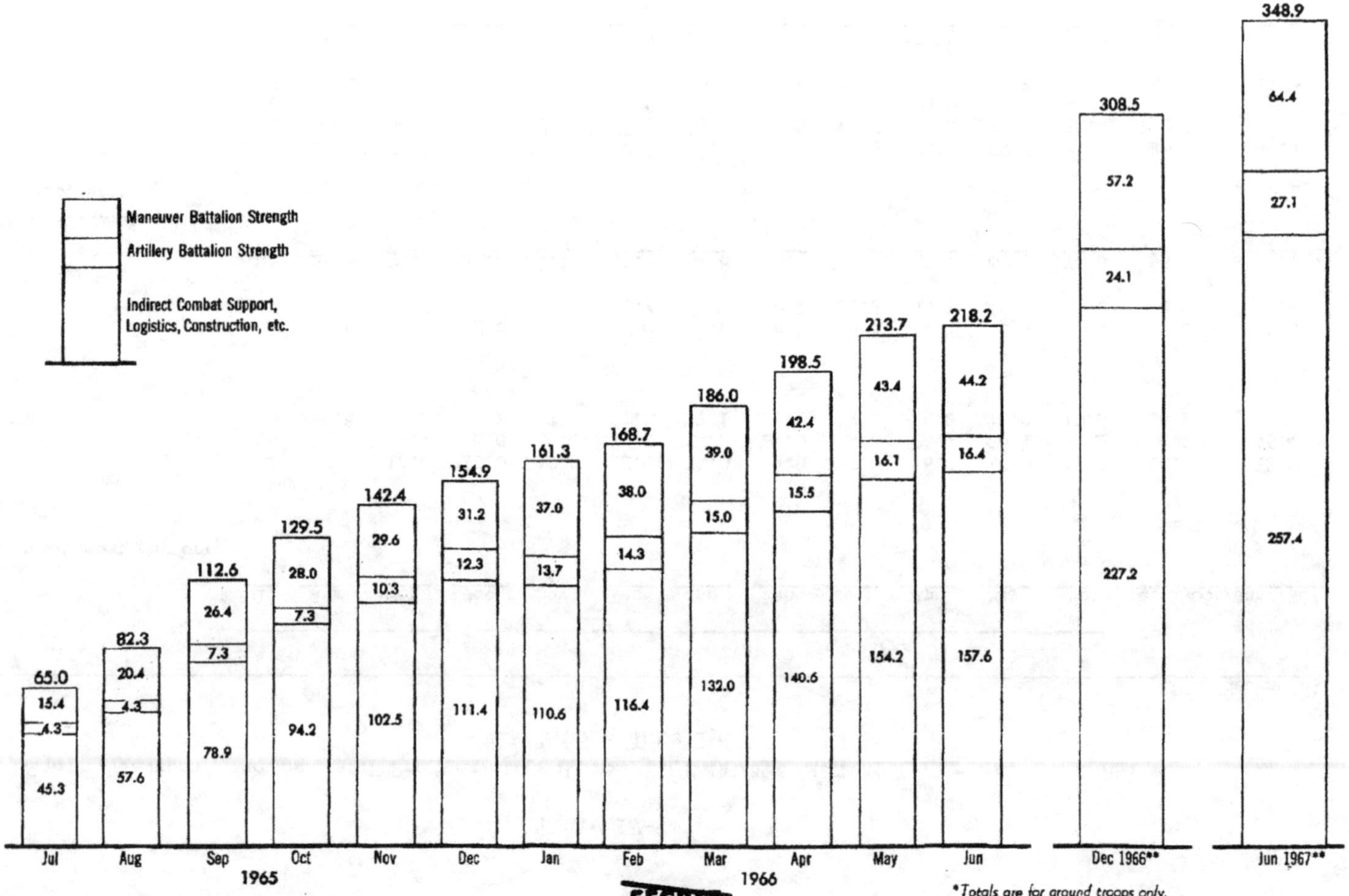

Month	Total	Maneuver Battalion Strength	Artillery Battalion Strength	Indirect Combat Support, Logistics, Construction, etc.
Jul 1965	65.0	15.4	4.3	45.3
Aug	82.3	20.4	4.3	57.6
Sep 1965	112.6	26.4	7.3	78.9
Oct	129.5	28.0	7.3	94.2
Nov	142.4	29.6	10.3	102.5
Dec	154.9	31.2	12.3	111.4
Jan	161.3	37.0	13.7	110.6
Feb	168.7	38.0	14.3	116.4
Mar 1966	186.0	39.0	15.0	132.0
Apr	198.5	42.4	15.5	140.6
May	213.7	43.4	16.1	154.2
Jun	218.2	44.2	16.4	157.6
Dec 1966**	308.5	57.2	24.1	227.2
Jun 1967**	348.9	64.4	27.1	257.4

*Totals are for ground troops only.
**Projections provided by the Department of Defense.

35,000 men in the Air Force, Navy and Marines are excluded. Approximately 16 percent of the total South Vietnamese Army strength is committed to maneuver battalions. (See Figure IV-6). As of June 1966, 21 percent of ARVN maneuver battalion strength was located in I Corps, 21 percent in II Corps, 30 percent in III Corps and Capital Military Region, and 28 percent in IV Corps. Projected deployments for June 1967 reflect no change in present troop size of deployment. (See Table IV-9).

  c. <u>NVA/VC Main Force</u>

    For purposes of this analysis regular enemy combat strength is considered to include all NVA/VC main force troops. Although it is recognized that not all of the troops in this classification are performing combat tasks, there are several justifications for making such an assumption. These regular enemy troops must be hunted down and destroyed or eliminated regardless of their operational functions. It is also recognized that the NVA/VC main force requirements in terms of endogenous support troops are but a small fraction of similar requirements needed by Western troops.

    The estimated strength of NVA/VC main force Corps areas as of June 1966 indicates that approximately 17 percent of NVA/VC main force strength is located in I Corps area, 38 percent in II Corps, 27 percent in III Corps, and 18 percent in IV Corps. (See Figure IV-7). North Vietnamese Army troops are predominantly deployed in the two Northern Corps while VC main force units are largely located in the two Southern Corps areas. Currently there are no known North Vietnamese Army units in the IV Corps.

  3. <u>Analysis of Critical Troop Ratios</u>

   a. <u>Aggregate Field Strength Ratios</u>

    It should first be pointed out that in the field, Allied forces as defined, do not have a distinct numerical manpower advantage over the regular enemy forces. In fact, Communist forces in certain Corps areas possess superior numbers. Strong objections could be raised to this observation. The high degree of Allied troop mobility, and essentially unlimited air and ground support

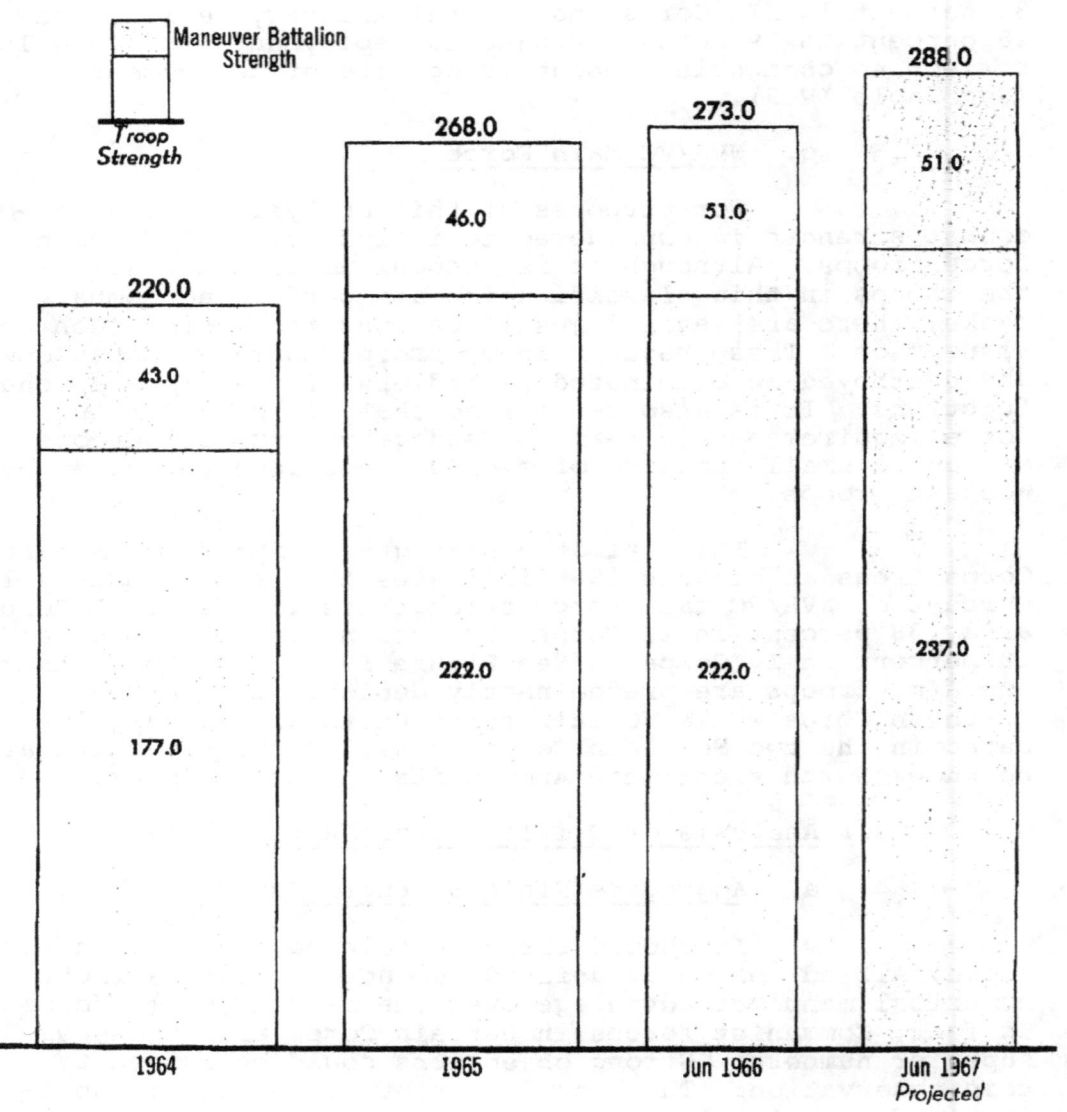

Figure IV-6

APPROXIMATE COMPOSITION OF ARVN MANEUVER BATTALION STRENGTH TO TOTAL ARVN TROOP STRENGTH
1964 - June 1967
(Thousands)

Table IV-9

South Vietnam: Actual and Projected Deployment
of ARVN Maneuver Battalions by Corps Area
February 1965 - June 1967

(In Thousands)

	1965											1966						Dec 1966	Jun 1967
	Feb	Mar	Apr	May	Jun	Jul	Aug	Sep	Oct	Nov	Dec	Jan	Feb	Mar	Apr	May	Jun		
I Corps																			
RVN	9.0	9.4	9.4	9.4	9.4	9.4	9.8	9.8	9.8	9.8	9.8	9.8	10.1	10.1	10.1	10.1	10.8	10.8	10.8
II Corps																			
RVN	8.6	8.6	8.6	8.6	8.6	8.6	9.4	9.4	9.8	9.8	9.8	9.8	10.5	10.5	10.5	10.1	10.5	10.5	10.5
III Corps																			
RVN	13.5	13.5	13.5	13.1	13.1	13.1	13.5	13.5	13.5	13.5	13.5	13.5	13.5	13.9	13.9	14.2	15.0	15.0	15.0
IV Corps																			
RVN	12.4	12.4	12.4	12.4	12.4	12.4	12.4	12.4	12.4	12.4	12.4	12.4	13.5	13.9	13.9	13.9	14.2	14.2	14.2
CMR	0	0	0	.4	.4	.4	.4	.4	.4	.4	.4	.4	.4	.4	.4	.4	.4	.4	.4
Total	43.5	43.9	43.9	43.9	43.9	43.9	45.5	45.5	45.9	45.9	45.9	45.9	48.0	48.0	48.0	48.7	50.9	50.9	50.9

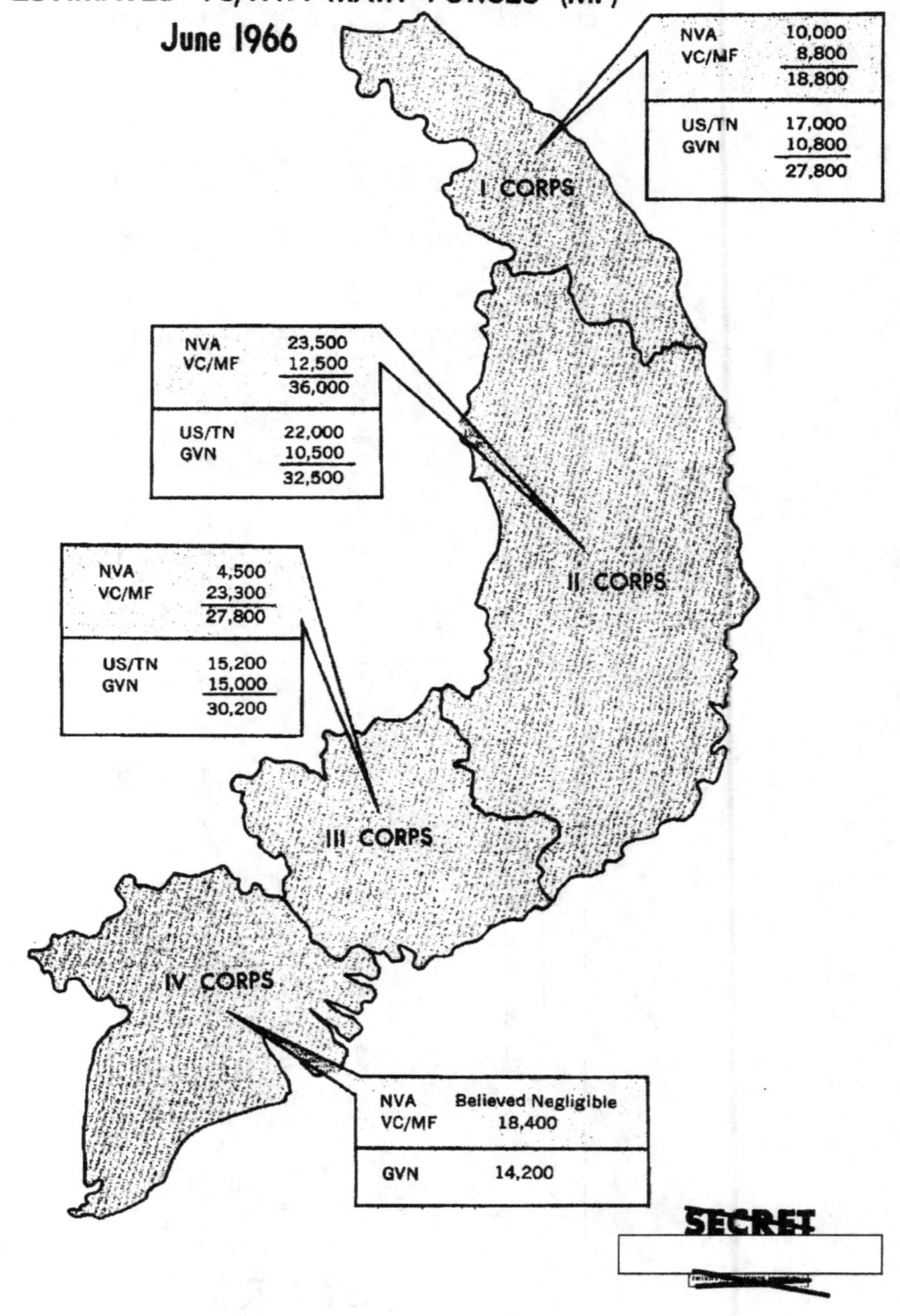

probably help to make the ratio of friendly to enemy field forces less critical than it appears in Table IV-10. The ratio of friendly to enemy field forces has increased slightly in favor of the Communists during the July 1965-June 1966 period. A friendly to enemy field force ratio of 1:.8 was observed in mid-1965 and a ratio of 1:.9 observed in mid-1966. Projections of enemy and Allied field strengths indicate that the Communists may achieve a 1 to 1 ratio with opposing field forces in December 1966 and a 1.1 to 1 ratio by mid-1967.

b. Qualitative Aspects of Increases in Field Force Strength

The contribution of South Vietnam to both the Allied and local Communist field troop strength has stabilized in the past year. In July 1965, GVN troops accounted for 73 percent of Allied field strength. In June 1966 GVN troops made up 48 percent of Allied field strength. In July 1965, South Vietnamese Communists accounted for 98 percent of the enemy field forces. By June 1966, local Communists accounted for 62 percent of the enemy field forces. United States/Third Nation field forces have increased by some 38,000 during the July 1965 - June 1966 period. Regular South Vietnamese Army field forces have increased by about 7,000 in the same period. Regular North Vietnamese Army force increased by some 37,000 troops in the July 1965 - June 1966 period. The endogenous Communist contribution to VC main force increased strength by an estimated 11,000 during the same period.

c. Corps Area Field Strengths

The critical ratio of opposing field forces in South Vietnam by Corps area as of mid-1966 indicates that Allied strength varies considerably from one area to another (See Table IV-11). The Allied field forces enjoy an estimated 1:.68 and 1:.92 manpower superiority in I and III Corps areas respectively. In II and IV Corps areas the Communists enjoy an estimate 1:1.1 and 1:1.3 manpower superiority in the field. Consequently, it is observed that while Allied forces enjoy an aggregate manpower superiority of 1:.96 in mid-1966, such an advantage is not held equally at each Corps level.

Table IV-10

South Vietnam: Ratio of Allied Maneuver Battalion Strength
to Estimated NVA/VC Main Force Troop Strength
July 1965 - June 1967

(In Thousands)

	1965						1966						Dec 1966	Jun 1967
	Jul	Aug	Sep	Oct	Nov	Dec	Jan	Feb	Mar	Apr	May	Jun		
NVA	1.2	1.2	5.2	7.7	10.7	11.1	11.1	13.1	18.3	24.5	30.9	38.0	60.0	75.0
VCMF	47.3	49.3	51.3	53.3	56.2	59.1	59.2	59.2	59.2	57.7	57.2	63.0	65.0	65.0
Total	48.5	50.5	56.5	61.0	66.9	70.2	70.3	72.3	77.5	82.2	88.1	101.0	125.0	140.0
US/TN	16.2	21.2	27.2	35.1	36.7	38.3	44.1	45.1	46.1	51.6	53.4	54.2	71.4	78.6
GVN	43.9	45.5	45.5	45.9	45.9	45.9	45.9	48.0	48.0	48.0	48.7	50.9	50.9	50.9
Total	60.1	66.7	72.7	81.0	82.6	84.2	90.0	93.1	94.1	99.6	102.1	105.1	122.3	129.5
Ratio Friendly to Enemy	1:.81	1:.76	1:.78	1:.75	1:.81	1:.83	1:.78	1:.78	1:.82	1:.82	1:.86	1:.96	1:1.02	1:1.08
Ratio US/TN to NVA	1:.07	1:.06	1:.19	1:.22	1:.29	1:.29	1:.25	1:.25	1:.40	1:.47	1:.58	1:.70	1:.84	1:.95

Table IV-11

South Vietnam: Ratio of Allied Maneuver Battalion Strength to Estimated NVA/VC Main Force Troop Strength by Corps Area, Mid-1966

		I Corps	II Corps	III Corps	IV Corps
NVA		10,000	23,500	4,500	--
VCMF		8,500	12,500	23,300	18,400
	Total	18,800	36,000	27,800	18,400
US/TN		17,000	22,000	15,200	--
GVN		10,800	10,500	15,000	14,200
	Total	27,800	32,500	30,200	14,200
Ratio Friendly to Enemy NVA/VC (US/TN + GVN)		1:.68	1:1.1	1:.92	1:1.29

C. Projected Critical Troop Ratios

We estimate that by the end of 1966 Communist field strength in South Vietnam will be about 125,000 and 140,000 by mid-1967 (See Table IV-12). North Vietnamese Army units will account for 54 percent of the total. Projected Allied deployments for the end of 1966 and mid-1967 show that approximately 122,300 and 129,500 troops respectively, will be allocated to maneuver battalions. About 58 percent of the projected Allied field strength will be accounted for by US/Third Nation forces. The projected increases in both forces will come largely from US/Third Nation troops and the North Vietnamese Army.

Table IV-12

South Vietnam: Projected Critical Troop Ratios:
Allied Maneuver Battalion Strength to
Estimated NVA and VC Main Force Strengths

(In thousands)

		June 1966	December 1966	June 1967
NVA		38.0	60.0	75.0
VCMF		63.0	65.0	65.0
	TOTAL	101.0	125.0	140.0
US/TN		54.2	71.4	78.6
GVN (ARVN)		50.9	50.9	50.9
	TOTAL	105.1	122.3	129.5
Ratio Friendly to Enemy $\frac{(NVA/VC}{US/TN + GVN)}$		1:.96	1:1.02	1:1.08

The ratio of NVA forces to US/Third Nation forces has grown from approximately 1 to .1 in July 1965, to 1: to .7 in mid-1966. Projections indicate that this ratio may increase to 1 to .8 in December 1966 and nearly 1 to 1 by mid-1967. The North Vietnamese apparently plan to match the buildup in US/Third Nation maneuver battalions. (See Figure IV-8). Thus, during the next 12 months Allied forces in South Vietnam will in a relative sense, face a larger enemy force than they have in the past.

Figure IV-8

COMPARATIVE, ACTUAL, AND PROJECTED ALLIED AND US/THIRD NATION MANEUVER BATTALION STRENGTH TO VC/NVA MAIN FORCE STRENGTH
July 1965 - June 1966 and Projected for December 1966 and June 1967

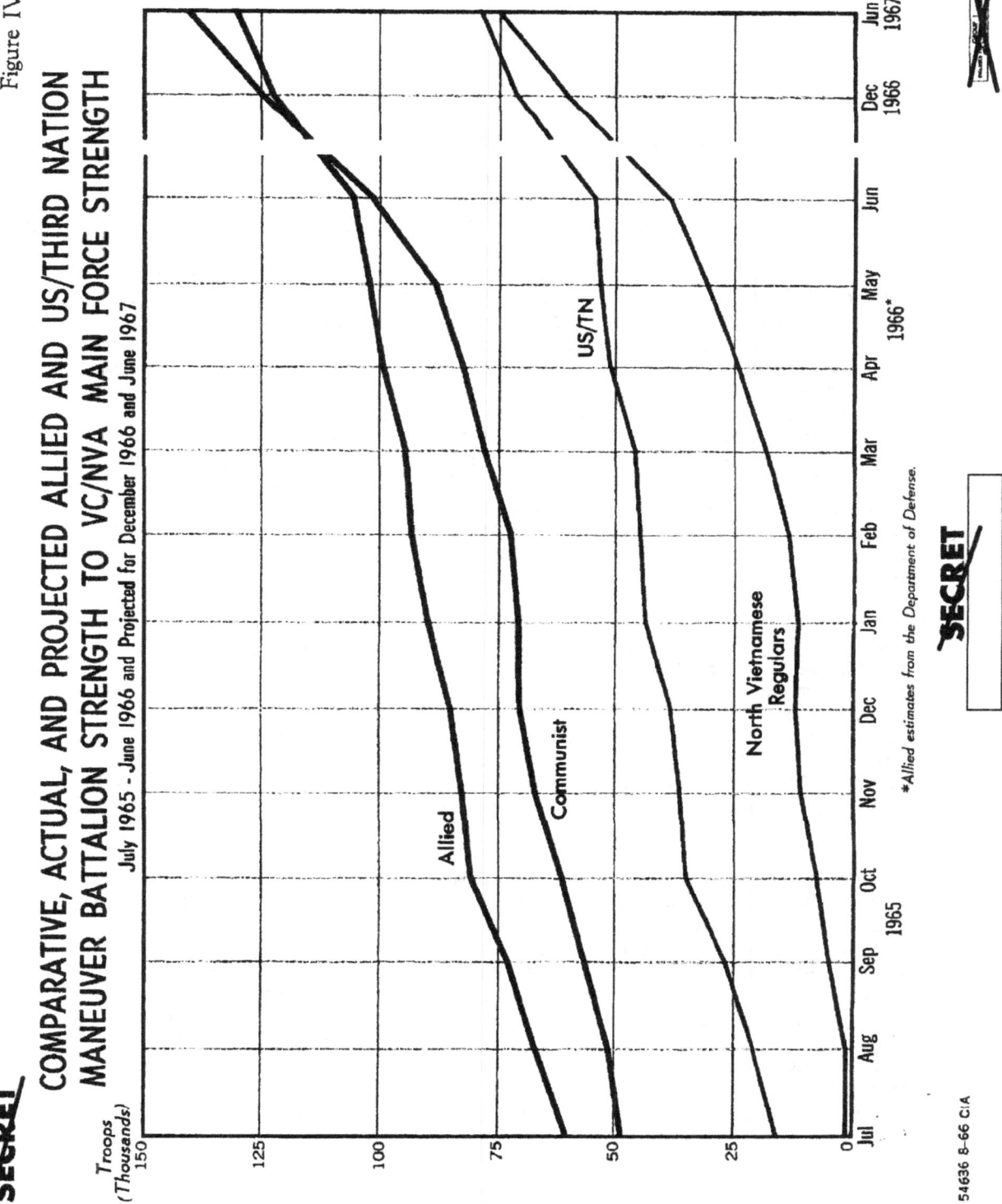

*Allied estimates from the Department of Defense.

III. Operations

   A. Assumptions and Methodology

   The statistics used to evaluate the intensity and course of the ground war in South Vietnam take on added meaning in a war without fronts. Several of the factors employed to assess the war in South Vietnam are subject to considerable margins of error, and as such require discussion. The number of Communist troops reported killed in action is both the most important and least reliable statistical measure used to assess the progress of the military aspects of the struggle. The figure is subject to error because of duplications, omissions, possibly inflated body counts, and the inability to identify non-military casualties. On the other hand, it is well known that Communist forces exert considerable effort to remove both their dead and wounded from the battlefields of South Vietnam. At present there appears to be no rational method for adjusting enemy body count figures. Consequently, the statistics on enemy dead are taken as received, subject to non-quantifiable reservations on their accuracy.

   The allocation of the reported enemy dead to the respective inflicting forces also presents a problem. Combined US/Third Nation and GVN operations are conducted in such a manner that an accurate accounting of enemy casualties by an inflicting force is difficult to achieve. A similar problem exists in trying to determine whether artillery, air support or ground forces inflicted the casualties. Statistical problems also exist in allocating casualties to large and small scale operations.

   To allocate the number of reported enemy killed in each engagement to the respective inflicting force, the number of Allied soldiers killed in each combined operation were weighted by their aggregate kill ratios. The number of Allied and enemy killed in action were also rounded in an effort to make the data consistent. It was observed that the majority of US/Third Nation inflicted and sustained casualties were results of maneuver battalion sized operations or greater. A similar assumption with far less certainty was made with respect to GVN forces. South Vietnamese casualties, both inflicted and sustained, were allocated to their respective corps areas for the July 1965 - May 1966 period on the basis of relative April and May data. The July 1965 - May 1966 period was examined with considerable emphasis because of the relative wealth of data and the increased involvement of US/Third Nation forces in the war.

B. Operations

1. Total GVN and US/Third Nation Operations

During the July 1965 - May 1966 period some 43,700 enemy troops were reported killed in action. Both in relative and absolute sense US/Third Nation forces are now playing a dominant combat role in the South Vietnamese war (See Figure IV-9). The number of US/Third Nation forces (maneuver battalions) capable of actively engaging Communist forces in combat operations has grown from 16,200 in July 1965 to 54,200 in mid-1966. The number of GVN forces capable of initiating offensive operations has remained relatively stable--from about 44,000 in July 1965 to 51,000 in mid-1966.

2. US/Third Nation*

During the July 1965 - May 1966 period US/Third Nation participation in ground operations increased directly with increases in US/Third Nation maneuver battalion strength. (See Figure IV-10). From July-December 1965, US/Third Nation forces accounted for 23 percent of the 23,600 enemy troops reported killed in action; during January-May 1966, US/Third Nation forces killed 56 percent of 20,100 enemy troops reported killed in action. (See Figure IV-11).

US/Third Nation field forces achieved a kill ratio of approximately 6 to 1 during the July 1965 - May 1966 period. Of the 16,800 enemy reported killed in action

---

*For purposes of simplicity Third Nation forces are combined with US. Combined operations are allocated to US/Third Nation and GVN operations respectively.

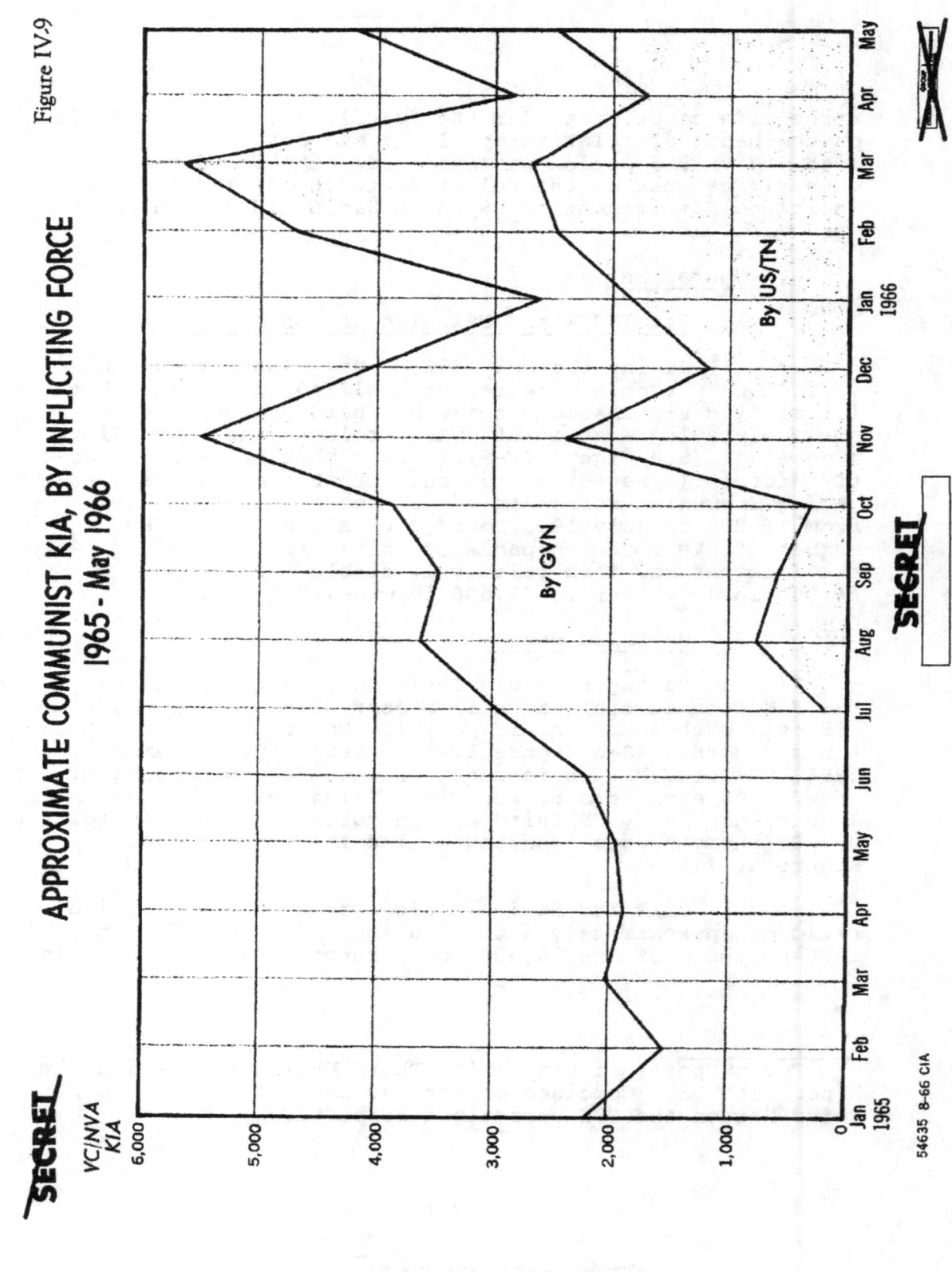

Figure IV.9
APPROXIMATE COMMUNIST KIA, BY INFLICTING FORCE
1965 - May 1966

Figure IV-10

RELATIONSHIP OF COMMUNIST AND US/THIRD NATION KIA TO BUILD-UP OF US/THIRD NATION MANEUVER BATTALION STRENGTH
July 1965 - May 1966

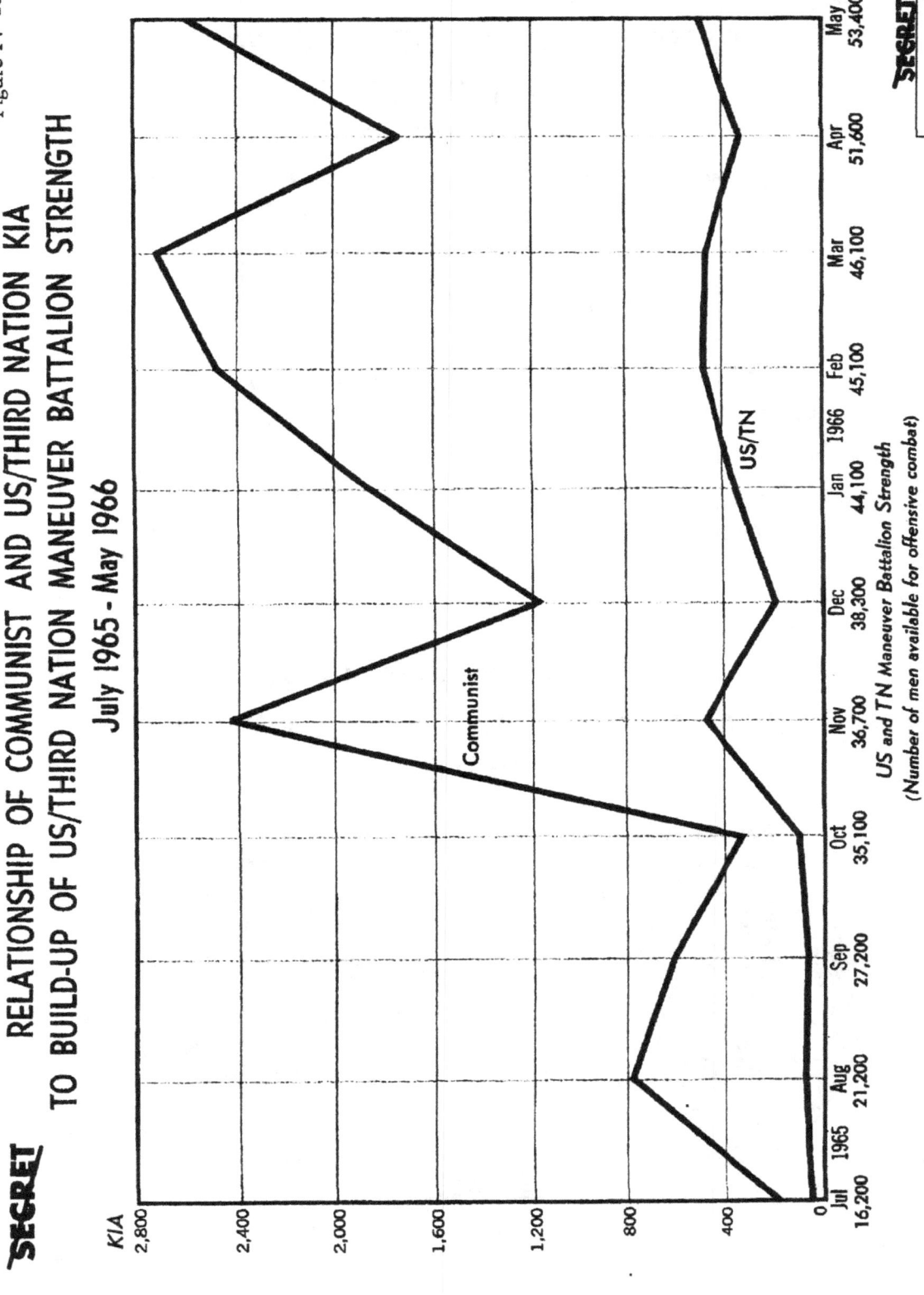

Figure IV-11

COMPOSITION OF REPORTED VC/NVA KIA BY INFLICTING FORCE
July 1965 - May 1966

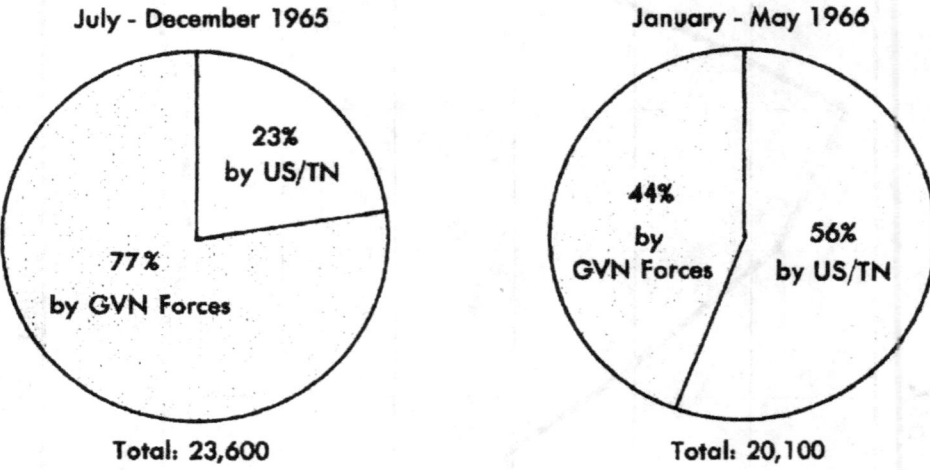

Figure IV-12

APPROXIMATE DISTRIBUTION OF REPORTED VC/NVA KIA, BY CORPS AREA
July 1965 - May 1966

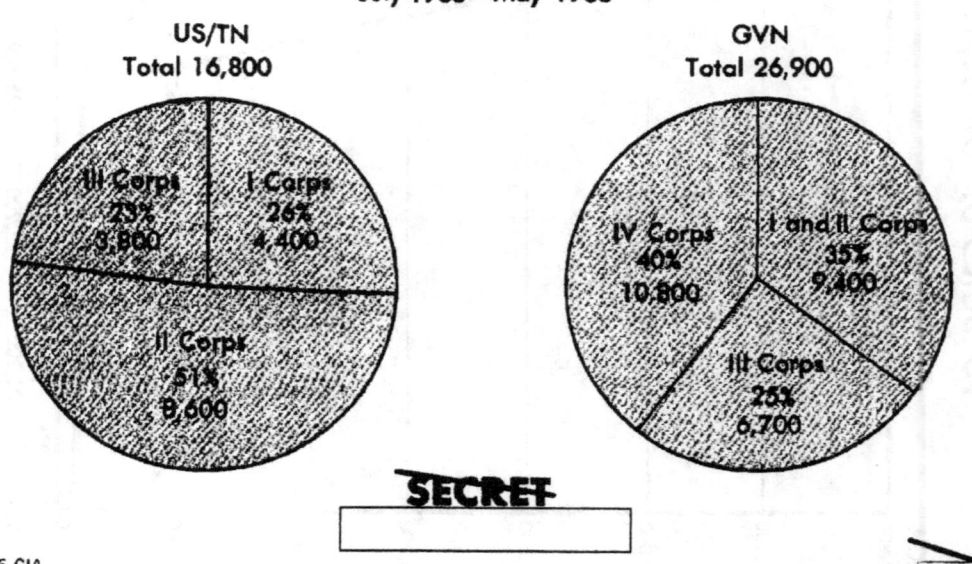

by them during the 11 month period, 26 percent were accounted for by US Marines in I Corps, 51 percent by US Army/Third Nation forces in III Corps. (See Figure IV-12). As a general rule US/Third Nation maneuver battalion kill ratios have been highest in I and II Corps areas and lowest in III Corps.

3. GVN

During the July 1965 - May 1966 period the South Vietnamese Army participation in ground operations decreased. From July-December 1965, GVN forces accounted for 7 percent of the 23,600 enemy troops reported killed in action, or approximately 3,000 enemy killed per month. (See Figure IV-13). High desertion rates, heavy casualties, and political instability have adversely affected the battlefield contributions of South Vietnamese military units.

South Vietnamese forces achieved a 2.7 to 1 kill ratio over Communist forces during the July 1965 - May 1966 period. Approximately 35 percent of these kills were recorded in I and II Corps, 25 percent in III Corps and 40 percent in IV Corps.

C. Communist Performance in Battle

The question of Communist troop morale is discussed in detail in Annex VII. Communist troop performance indicates that the enemy troops are not yet experiencing morale problems that adversely affect their behavior on the battlefield. However, the number of captured Communist weapons, personnel, and desertions have increased considerably since 1964. (See Table IV-13). These losses can be explained by the increasing scale of combat and do not necessarily reflect a decline in Communist battlefield performance.

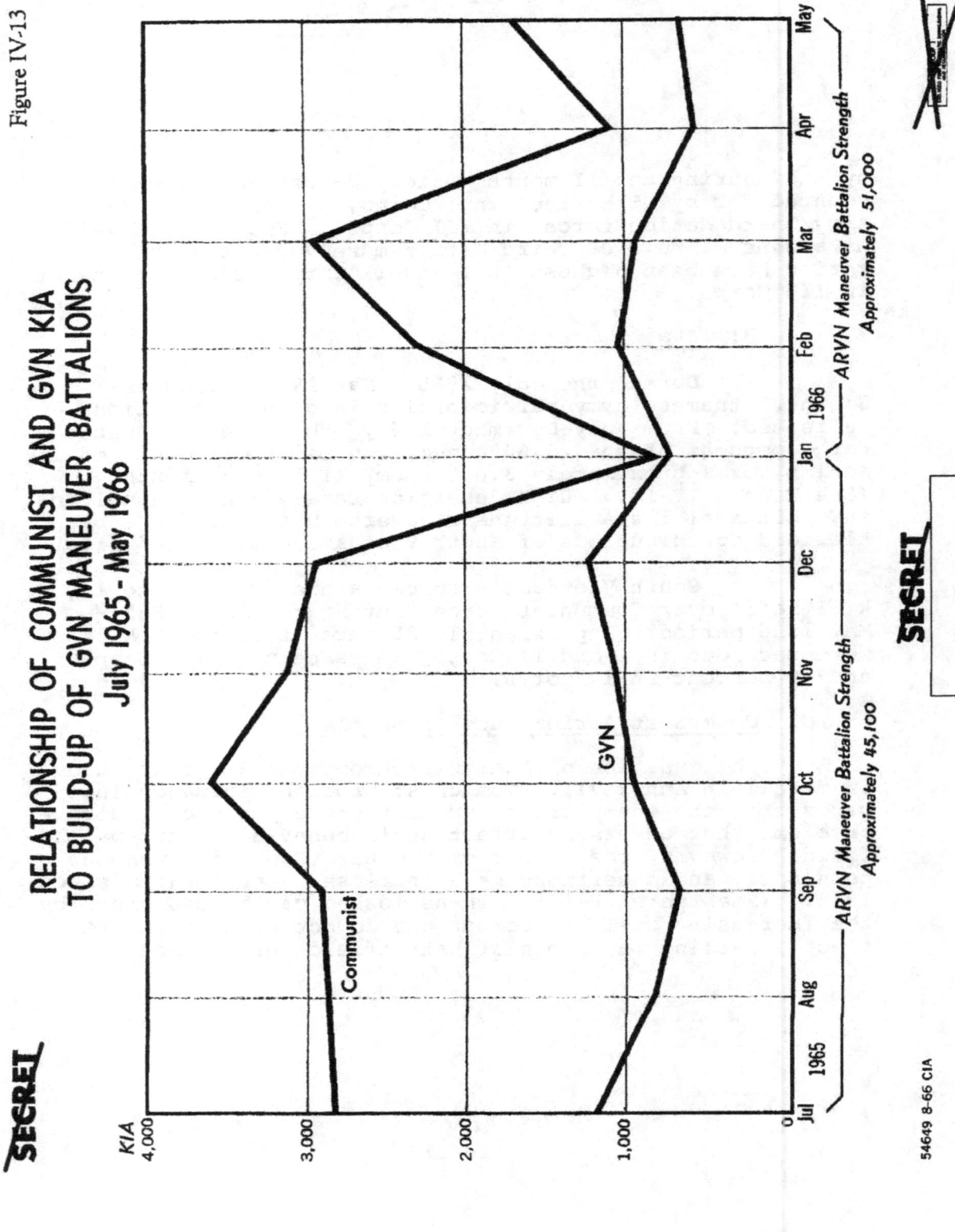

Table IV-13

South Vietnam: Absolute Indicators of Communist Performance in Battle

	1964	1965	1966*
Communist "Chieu Hoi" Military Desertions**	1,900	9,500	12,000
Captured	4,200	6,300	7,000
Communist Weapons Captured	5,900	11,800	N. A.

*Estimate for entire year.
**GVN amnesty program for Communist deserters.

By relating the selected indicators to the scale of combat (the number of enemy reported KIA and captured) it is possible to illustrate that in a relative sense Communist forces are essentially performing as well as in battle today as they were in 1964 and 1965.

Table IV-14

Relative Indicators of Communist Motivations in Battle Expressed in Terms of the Scale of Combat, 1964-66

	1964	1965	1966*
Captured - as a Percent of KIA	$\frac{.24}{1}$	$\frac{.19}{1}$	$\frac{.14}{1}$
Weapons Loss - as a Percent of KIA and Captured**	$\frac{.29}{1}$	$\frac{.30}{1}$	$\frac{.32}{1}$
"Chieu Hoi" Desertions - as a Percent of KIA	$\frac{.11}{1}$	$\frac{.27}{1}$	$\frac{.26}{1}$

*Ratios calculated on January-June data.
**Also includes weapons captured on junks and other infiltration craft, consequently this ratio overstates the true battlefield weapons loss.

It is observed that Communist battlefield performance has not changed in spite of the growing scale of combat and increased US/Third Nation participation. At present, the magnitude of Communist morale problems in terms of influencing battlefield performance, seems to be a minor hindrance to enemy operations in South Vietnam.

D. An Approximate Allocation of NVA/VC Battle Fatalities January-May 1966

1. Methodology

One of the most difficult intelligence problems faced in South Vietnam is that of allocating enemy casualties to their respective fighting units. The characteristics of guerrilla warfare make it impossible to distinguish between civilians, irregulars, VC main force and PAVN troops killed in action. Lack of uniforms and unit insignias are some of the basic problems encountered. The time alloted to body identification of the battlefield is influenced by the pressures of combat and undoubtedly is far too short to allow for accurate body counts, let alone extensive investigations of enemy unit identification. The importance of allocating enemy casualties to their respective units is crucial in assessing the present and probable course of the war in South Vietnam. The extent to which the Communists must rely on internal recruitment and North Vietnamese regulars can best be determined by arriving at an approximate allocation of enemy casualties.

It was initially assumed that all enemy reported killed in action were members of the Communist military establishment. Such an assumption obviously overstates enemy losses since it includes civilians inadvertently killed in and around the battlefields and counted as enemy dead. The inclusion of considerable numbers of South Vietnamese Communist irregulars and combat support troops helps to relax this assumption to a certain degree. However, the lack of any definitive study on such civilian casualties makes it impossible to adjust enemy casualties with any degree of precision. Consequently the killed in action figures are taken as given.

In order to allocate enemy battlefield fatalities to NVA/VC units, it was assumed that enemy casualties were sustained in proportion to their respective troop strength in the various Corps areas as of mid-1966. In the case of irregular and combat support troops it was assumed that these forces were half as likely to engage in major combat operations as were the NVA and VC regular forces. Reported enemy battlefield fatalities were allocated on a corps basis during the January-May 1966 period. Enemy losses and respective strength by corps area were then compared. Since there were no known NVA troops stationed in IV Corps during January-May 1966 it was concluded that all of the reported battle fatalities were sustained by local Communists. NVA strength in III Corps during the relevant period accounted for a small portion of the enemy main force strength - 15 percent in III Corps by mid-1966. The preponderance of enemy casualties in III Corps during the relevant period were assumed, therefore, to be sustained by local Communists. The bulk of the NVA strength in South Vietnam is stationed in II and I Corps respectively. Communist losses during the January-May 1966 period in the two upper Corps were allocated to NVA/VC on the basis of regular enemy troop strength as of mid-1966. By employing this methodology it was deduced that at a maximum 25-30 percent of Communist battlefield fatalities were inflicted on NVA troops during January-May 1966. Projected enemy troop strengths indicate that about 40 percent of the enemy battlefield fatalities during the next year will be sustained by NVA forces.*

The use of Communist regular troop strength as of mid-1966 weights the casualties heavily toward NVA forces during the January-May 1966 period. NVA troop strength has rapidly increased in recent months, thus overstating probable NVA losses during the early months of 1966. Such a bias should counter arguments that NVA forces are employed more intensively in combat than are local Communist forces. The use of total South Vietnamese Communist

---

*It is not possible at this time to refine the allocation of fatalities by considering the actual frequency with which VC NVA units engage in combat.

troop strength may also overstate local enemy casualties since it implicitly assumes that local forces have and will be engaged as often as North Vietnamese troops.

2. Analysis

This distribution provides some insights into probable future trends in the growth and composition of enemy forces in South Vietnam. It is estimated that Communist battlefield fatalities averaged approximately 4,000 a month during January-May 1966. Average monthly North Vietnamese and VC battlefield fatalities were 1,600 and 2,400 respectively. Accepted aaverage monthly Communist infiltration during the same period was 4,200. Combined accepted and reported NVA infiltration averaged 7,000 a month.

It is obvious that during January-May 1966 North Vietnamese troop strength grew at a more rapid rate than did direct sustained battlefield fatalities. Considerable increases in estimated North Vietnamese Army strength in South Vietnam during the same period confirm this trend. The relatively stable size of the VC main force during the period probably indicates that the local Communists have been able to offset battlefield deaths by recruitments from the irregular forces and the populace.

IV. Communist Losses

A. Total Communist Losses

During 1965, it is estimated that some 79,300 to 90,300 Communists (See Table IV-15) were effectively put out of action. Projections indicate that from 105,000-120,000 enemy forces will be effectively lost in 1966 and from 65,000-75,000 will be lost during the first half of 1967. Battle fatalities account for approximately 40 percent of the losses, seriously wounded, estimated on the basis of captured documents, account for 32 percent, and captured and deserters the remaining 28 percent.

Table IV-15

South Vietnam: Estimate of Communist Losses
1965 - June 1967

	1965	1966	Jan-June 1967
KIA	35,000	48,000	30,000
Captured	6,300	7,000	4,300
("Chieu Hoi" Returnees)	9,500	13,000	8,000
SUB TOTAL	50,800	68,000	42,300
Seriously Wounded	19,000-30,000	24,000-39,000	15,000-24,000
Deserters	9,500	13,000	8,000
TOTAL	79,300-90,300	105,000-120,000	65,300-74,300

1. Killed in Action

Average monthly reported Communist battle fatalities increased from less than 2,000 during the first 6 months of 1965 to approximately 3,900 each month in the second half of the year. During January-May 1966, Communist battle fatalities averaged 4,000 per month. Some 35,000 Communist troops were killed in action in 1965. Approximately 20,000 enemy troops were reported killed in action during January-May of this year, and current estimates indicate that approximately 48,000 Communists will probably be killed in action by the end of 1966.

2. Wounded in Action

   a. Methodology

Few if any official figures are released that give an indication of the total number of Communist soldiers wounded in action. The primary reason for the lack of such information is that the enemy remove a considerable number of their dead and wounded from the battlefield in an effort to conceal their losses and prevent the capture of additional personnel.

IV-22

Three basic components went into derivation of an estimate of NVA/VC wounded in action. Consideration was given to historical factors such as: (1) US, ANZAC, and Japanese experience in Burma, Malaya, and the Pacific Islands in World War II; (2) the experience of South Vietnamese, and US/TN forces in Vietnam; and (3) Communist prisoner interrogation reports mentioning casualties and captured enemy documents such as medical reports and unit combat records. The observed ratios of wounded to killed during World War II and in Vietnam are summarized in Table IV-16 below.

Table IV-16

Selected Wounded to Killed Ratios

World War II	Wounded to Killed
Papuan Campaign (Australian)	2.04/1
Papuan Campaign (US)	2.79/1
Philippines (US)	3.52/1
Okinawa (US)	4.31/1
Burma 1949 (Japan)	2.47/1
Burma 1943 (Japan)	3.23/1
Vietnam	
South Vietnam, 1963-65, (GVN)	2.17/1
US/Third Nation, 1965	4.1/1

Prisoner interrogation reports and captured enemy documents provided 15 quantifiable observations on the relationship between Communist troops killed and wounded in action. Enemy casualties ranged from some 700 in large unit actions to 20 casualties or less in small group actions. All of these losses were sustained while fighting against South Vietnamese forces during 1964 and 1965. The observed ratios of wounded to killed in action ranged from 1.07:1 to 2.4:1, with a weighted average ratio of 1.62:1. Since these figures are not biased by enemy removal of dead troops from the battlefield they may better reflect the distribution of enemy killed to wounded than those ratios which employ Allied body counts as a base figure.

An enemy document captured by the 1st Cavalry Division on 17 March 1966, in central Binh Dinh Province, revealed regimental data on Communist troops wounded in action during 9 April 1965 - 1 March 1966. The 2nd VC, 18th NVA, and Quyet Ram regiments which were estimated to be the major enemy elements stationed in Binh Dinh were listed in the document. The security of Binh Dinh is predominantly maintained by US and ROK forces. Consequently, a comparison between Communist troops killed in action (US/ROK body count) and enemy accounts of those wounded in action in Binh Dinh during the relevant period provides some indication of an enemy $\frac{(WIA)}{(KIA)}$ relationship between US/Third nation forces and the enemy.

US/ROK forces killed 628 Communists in Binh Dinh during the relevant period according to body counts. Enemy documents indicate that 1,135 troops were wounded. Some 85 Communists wounded in action were captured by US/ROK forces. It is assumed that: (1) US/ROK forces did most of the fighting in Binh Dinh Province; and (2) that the above mentioned Communist regiments comprise most of the enemy strength in Binh Dinh. The resulting ratio is $\frac{WIA}{KIA} = \frac{1,135 + 85}{628} = 1.94$ for Communist forces engaging US/Third Nation forces in South Vietnam. The US/ROK body count probably understates the number of enemy killed and consequently results in higher wounded to killed ratio than was probably experienced.

A general relationship between the number of troops killed in action and those wounded in action was observed in the samples examined. Troops with high kill ratios $\frac{\text{(Enemy killed)}}{\text{(Friendly killed)}}$ also experienced high wounded to killed ratios $\frac{\text{(Friendly wounded)}}{\text{(Friendly killed)}}$. Conversely, troops with relatively low kill ratios tended to have low wounded to killed ratios. Troops (such as NVA/VC) with low kill ratios probably sustain a large number killed and a relatively smaller number wounded, while troops (such as US/Third Nation forces) with high kill ratios sustain a smaller number killed and a relatively larger number wounded. This relationship can be rationalized by the fact that better trained and organized troops with superior support fire from artillery and aircraft sustain fewer fatalities in obtaining or defending an objective than do forces that lack such support fire.

Captured enemy documents further indicate that approximately 50 percent of the wounded received serious injuries--broken bones and damage to internal organs that required immediate surgery. About 30 percent of the wounds were classified as light, and most of these cases were immediately returned to the battlefield. The remaining 20 percent suffered slight wounds that required little medical attention and were also immediately returned to the field.

It is difficult to estimate the number of seriously wounded Communist troops who die or cease to be effective fighting men. However, most of the seriously wounded are moved considerable distances by primitive means of transportation to surgical centers where, undoubtedly, the facilities and the quality of the medical personnel are far below Western standards. These factors coupled with the consideration that many Communist troops are already affected by debilitating tropical diseases suggest that the majority of the seriously wounded troops are out of action for considerable lengths of time or indefinitely.

b. <u>Estimate</u>

Some 19,000 to 30,000 Communist troops were seriously wounded in 1965. End of year estimates indicate that from 24,000-39,000 enemy troops will be seriously wounded in 1966.

3. Captured

Some 6,300 Communist military personnel were captured in action during 1965. Given the current scale of operations it is estimated that approximately 7,000 enemy troops will be captured in 1966.

4. "Chieu Hoi" Returnees and Deserters

Some 9,500 Communist soldiers defected under the GVN "Chieu Hoi" program during 1965. Current estimates indicate that about 13,000 enemy military personnel are expected to defect under the "Chieu Hoi" program this year. No information exists on the number of enemy personnel who simply desert and return to their villages. We estimate that unrecorded enemy desertions are at least equal to the number of defectors under the "Chieu Hoi" program. This is admittedly a conservative approach and the actual numbers of deserters could be significantly higher than the estimates used in this annex.

B. Allocations of Present and Future Communist Military Losses in South Vietnam

It is estimated that a maximum of some 25,000 to 30,000 North Vietnamese troops will be effectively put out of action in South Vietnam during 1966. An additional 25,000 to 30,000 will be lost in the first half of 1967 if current rates of combat are maintained and projected troop strengths are realized. The bulk of the North Vietnamese losses will result from troops killed and seriously wounded in action. Relatively few North Vietnamese losses will be accounted for by captures, desertions, or defections.

Local Communists (including main forces, irregulars and combat support troops) will at a maximum sustain some 80,000 to 90,000 effective losses in action during 1966. An additional 40,000 to 45,000 will be lost in the first half of 1967. Approximately two-thirds of the local Communist losses will result from battle deaths and serious wounds. The remainder will be accounted for by captures and desertions. The relative shift in casualties from local to North Vietnamese Communist forces in 1967 reflects the expected increase in the role of PAVN troops in the South Vietnamese war. In terms of comparative battlefield losses the Allied forces have a distinct advantage over the Communists. It is estimated that some 16,000 Free World soldiers will be killed in action during 1966, (6,000 US/TN, 10,000 GVN), compared to 48,000 Communists. An additional 9,000 Allied soldiers will probably be killed by mid-1967, reflecting the same loss composition, compared to some 30,000 Communists.

In a country with an abundant population, where some 270,000 natural deaths and 20,000 accidents occur each year, the loss of some 40,000-60,000 youths annually for the sake of "National Liberation" does not, in an oriental sense, seem too high. The increased North Vietnamese commitment in South Vietnam is not, however, entirely based on patriotism. VC units have borne the brunt of enemy casualties to date and appear pressed to maintain their current strength in face of growing Allied strength. The squeeze on VC manpower is becoming more apparent, and the necessity of outside help more acute if the war is to be waged at the present level. North Vietnam appears both willing and able to take on this task in the hope that a protracted struggle will give them ultimate victory. It may, however, find this commitment to be increasingly burdensome particularly as it required increasing numbers of the country's limited resources of skilled manpower and leadership cadres.

~~TOP SECRET~~

ANNEX V

THE RESOURCES AND LOGISTIC CAPABILITIES
OF THE COMMUNISTS IN SOUTH VIETNAM

~~TOP SECRET~~

~~TOP SECRET~~

ANNEX V

THE RESOURCES AND LOGISTIC
CAPABILITIES OF THE
COMMUNISTS IN SOUTH VIETNAM

I. The Viet Cong Economy and Its Manpower

   A. The Viet Cong Economy

The Viet Cong have successfully organized and expanded an economic organization to meet the basic task of funding VC revolutionary activity. The basic economic organization, operating through the Finance and Economic Section of the People's Revolutionary (Communist) Party is assisted by the National Liberation Front and Communist military components in acquiring, transporting, and storing within South Vietnam almost all the non-military supplies required by the Viet Cong. During the past five years, the VC economic organization has expanded with the development of VC forces. Starting as a local self-production unit, the economic structure progressed, first, into a voluntary fund drive, then, into an organized taxation and finance mechanism and, finally into an organization activity supporting enlarged base and battlefield requirements.

Taxation appears to be the principal means used by the Viet Cong to acquire financial and material resources within South Vietnam. Agricultural taxation remains the most important source of VC tax receipts and is clearly dependent on continuing Viet Cong access to or some measure of control over the rural population. The Viet Cong currently exercise predominant political influence over 25 to 30 percent of the rice-cultivated area of South Vietnam which produces between 750,000 and 900,000 metric tons of rice per year. Annual consumption of rice by Communist regular forces could be obtained by an average tax of about 3 percent of total production in VC areas alone. The Viet Cong usually tax at a substantially higher level (12 to 15 percent). There is no indication that resentment by the rural population against taxes of this magnitude has reached levels adequate to stop rice collections. Plantation taxes--either in money or in kind--continue to be

V-1

collected and are an important source of supply for Viet Cong forces in the northern III Corps. Internal transportation, business establishments, and commercial activities are also widely taxed.

VC-initiated economic activities, seizures, and clandestine operations supplement VC tax receipts. Bond drives, food production, and simple manufacturing units have been initiated by the VC to support military personnel. Significant supplies of war booty continue to be accumulated by the Viet Cong. Clandestine front business operations and discreet purchases by civilians acting for the Viet Cong, provide access to resources from GVN-controlled areas, including imported manufactured goods.

For specific goods in certain areas of South Vietnam, the Viet Cong have utilized traditional smuggling along the South Vietnam - Cambodia border. During recent months, however, Viet Cong use of Cambodia as a source of non-military supplies has increased and been organized in a systematic fashion. Although this logistic support is more costly than domestic acquisition and evidently requires external financial arrangements with banks in Hong Kong, the immunity and proximity of such logistic support to large VC/NVA forces along the Cambodian border apparently has made this source of supplies increasingly valuable. On an annual basis, it is estimated that at least 5,000 and probably as much as 10,000 metric tons of rice are being acquired from Cambodia and a frequently reported figure of 20,000 metric tons appears to be possible. Some of this rice is also acquired to support Communist forces in Laos. In addition, the VC are acquiring in Cambodia substantial quantities of cloth, pharmaceuticals, salt, fish and fish sauce, gasoline, communications equipment, explosive chemicals, and other supplies.

B. The Economic Impact of Increased Military Pressure

The build-up in VC/NVA forces in South Vietnam during the last year has placed a heavy strain on VC logistic operations. Confirmed VC/NVA main force strength has approximately doubled during the last year. Whereas guerrilla personnel, like the civilian population, are expected to be self-sufficient in basic supplies, main force units require extensive logistic support. Food supplies, especially rice, remain the principal bulk commodities required by these forces. The entire increase in main force strength has been recorded in rice-deficit areas--I and II Corps and northern III Corps. There has been no increase in VC main force strength in the rice-surplus IV Corps where logistic requirements for food supplies are relatively small.

With the concentration of VC/NVA main force strength in I and II Corps and in northern III Corps annual rice requirements clearly exceed the total rice production under VC control in the provinces of Pleiku, Kontun, Phu Bon, the western districts of the coastal provinces of central Vietnam, and the rice-deficit areas of VC military region 7. In all of these areas, there is evidence that the VC are experiencing food supply problems. For example, a recently captured document cited the logistical difficulties experienced by the VC during an early 1966 campaign in rice-deficit Quang Duc Province that did not have sufficient rice for its own provincial force; region forces assigned to the campaign were required to arrange their own rice supply "through the border," presumably the Cambodian border. During the course of the campaign, one-third of VC combat strength was diverted to the transportation of rice.

The increase in allied military action has continued to hamper the logistic system of the Viet Cong. Allied military actions have had an adverse effect on agricultural production in VC controlled areas and on the percentage of the harvest that the VC can acquire and transport to their base areas. The area covered and percentage of crop harvested in these rice-harvesting operations is not reported, and no aggregative estimate of their impact is possible. Even with continued VC access to rice-producing areas, the Viet Cong face a second major difficulty in transporting this commodity. The major portion of this movement has been carried out by civilian laborers, but the danger of involvement in military action has caused serious disaffection among the VC-controlled population as the tempo of military activity has increased. A third major difficulty caused by allied military activity has been the disruption caused by allied destruction of VC supply caches.

C. The Manpower Situation

The South Vietnamese population in VC controlled areas is at least 3.5 million people and could be as much as five million people depending on the extent to which the VC have access to contested areas. Most of the VC controlled population live in the delta region. This controlled population probably contains some 500,000 physically fit young males. An additional 30,000-35,000 youths annually become old enough to fight. In addition to this controlled population the VC also draw on the population of military age in contested areas, on GVN deserters and on recruits from urban areas.

An increasing requirement for manpower during 1965 forced the VC to resort to monetary inducements and to forced conscription and returnee programs to obtain local personnel. With these new methods VC have been able to attain a significantly higher level of local recruitment--over 80,000 in 1965 compared to 30,000-40,000 annually during 1961-64. We estimate that the VC have a capability in 1966 to recruit and train some 7,000 to 10,000 personnel a month.

Recruitment at this scale must be regarded as close to the maximum capabilities of the VC, particularly if these recruits are to receive adequate training. There have been increasing signs of a growing squeeze on VC manpower during 1966. This is reflected in the growing dominance of North Vietnamese troops as the NVA/VC force expands. There are also frequent prisoner reports of manpower shortages and the poor quality and training of new recruits.

In addition to making up for their own losses of an estimated 80,000-90,000 in 1966, we estimate that VC forces will increase by about 5,000 troops in 1966. The VC are also required, however, to provide replacements for a growing number of NVA losses. During 1966 we estimate that the NVA will infiltrate from 55,000-75,000 troops at the same time that they are expanding the NVA troop level by an estimated 49,000 troops. NVA losses during the year, however, will range from 25,000-30,000. Thus the VC could have to make up for 5,000-20,000 NVA losses, depending on the rate of infiltration and expansion of NVA forces. This indicates a total VC military manpower requirement in 1966 of from 90,000-115,000. This requirement is within the higher end of the range of current estimates of VC recruitment capabilities.

If the casualty rate increases as expected during 1967 to an annual rate of 130,000-150,000 Communist losses will be beyond the estimated recruitment and training capabilities of the VC. More of the manpower burden will then be placed on North Vietnam creating additional pressures on its manpower resources.

II. <u>Communist Logistic Operations in South Vietnam</u> (See Appendix A)

The Communist forces in South Vietnam have created a highly centralized system of Supply Councils to meet the logistics requirements of the VC/NVA forces. This organization operates at each administrative level in South Vietnam working closely with counterpart economic and service organizations of the Central Office for South Vietnam (COSVN) and the Rear Services Staffs of the military command. This elaborate system controls from 40,000-50,000 personnel engaged full-time in logistic support activities. Additional thousands of personnel are conscripted on a part-time basis to assist in transporting supplies, the construction of logistics bases, and the maintenance of supply routes. The VC use an elaborate system of land routes, trails, and inland waterways connecting the infiltration routes from Laos and Cambodia with the major COSVN base areas.

The VC storage system is greatly decentralized working from a large number of small depots, storing generally only 5-10 tons of supplies each. This dispersed system provides maximum protection against large scale destruction or capture of supplies but also serves as a major constraint to the initiation of large sustained enemy actions.

The logistics system used by the Communist forces in South Vietnam has been able to satisfy adequately the minimum requirement for movement and storage of supplies.

This capability has been weakened and made more difficult as the scale of combat has increased and Allied ground operations have disrupted normal logistic movements and overrun storage areas. Difficulty in effectively maintaining the internal distribution of supplies has also been compounded by the manner in which VC/NVA forces are dispersed throughout South Vietnam.

In mid-1966 one-third of the enemy combat and combat support troops was located in the II Corps Area, one third in the III Corps, and the remainder about equally between the I and IV Corps. The IV Corps area with only 15 percent of total VC/NVA regular forces, is the area in which the VC have the greatest self-sufficiency in logistic supplies, particularly foodstuffs. The predominant share of VC/NVA forces is concentrated in food-deficit areas. Thus the II and III Corps areas which are the predominant rice-deficit areas account for almost two-thirds of the total daily logistic requirement.

The inability to transport food from rice surplus to deficit areas has become more severe as Allied ground actions intensify. The Communists have been compelled to turn to Cambodian sources in order to provide rice to the forces in the central highlands. Use of this source of supply has increased in the last half year and may now be as much as 15 tons a day. The need to turn to sources outside the country for rice indicates that internal distribution is one of the most pressing problems faced by the Communists and is probably the most vulnerable aspect of their entire logistics operation.

If the disposition of Communist forces in South Vietnam remains unchanged during the build-up projected through mid-1967 and internal distribution of food is impossible, their dependence on external sources for supplies could double. Our present estimates indicate a maximum external requirement of about 55 tons a day. But if internal distribution of food to the food-deficit areas cannot be effectively accomplished, this requirement could be increased to at least 100 tons a day.

This added logistic requirement would not be critical, particularly if it were met from Cambodian sources. It would not even tax the Laotian infiltration route very severely but would aid substantially in reducing the excess of road capacity over logistic requirements.

The present disposition of Communist forces is much more favorable for the internal distribution of supplies infiltrated into South Vietnam. Over 85 percent of the NVA forces and 35 percent of the VC forces are in the I and II Corps areas in close proximity to the Laotian infiltration corridor and the northern infiltration routes from Cambodia. These forces account for almost three-fourths of the supplies which must be infiltrated from external sources.

The data available on the destruction and capture of supplies by Allied forces during the past year are quite incomplete. Food supplies amounting to at least 10,000-12,000 tons and over 21,000 weapons and 180,000 rounds of ammunition are the major amounts known to have been captured or destroyed. We lack almost completely any meaningful data on Communist stock-piles and are therefore unable to assess the impact of these losses. But as minimum losses, the food stocks may be relatively significant, particularly as Allied operations uncover more storage areas and interfere more with the internal distribution of supplies.

The substantial increase in incidents of Communist terrorism and harassment of local population may indicate that the enemy is finding it increasingly difficult to obtain local support in terms of food and/or labor for its war effort.

APPENDIX A

THE COMMUNIST LOGISTICS SYSTEM IN SOUTH VIETNAM

I. Organization

VC/NVA* logistic operations are under the control and supervision of Supply Councils found at every echelon of command from the Central Office for South Vietnam (COSVN) to the village level. (See Figure III-1)** Village Forward Supply Councils are responsible for procurement and for the distribution of supplies to troops in the field. The province level controls the planning and regulatory agencies which furnish logistic data to the military Rear Service Staffs at the various levels of command. Communications and liaison sections, under the Supply Councils, exercise an important role in safeguarding all types of logistic operations. Party cadre associated with the communication and liaison sections serve as guides, security personnel, station attendants, and supervisory personnel.

Supply Councils also supervise the work of two basic transportation organizations--the People's Revolutionary Party (PRP) Finance and Economic Section transport elements and the military Rear Service Section transport elements.

Transport and supporting elements under the jurisdiction of military Rear Services Sections are organized

---

*The organization structure outlined in this section is estimated to apply generally to both VC and NVA forces. Some of the material appearing in this section is based on an analysis of a captured document discussing the VC Sao Vang Division, a division containing both VC and NVA elements.

**Figure III-1 follows page III-5 in Annex III.

into (1) transport elements of the Rear Services Sections which are organic to the various echelons of the VC/NVA regular military forces, (2) separate military transport units (not found below military region level) responsible for the receipt and redistribution of supplies, and (3) ordnance sections and armament sections. The Rear Service Staff organic to the VC/NVA Division is organized into four functional sections: a quartermaster section for procurement, storage, and distribution of food and clothing; an ordnance section for procurement, storage, maintenance and distribution of weapons and ammunition; a medical section for medical support and evacuation; and a finance section for financial support.

A. Personnel

Enemy forces in South Vietnam in mid-1966 amounted to 260,000-280,000 including from 40,000-50,000 personnel engaged in logistic support. The composition of important VC supply elements is shown in the following tabulation:

Combat Support

Separate Military Transport Units	5,800
Region/Province/District Ordnance and Ammunition Sections	3,000
Other Combat Support Troops	8,800
Total	17,600

Other Forces

Finance and Economic Transport Units	2,000
Infiltration Corridor Personnel	3,000
Communications and Liaison Units	2,000
Organic Military Transport Elements	7,400
VC/NVA Crewmen on Water Craft	12,000
Total	26,400
TOTAL	44,000

In addition to these regular employees the VC have conscripted thousands of temporary, civilian workers to assist in logistic activities. Recruiting is carried out among men between the ages of 18 and 50 and women between the ages of 20 and 41, with the annual period of service usually being from 1 to 3 months. This conscripted labor is given both political and security training. It is then organized into platoons and companies, and assigned by village and district forward supply councils to the combat units or to a rear services staff. Front line or Class A laborers are used by combat units to transport ammunition and food supplies; to evacuate battle casualties; to remove captured supplies to collection points, and to construct supply depots and defensive positions, as well as in other miscellaneous tasks. Local inhabitants have been conscripted to carry weapons and ammunition inland from coastal areas and to transport food to the mountainous regions. Special groups are assigned to carry supplies and ammunition from the Cambodian border area to enemy base areas.

II. Storage and Distribution

The VC supply system is designed to satisfy both normal, continuous troop requirements and those requirements imposed by rapidly changing battlefield conditions. The VC have established an area supply system which incorporates a large number of small depots--each generally having a capacity of five-ten tons--dispersed throughout areas in which VC units operate. Although classes of supplies in depots are usually mixed, some depots store food exclusively and others contain only weapons and ammunition. Even in the larger war zones, supplies are dispersed throughout the area. Villages that are located close to combat units may also act as supply points. In certain areas, only one-third of the prescribed stock is allocated to depots, with the remaining two-thirds dispersed among civilians for custody. This system limits the damage that can be caused by the destruction of one large depot or supply cache, but it also acts as a major constraint to the initiation of large, sustained enemy actions when large amounts of supplies need to be concentrated in relatively small areas.

A. Distribution of Food

Regiments are given an initial issue of rice corresponding to a 30 day supply, which is to be replenished when half of the supply is consumed. Rear service staffs are charged with maintaining a stock equivalent to one month's supply for all forces operating in their area of jurisdiction. When a regiment leaves the area the remaining rice must be returned to these staffs. Troops usually have a seven-day supply of rice in their individual packs as a reserve for emergencies; the unit draws rice from supply points located along the line of movement. This method reduces the supply train and the requirement for porters. Each regiment is assigned an area from which food is purchased. A rear supply element of the regiment normally sends out purchasing teams to the area to contact local VC authorities and to arrange for purchase in the prescribed quantities.

III. Transportation Routes

The enemy in South Vietnam makes use of a very large number and variety of lines of communication. These include major South Vietnamese highways, secondary roads, waterways, trails and innumerable footpaths. (See Figure V-1). Many of the land routes, especially in the north, are narrow, unimproved trails, negotiable only by foot, animal, or small two or three-wheeled vehicles, but trucks are sometimes used on segments of the major routes when they are under Communist control, and sometimes on routes nominally under GVN control. Extensive use is made of water craft in the Delta area.

A. Land Routes

The most frequently used land routes for the movement of personnel are probably the two in a north-south orientation connecting the Laotian and Cambodian infiltration corridor with the large established enemy base areas in Tay Ninh Province northwest of Saigon. The first route, which runs just inside South Vietnam along the Cambodian border, consists for the most part of a connecting group of trails although it follows or parallels existing roads in its southern segments. The second

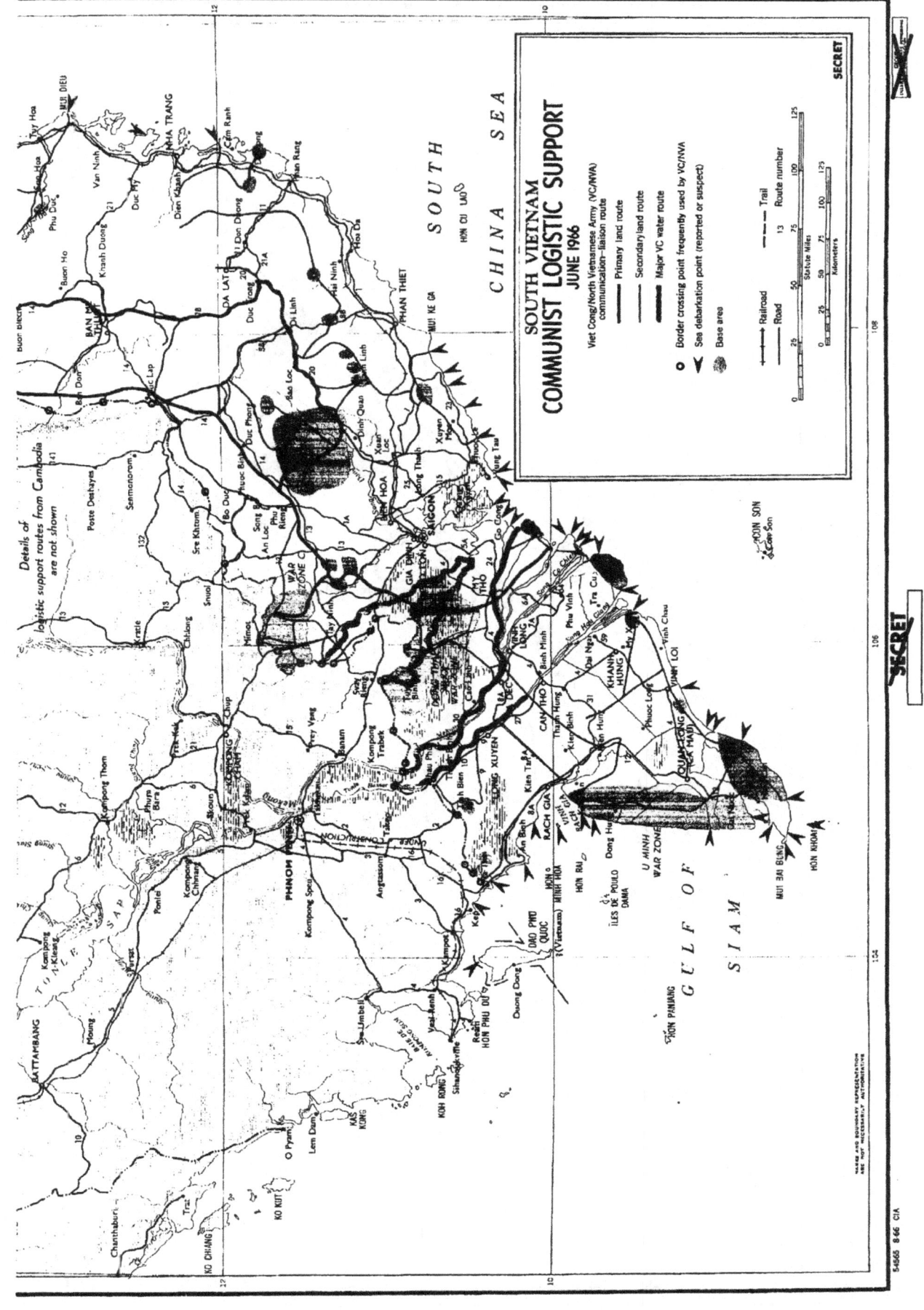

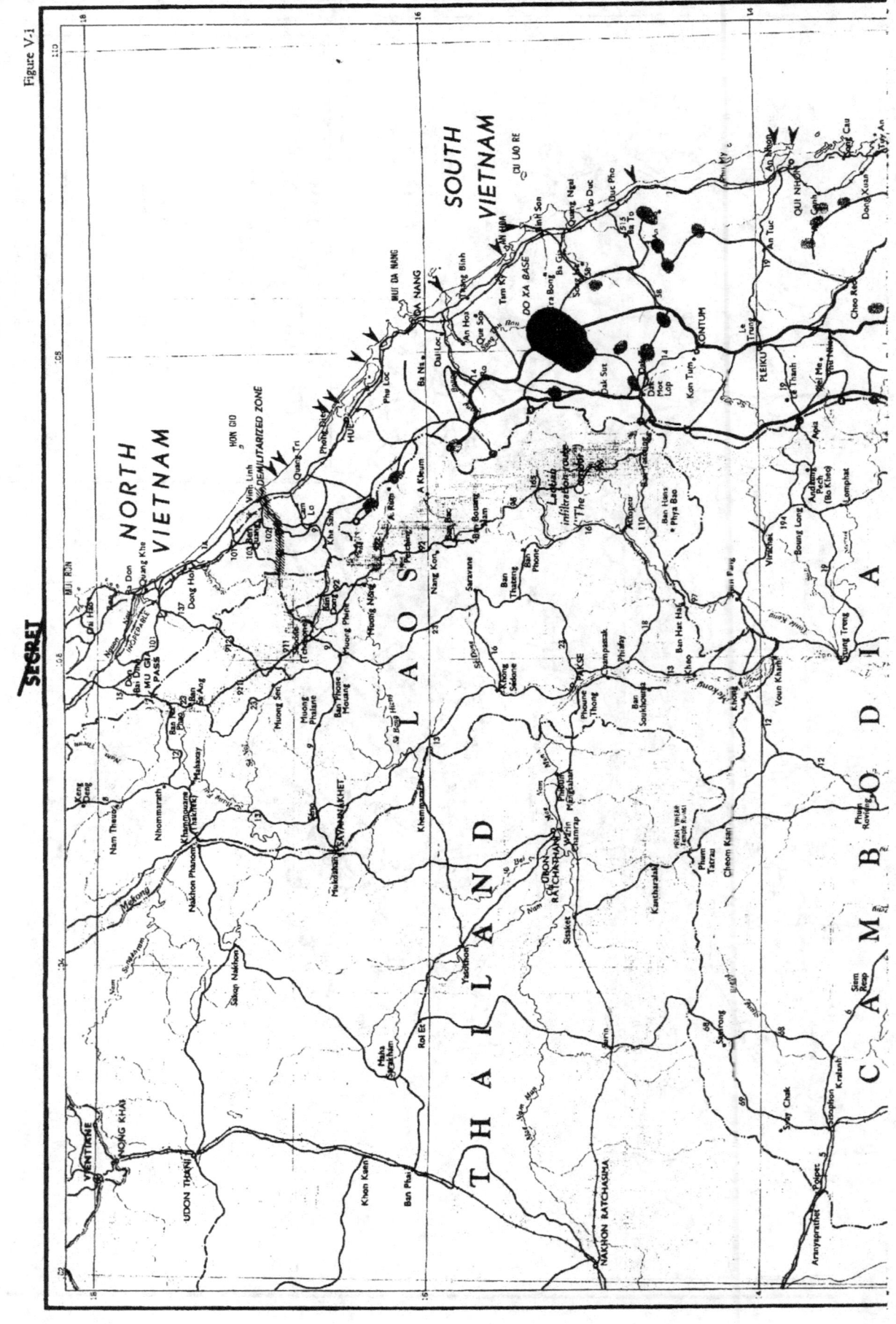

Figure V-1

route runs between the first route and the coast and follows route 14 for many miles. Many lateral routes connect the two major north-south routes and with coastal points. Some of the north-south routes in the eastern section of the country running roughly between route 19 and the Saigon area are used mainly as supply routes.

Enemy forces attempt to use major South Vietnamese highways to the maximum extent possible. When such roads are only partly under their control, personnel and/or supplies move parallel to the uncontrolled sections. A large portion of the network is located near South Vietnamese provincial and military boundaries where surveillance may be least effective. The enemy selects routes in many cases which are just outside the fire envelope of static GVN artillery units.

Besides Route 14, the VC probably make extensive use of Route 20 north from Saigon, Route 21 west from Khanh Hoa to Darlac, Route 22 through Tay Ninh, Provincial Routes 12 and 8 in the Delta region, Provincial Route 7 west from the coastal province of Phu Yen, and Provincial Routes 13, 4, 1, and 8 north of Saigon. Most of the use of trucks occurs on these roads.

B. Waterways

The VC depend on water craft as the basic means of transportation in the Delta region of South Vietnam. The VC main and local force units in IV Corps alone probably possess about 4,000 craft of varying sizes; the approximately 40,000 militia in IV Corps probably use additional thousands of vessels.

Troops usually are transported in small three-man sampans, and supply movements vary from organized convoys of medium-sized craft capable of carrying loads of one ton or more to small individual craft. The average load per water craft is estimated at 1 3/4 tons but the enemy also has much larger types at his disposal.

Several factors permit Communist forces to make extensive use of waterways in the Delta. There is no registration of civilian boats, so that Communist boats are difficult to identify. Curfew restrictions cannot be imposed or enforced except on some major waterways because of the lack of adequate communications and patrol craft. Moreover, security is maintained by moving primarily at night, by taking advantage of foliage near river banks, by maintaining advance and rear units to warn of nearby flight activity and by sinking boats for later recovery when detection seems imminent.

IV. <u>War Zones</u>

War Zones usually consist of a group of dispersed and relatively primitive supply caches, command posts, arms workshops, training facilities, and troop bivouacs linked by a network of unpaved roads, trails, and paths. They generally are located on major transport routes used by the enemy in areas which are sparsely populated and/or populated by ethnic or religious minorities hostile to the South Vietnamese government. The war zones located near planned Communist areas of combat probably serve as staging areas, while those located well away from friendly forces most likely contain facilities for weapons repair and manufacture, training, and rest. Areas, such as War Zone C, adjacent to the Cambodian border also serve as access to sanctuary and as transit points for movement of supplies and troops. Until late 1962, the enemy operated in these zones with relative impunity, but the areas have been coming under increasingly heavy ground and air attack in recent months.

V. <u>Logistic Resupply Requirement for Communist Forces in South Vietnam</u>

The VC/NVA forces in South Vietnam have a daily total logistic requirement of 150 tons. This logistic requirement is divided into 5 classes: Class I (food), Class II (weapons), Class III (petroleum), Class IV (quartermaster, engineer and medical) and Class V (ammunition). Figure V-2 shows the daily volume of each class of supply and the amounts supplied from internal and external sources.

A. <u>Class I (Food Supplies)</u>

The Communist forces in South Vietnam obtain most of their food supplies within the country. Although

Figure V-2

SOUTH VIETNAM
DAILY VC/NVA LOGISTIC REQUIREMENTS AS OF MID-YEAR 1966 BY CLASS AND SOURCE OF SUPPLY*

(Short Tons)

☐ Internal Supplies
☐ External Supplies

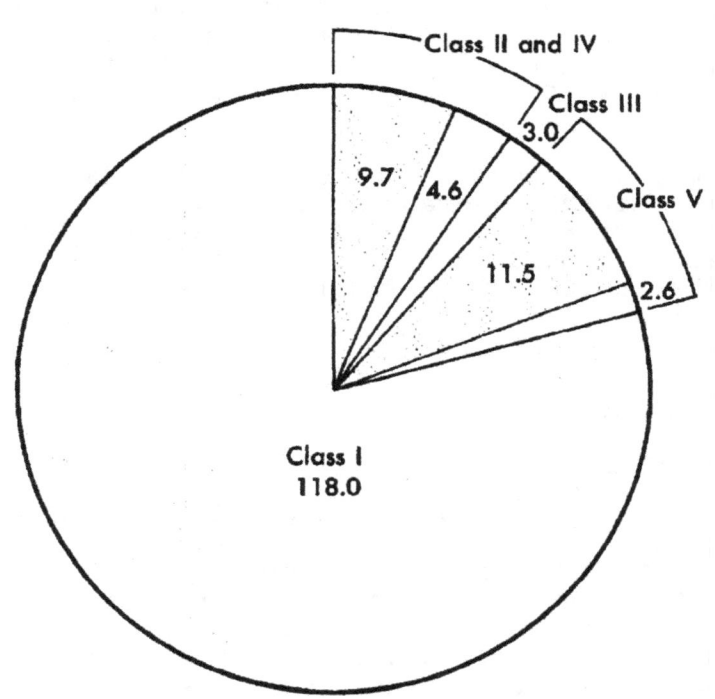

*Requirements as calculated by CIA and contained in ranges presented in NIE 14.3-66.

54638 8-66 CIA

these forces control sufficient rice production to satisfy all VC/NVA food requirements, large quantities of rice apparently are being transported from Cambodia to enemy controlled rice-deficit areas in South Vietnam. This is because of the difficulty in sustaining internal distribution of large amounts of bulk commodities.

The principal rice-deficit areas with large troop concentrations include the provinces of Kontum, Pleiku, Darlac, Phu Bon, and Quang Duc, all in the II Corps area, and Phuoc Long, Binh Long and the northern part of Tay Ninh in the III Corps. If the main and local force VC and NVA troops in these areas were made completely dependent on Cambodian sources for food, Cambodia would be providing about 25 percent of the total daily food requirement for all Communist forces in South Vietnam.

Enemy incidents of terrorism and harassment have risen from a monthly average of 1,629 in 1964 to 2,233 during the first four months of 1966. Although these increases are attributable to various factors they may indicate that the enemy is finding it increasingly difficult to obtain local support in terms of food, and/or labor, for the war effort.

B. Class II and Class IV Supplies

1. Weapons

The enemy stock of weapons has been accumulated from several sources. These include weapons which have been captured, locally-produced, buried or left behind in South Vietnam from the Indochina War, and infiltrated from North Vietnam. Local manufacture of military supplies, however, presently emphasizes ammunition, hand grenades, and mines rather than the fabrication of individual weapons.

Significant quantities of Soviet and East European weapons and Chinese Communist copies of these weapons have been infiltrated into South Vietnam from North Vietnam. About 30 percent of the VC main force is estimated to have been at least partially equipped with the new family of Chinese 7.62 mm weapons by January 1966.

With respect to heavy weapons, the crew-served 60/61 mm and 81/82 mm mortars are now found in most main force battalions. The recent introduction of 120 mm mortars also has added to the firepower of Communist forces in the south. Other heavy weapons known to have been used by Communist forces include the 75 mm recoilless rifle, the 70 mm pack howitzer, and possibly the 105 mm howitzer, the latter having been captured from friendly forces or dating from the war with the French.

The flow of weapons from outside South Vietnam has enabled the VC to achieve some progress in weapons standardization within main force units. However, nonstandard weapons are used by a large number of VC local forces and guerrilla forces. Data on weapons captured in 1963, 1964, and 1965 show that the use of Chinese-manufactured arms is increasing as seen in the following tabulation:

(Percentages based on captured items)

	Chinese	U. S.	French	Home made and other
1963	8.4	27.7	49.8	14.1
1964	22.7	29.1	32.6	15.6
1965	27.0	50.0	8.0	15.0
1966 (estimate)	35.0	30.0	15.0	20.0*

*Includes 5 percent from USSR.

Of the nearly 1,000 weapons captured by Allied troops in clashes with the NVA near Plei Me last November, 86 percent were of Chinese Communist manufacture, 11 percent of North Korean manufacture, and 3 percent of Soviet manufacture. These arms represent the most modern weapons used by Chinese and North Korean forces, suggesting that NVA units are well equipped.

2. Clothing

Enemy requirements for clothing and other textile products are not extensive, and most of it is obtained locally by a special VC clothing unit. However, a number of clothing items such as khaki uniforms, underwear, and winter clothing for the mountainous regions have been produced in North Vietnam and are issued to infiltrators. Some clothing is also required in Cambodia.

3. Medical Supplies

Medical supplies are obtained both locally and from various Communist and Free World countries through Cambodia and North Vietnam. Antibiotics, plasma, and quinine are the principal items acquired from external sources. Medical supplies are in fairly tight supply so that their external procurement has a high priority.

4. Transportation Equipment

Trucks, water craft, and other transportation equipment used by enemy forces in South Vietnam usually are acquired in the country, sometimes by confiscation, but also by purchase or borrowing.

5. Signal Supplies

Most VC communications equipment has been supplied by East European Communist countries or Communist China or is of US, Japanese, or French manufacture and has been captured on the battlefield. NVA equipment is infiltrated with military personnel.

6. Engineer and Chemical Supplies

Most VC/NVA chemical and engineer supplies are estimated to be obtained from within the country, although some chemicals are also smuggled in from Cambodia. A large share of the chemicals is used for the production of filler for locally-produced ammunition.

C. **Class III (Petroleum)**

The total requirement for petroleum products for VC/NVA forces in South Vietnam is small, being needed primarily for confiscated vehicles, motorized junks in the Delta region, generator equipment at command posts, and in some crude arms factories. The VC obtain supplies from taxation of the content of petroleum tank trucks in VC/NVA-controlled areas of South Vietnam, seizure of petroleum supplies, and purchase from local gasoline stations or in Cambodia.

D. **Class V (Ammunition)**

In the present situation of relative independence from external sources for most supplies, ammunition is the principal determinant of the volume of supplies which must be infiltrated from North Vietnam. The supply of ammunition is particularly important to the major combat elements equipped with the new family of weapons who are completely dependent on outside sources for their ammunition. Due to the extensive use of a variety of weapons, however, the enemy utilizes both internal and external sources for the supply of ammunition. Standard ammunition is generally manufactured in the Communist countries. The remainder of the supply is from captured stock or is manufactured locally in VC engineer workshops. Viet Cong munition factories are not estimated to have a present capability to manufacture 7.62 mm ammunition. There is no evidence that expended shells are reloaded, and captured U.S. 7.62 mm ammunition is not compatible with Communist weapons.

The heavier ammunition employed by the enemy includes 40 mm antitank grenades, 57 mm and 75 mm recoilless rifle rounds, 60 mm, 82 mm, and 120 mm mortar rounds, and 70 mm, 75 mm and 105 mm howitzer ammunition. All heavier ammunition is either captured or obtained from external sources.

VI. **Geographic Distribution of Logistic Requirements for VC/NVA Forces in South Vietnam**

As of mid-year 1966 the strength of VC/NVA regular forces in South Vietnam stood at 118,000 personnel. The disposition of these forces by Corps area is shown in Figure V-3 which also shows the major areas of rice cultivation. The predominant share of these forces is located in rice-deficit areas.

In Figure V-4 we show by Corps area the current allocation of total logistic requirements--150 tons a day--and that portion--some 20 tons a day--which must be supplied from external sources. The distribution of Communist forces reflects an unevenness in daily logistic requirements by Corps area and leads to internal distribution problems.

Thus the forces in the I and IV Corps areas require only 19 and 15 percent respectively of total daily requirements. The IV Corps, with the smallest concentration of forces, is also the area in which the Communists have the greatest self-sufficiency in food. The II and III Corps areas, in which most of the Communist forces are concentrated, account for almost two-thirds of the total daily requirement. These areas are also the predominant rice-deficit areas.

The inability to transport food from rice surplus to deficit areas is apparently becoming more severe. The Communists consequently have had to turn to Cambodian sources as a logistic expedient to provide rice to some of the forces in the central highlands. This movement has increased in the last half year and has reached an estimated 15 tons a day. The need to turn to Cambodian sources for rice indicates that internal distribution is one of the most pressing problems faced by the Communists and is probably the most vulnerable aspect of their entire logistics operation. As US/GVN and allied forces have increasing success in capturing or destroying Communist stockpiles and in disrupting Communist control of transport routes this problem would be even more aggravated. It would not, however, be critical, particularly as long as food supplies could be obtained and infiltrated from Cambodia. Even if they had to be provided by North Vietnam through Laos the volumes which we estimate would be required could be accommodated on the Laotian infiltration network.

Figure V-3

SOUTH VIETNAM
DISPOSITION OF VC/NVA REGULAR FORCES BY CORPS AREA, MID-1966

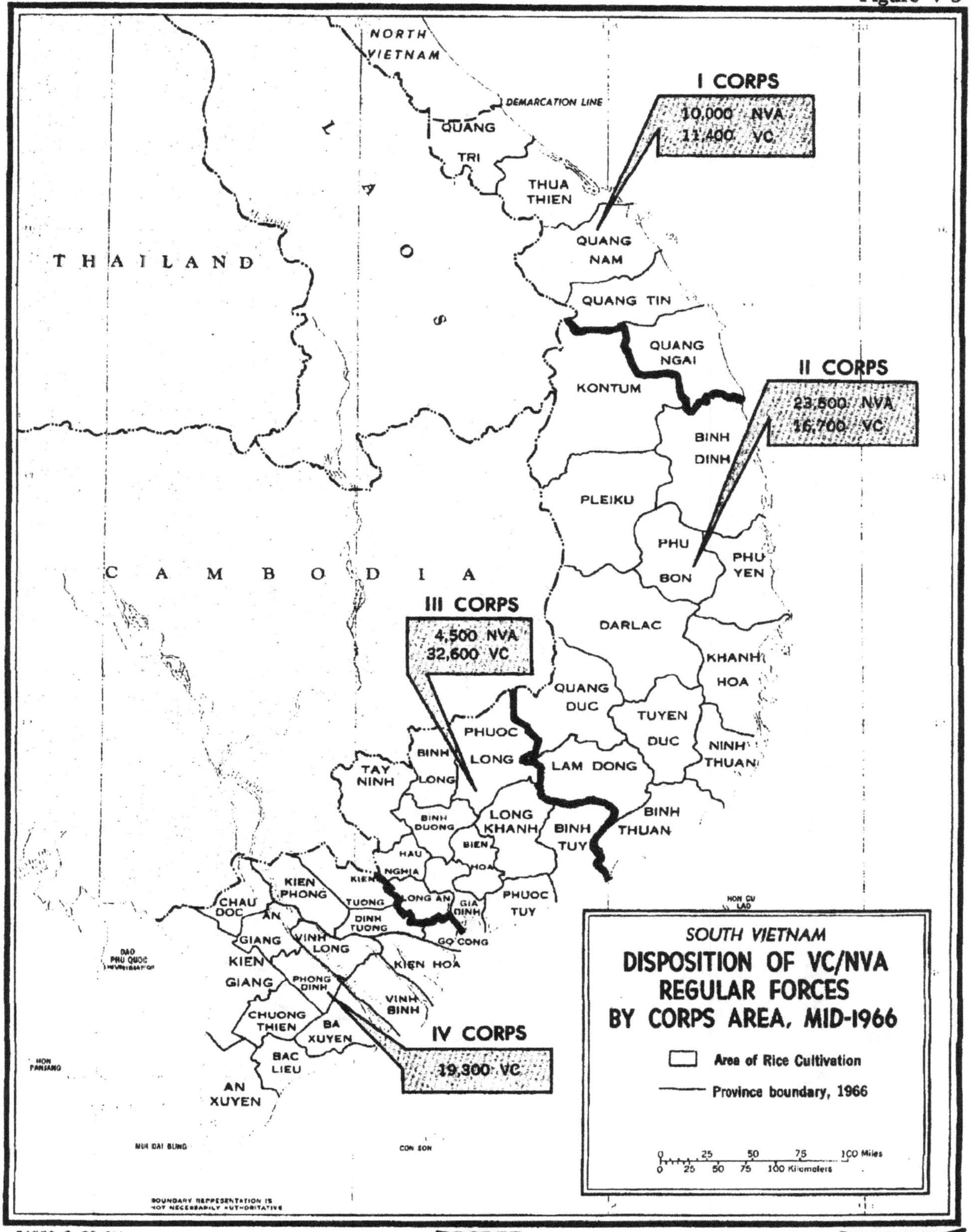

I CORPS
10,000 NVA
11,400 VC

II CORPS
23,500 NVA
16,700 VC

III CORPS
4,500 NVA
32,600 VC

IV CORPS
19,300 VC

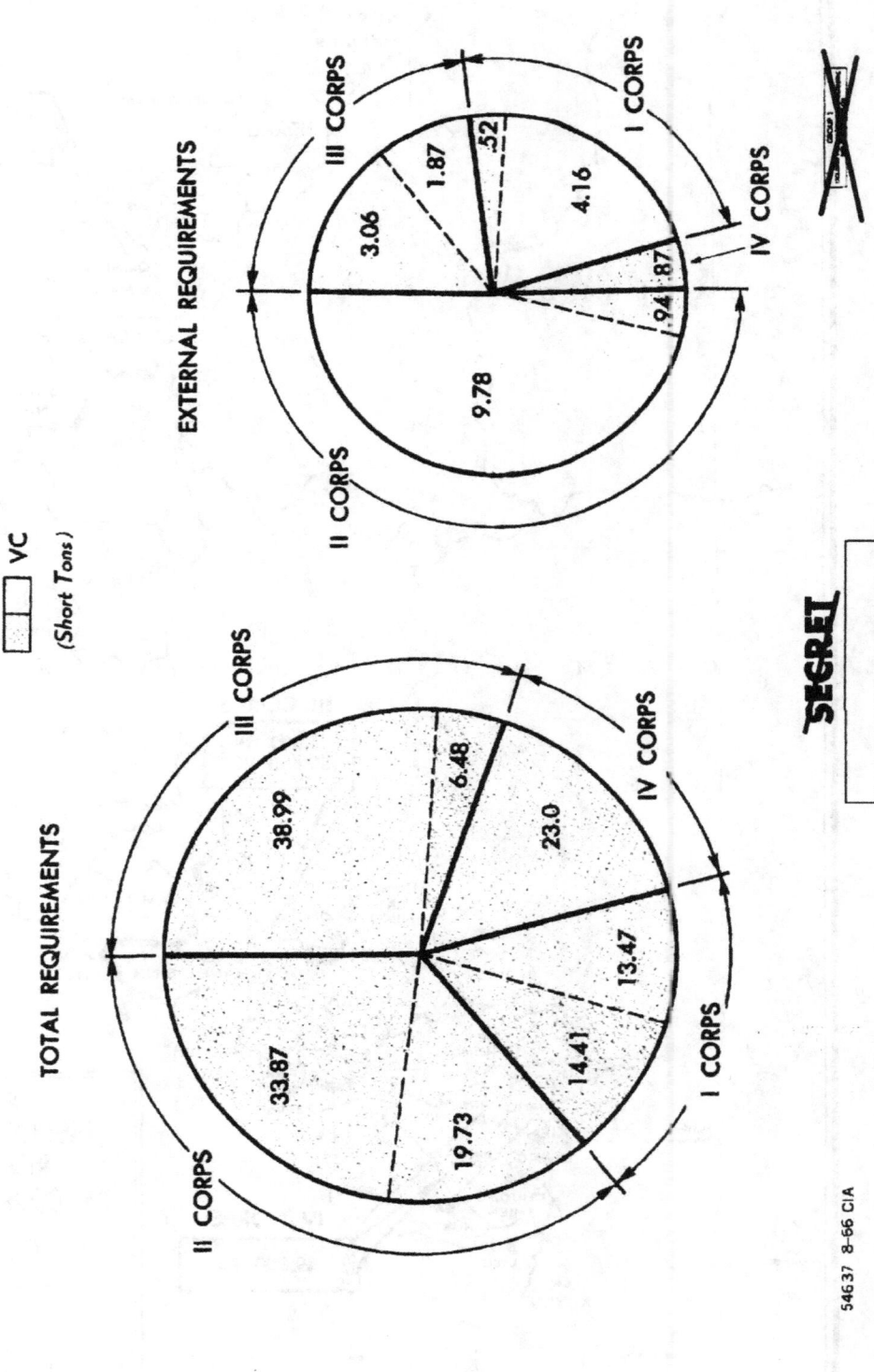

Figure V-4

SOUTH VIETNAM
DAILY VC/NVA LOGISTIC REQUIREMENTS AS OF MID-YEAR 1966, BY CORPS AREA
(Short Tons)

The current estimates of the build-up of Communist forces and the highest probable levels of combat through mid-1967 yield an external logistic requirement for Class II and IV and Class V supplies of 55 tons a day. If the disposition of Communist forces remains the same and internal distribution of food is impossible, an additional 45 tons of food could be required daily in the food-deficit areas (See Figure V-5). This added logistic requirement would not tax the infiltration route through Laos very severely, but it would aid substantially in reducing the excess of road capacity over logistic requirements. But as the Communist build-up continues and the level of combat increases the excess of road capacity in Laos over logistic requirements could be diminished substantially.

The present disposition of Communist forces in South Vietnam is much more favorable for resupply from external sources. Over 85 percent of the NVA forces and 35 percent of the VC forces are in the I and II Corps areas in close proximity to both the Laotian infiltration corridor and the infiltration routes from Cambodia. These forces account for almost three-fourths of the supplies which must be infiltrated from external sources.

VII. Effect of Destruction and Capture of Supplies

The destruction and capture of Communist supplies by US and Allied forces during the past year as compiled from available data for selected categories of supplies are shown below. The data for food, ammunition, and POL basically represent losses incurred in the provinces of Binh Duong, Bien Hoa and Tay Ninh in III Corps area, and Quang Duc, Binh Dinh, Phu Yen, and Pleiku in II Corps--areas where US forces engaged in large search and destroy operations. Weapons losses include those inflicted by South Vietnamese troops as well as US and Allied forces.

Food (tons)	10-12,000
Ammunition	
Small arms and 12.7 mm machine gun (rounds)	180,000
POL (gallons)	7,700
Weapons	21,284

Figure V-5

SOUTH VIETNAM
DAILY LOGISTIC REQUIREMENTS OF VC/NVA FORCES
AT VARYING LEVELS OF COMBAT
June 1966 and Projected June 1967

(Short Tons)

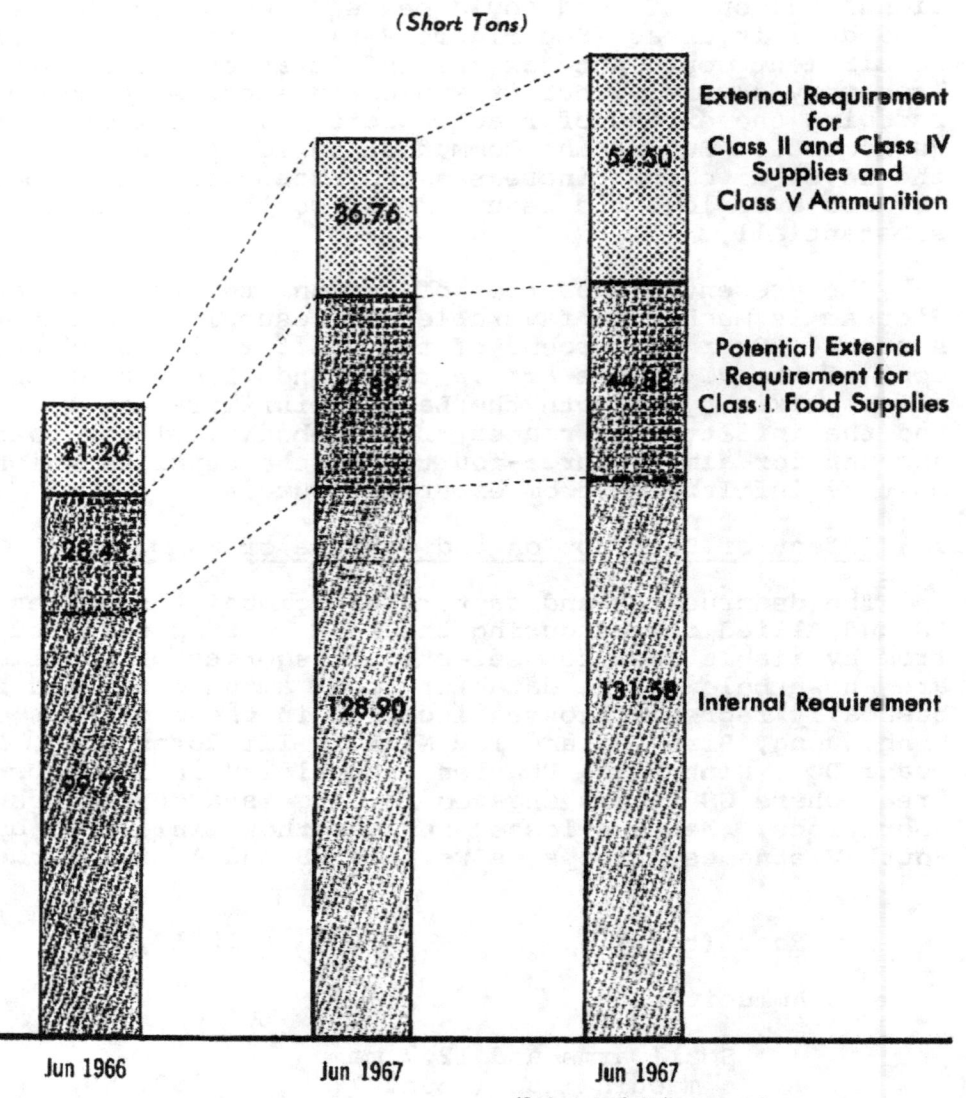

The quantity of food known to have been captured or destroyed represents an amount sufficient to feed the current Communist main and local forces in South Vietnam for a period of about three months. This quantity becomes relatively significant when considered as the minimum loss of food to the enemy. Moreover, recent allied operations have not only destroyed enemy food crops and uncovered VC food storage points, but protected rice harvests from enemy acquisition and interdicted the movement of some food to VC distribution points.

Known losses of small arms and heavy machine gun ammunition, however, represent only about three days' supply for the current order of battle of VC/NVA troops at present levels of combat. Although the magnitude of losses sustained in engagements with ARVN forces or as a result of air strikes cannot be determined at the present time, such losses to date have had little discernible effect on the enemy's ability to initiate attacks or on the rate with which he expends his ammunition.

Known losses of POL in South Vietnam represent less than a two week supply for VC/NVA forces. Losses inflicted against POL stocks by ARVN forces and air strikes probably have added to the quantity of such supplies denied the enemy, but due to the small requirement estimated for VC/NVA forces operating in South Vietnam these losses probably have no effect on enemy capabilities.

The known number of weapons captured or destroyed by friendly forces through June 1966 was sufficient to equip some 40 battalions. Losses incurred as a result of air strikes have raised the total weapons loss, but again, if such losses are examined in the context of the number of VC-initiated attacks over recent months, it becomes clear that total weapons losses have not been prohibitive.

The quantities of destroyed and captured Communist supplies undoubtedly have added to the logistic problems faced by VC/NVA forces in South Vietnam but the extent of these adverse effects cannot be estimated since we are almost totally lacking in knowledge of Communist stockpiles in South Vietnam. The data presently available do not include losses inflicted by South Vietnamese forces (with the exception of losses of weapons); supplies lost as a result of B-52 strikes; or supplies destroyed as a result of numerous strikes by U.S. tactical aircraft.

~~TOP SECRET~~

ANNEX VI

THE MORALE OF THE COMMUNIST FORCES

~~TOP SECRET~~

year. There is little hard evidence on the extent of simple desertion or "resignation" from irregular ranks.

Southbound NVA units apparently lose a few deserters in North Vietnam and Laos, and some also in South Vietnam. By mid-1966, there had been about 100 defections and 500 surrenders from NVA units.

The continued resolution of the NVA is in sharp contrast to the decline in morale of the southern Viet Cong Army in part because its cadres are good, but also because NVA soldiers who want to quit believe they have no place to go.

Barring a marked improvement in Viet Cong military fortunes or another round of political instability in Saigon, Southern Viet Cong morale seems likely to continue its downhill course. The deterioration in morale seems likely to accelerate as the quality of low level cadres continues to decline and as the proportion of poorly motivated draftees in army ranks increases. The erosion of morale will probably be reflected by rising rates of defection and desertion. Desertion rates could begin to hurt the Viet Cong seriously in the not too distant future.

The NVA troops in South Vietnam are likely to remain resolute, in large part because they see no alternative to fighting. If the resolution and quality of the southern Viet Cong continue to deteriorate, the NVA units will probably assume an even greater share of the fighting.

A. The Viet Cong View of Morale

The Viet Cong, like Napoleon, consider morale far more important than materiel. According to a Viet Cong document written in 1965, apparently by an official on the COSVN staff, "the Americans fail to realize that neither the size of an expeditionary force nor the quantity of modern weapons can be a decisive factor in any liberation war. They (the Americans) are not aware or not willing to admit the fact that the key factor that leads to victory in any war is the determination of the people to fight and win."* The Communists do not leave the maintenance of morale to chance.

A Viet Cong document which discussed several missions of training italicized only one: that of heightening "the will to fight and morale of our organization." It prescribed "reindoctrination" courses, 60-70 days long for Viet Cong regulars, and 20-30 days long for village guerrillas. Such courses are supplemented by frequent spot lectures, several drafts of which have been captured, and by attempts by the Viet Cong to exclude government propaganda from their territory.**

The Viet Cong constantly assess the state of their own morale. For example, a captured memorandum, dated 14 April 1965, concerning the censoring of personal letters stated "the purpose of censorship is to detect anti-revolutionary thoughts or loss of morale...." A more recent memorandum, dated 27 February 1966, asked subordinate units to report on the "status of political ideology" together with "the number of North Vietnamese, and South Vietnamese (Viet Cong) deserters, stragglers, ralliers and missing."

While determined to preserve their own morale, the Viet Cong are equally resolved to undermine their enemy's. Government officials are assassinated not simply to eliminate specific officeholders, but to sow panic and confusion. Attacks are often launched for psychological effect rather than for purely military reasons. Viet Cong psychological warfare efforts are massive, much larger in proportion to resources available than those of the allies. All PRP Committees, from

---

*North Vietnamese Minister of Defense Giap reiterated the theme in the January issue of Hoc Tap, the party's theoretical journal in North Vietnam.

**One Viet Cong document even suggested that people in the "liberated zone" be forbidden from listening to "plays and soap operas" broadcast by government radio.

COSVN down to village levels, have Military Proselyting Sections to induce GVN defections.*

The Viet Cong hierarchy is aware that the morale of its rank and file has been gradually eroding, but it apparently believes that allied--particularly South Vietnamese--morale is deteriorating even more rapidly. Because the Viet Cong view the war primarily as a contest of wills, evidence of crumbling or lowered morale on the part of their adversaries takes on particular significance. Tales of South Vietnamese ineptitude and lack of motivation are frequent and often well-grounded. ARVN desertion rates may give the Viet Cong considerable grounds for hope.** The recent Buddhist upheavals may have reinforced the Viet Cong's opinion that the fabric of the South Vietnamese government is weak, and that its will to continue over the long run is questionable.

B. Morale of the Cadres

The Viet Cong's greatest strength lies in the organization and in the cadres who keep it going. As long as the cadre structure remains intact and cadres are determined and willing to impose discipline, the rank and file, who may become individually disheartened, are unlikely to give up in large groups.

The level of cadre spirit, although generally high, varies from echelon to echelon. Among the leaders of the party, there is little evidence of a slackening of resolve, and mid-level cadres also appear resolute. Low-level cadres, although they continue to get the jobs done, are often less sanguine than their superiors, however, and there is considerable evidence that many are discouraged. A moderate but increasing number of assistant platoon leaders, squad leaders, assistant

---

*The proselyters aim at US as well as Vietnamese soldiers. A study of US troops, written late last year by COSVN's Military Proselyting Section, asserted that while US officers were well-indoctrinated, most US enlisted men in South Vietnam "dread a large-scale and protracted war, and favor negotiations." Thus far, no American soldiers have defected.

**ARVN desertion rates per thousand:
Monthly average, 1964: 8.3
Monthly average, 1965: 14.2
Monthly average, 1966: 20.1 (1st quarter)

squad leaders, and hamlet village officials, have appeared at government Chieu Hoi centers,* and many others have deserted or "resigned."**

North Vietnamese formations apparently are not immune from cadre desertions. Captives from an antiaircraft unit established in North Vietnam in April 1965 said that the unit had had "many sudden changes in command" because cadre deserted before arriving in the south. Cadre desertions from North Vietnamese units are probably not numerous, however. Interrogations, RAND studies, captured diaries, and letters indicate that most NVA cadres, despite hardships, are resolute. A recent MACV study on the NVA states that "the quality of its cadre is one of the NVA's strongest assets."

The lowering quality of Southern Viet Cong cadres probably accounts to a large degree for recent increases in cadre desertion. A captured party directive from the Viet Cong province of Can Tho, dated 30 April 1966, complained of the party cadres' "inability to cope with hardship," and ascribed "the drop in quality.. [to] recent heavy recruiting, which resulted in members' putting too much stress on quantity..." The directive stated that "at present we have a number of comrades who have not

---

*A RAND researcher has noted that out of 1,274 ralliers who defected in the last six months of 1965, 164 (13%) claimed to be cadres. Surprisingly, a larger percentage of regulars (26%) than irregulars (9%) said they were cadres. The same researcher said in June 1966 that the overall ratio of cadres to total defectors is rising. Exact figures are unavailable.

**Captured documents indicate that on some occasions cadres have been about as prone to desert as the rank and file. For example, a Viet Cong report dated 3 April 1966, stated that an ARVN operation in the delta had induced "32 cadres and 42 troops" to "resign."

yet been able to eradicate their bourgeois mentality...
When the going gets rough, they drag their feet.*

The shortage of experienced cadre has become an increasingly common theme in Viet Cong documents. The shortage--particularly in the delta where many have been withdrawn to reinforce units outside the area--has forced the Viet Cong to employ what may turn out to be unpopular expedients. A RAND researcher in Dinh Tuong Province in the delta has reported that in a number of cases, women are now being employed as party officials. Despite the Communist doctrine of the equality of sexes, this is probably deeply resented by Vietnamese men. The same researcher states that in some instances, "outsiders" are being put in charge of local units in Dinh Tuong. Although many reports have been received about "dissension" arising from the use of outsiders, there are no hard indications as yet that the disagreements have reached serious proportions.

C. *Morale of the Soldiers*

1. *The North Vietnamese Army (NVA)*

By most objective measures, the fighting spirit of the North Vietnamese soldier is good. As of 1 July 1966, only about 100 NVA soldiers had defected, and allied soldiers had captured only about 500, despite frequent engagements and heavy fighting. No NVA infantry unit as large as a squad, has surrendered en masse. Allied field officers report that with few exceptions, North Vietnamese soldiers fight tenaciously and are well disciplined in battle. On the basis of interviews of 39 North Vietnamese soldiers, the RAND Corporation has concluded that "most NVA soldiers see no option but to go on fighting."

---

*Other captured documents make reference to the poor quality of new cadre. For example, a 1965 "Top Secret" document from Phu Yen Province complained that the "new cadres used for replenishment of our VC units cause serious security problems due to their low political experience." A later document from the same province contrasted the "old time cadre," who were "experienced but somewhat tired," with the "new cadre" who were "ardent but inexperienced." The document added, however, that "poor cadre are better than none."

Available evidence, however, indicates that many of the rank and file, and some cadres, are in low spirits. The level of an NVA soldier's morale, of course, depends on where he is and what he has experienced. Before starting the trip south, most North Vietnamese are in good spirits. Interrogations of prisoners and ralliers, and captured NVA diaries, of which there are at least 30 examples, indicate that most feel their cause is just, and that their mission is to rid South Vietnam of American "imperialists" and "puppets."

With some exceptions, the NVA soldiers retain their spirit as they march through the southern part of North Vietnam toward the Laotian corridor. After they cross into Laos, however, their mood begins to shift. Steep hills, tight marching schedules, bombing raids, mosquitoes and leeches help induce the change. Diarists frequently become eloquent about their troubles during the march through the corridor, which takes from one to three months. An NVA sergeant wrote in his diary, after three weeks in Laos, that "twelve days had passed with innumerable hardships. Marches and marches. Rains and rains." Another diarist wrote, after a month on the trail, that he was going through "the deepest sorrow and utmost hardship" he had ever experienced. A third diarist, also on the trail for a month, wrote on 25 January 1966 that he was "lying on the ground, suffering from the stings of Laotian flies and bleeding...." A fourth declared that "no word is enough to depict the rigor and hardship we have been experiencing."

Once he reaches South Vietnam, an NVA soldier's morale often rises, particularly if his unit is allowed to recuperate. One infiltrator, on reaching the South, wrote a friend that although "the infiltration trip to South Vietnam was filled with rigors and hardships," he was now "eager to do his duties." Not all of them can rest, however. Many NVA soldiers who fought at Plei Me last November or at A Shau this March were relatively fresh from the trail.

Once in South Vietnam and committed to campaigning, the average NVA soldier lives a life of hardship and danger. Frequently, he is sick. A 23 January 1966 entry in a medical record picked up by the Air Cavalry in Binh Dinh Province noted that in a 519-man NVA battalion, "sick personnel accounted for 45% of the assigned strength." The sick included 133 men who had malaria, 10 suffering from "debility," and two who contracted beri-beri. More recent documents indicate that the NVA sick rates continue high.*

Hardships, fighting, and air and artillery harassment sometimes combine to dishearten individual NVA soldiers, even units. A diary captured in February 1966, kept by a soldier in an antiaircraft detachment infiltrated into South Vietnam late last summer, indicated that the "morale of cadres and soldiers" in his unit "continued to be unstable." Another diarist wrote on 2 January 1966 that "I have been 5 months in the battlefield... I began to wilt under the strain of privations, hardships, and loneliness in the heart of the jungle... I have seen nothing but... jungle, stream water, and bombs and bullets. What a bitter truth! Now I am hoodwinked at the point of no return... I have a deep distaste for the war and I am really fed up with the liberation undertaking, which has been heralded as a 'turning point of history' and a 'golden opportunity'... Instead there exists only illusion, a political trick to appease those who are engaged in the fight." Not all diarists, of course, react to their hardships the same way. One had written earlier, "Damn the Americans! They force us to sleep in forests and eat nothing but rice and salt. I am determined to fight and serve my people until my last breath."

Although NVA units continue to perform well, there is considerable evidence that their composition has been changing, probably for the worse from their point of view. The ratio of recruits to veterans is rising.** Moreover, as NVA units suffer heavy casualties, they are taking

---

* The 324B Division, which infiltrated in May directly through the DMZ, has had a much lower malaria rate than other NVA units. A POW said that only about 10% of the division suffered from malaria. The trip across the DMZ, of course, is far shorter than that through Laos.

** A document captured late last year indicated that 59% of the soldiers in one NVA battalion had been conscripted in 1965. NVA units infiltrated earlier in the year had a much higher proportion of veterans.

in southerners as replacements. As a general rule, South Vietnamese fillers are less eager than their northern counterparts.*

On balance, however, neither the rising percentage of draftees nor the inclusion in NVA units of poorly motivated southerners seems likely in the near future to affect seriously NVA combat performance. The quality of NVA cadres is still too high, and the base rates of defection, desertion, and surrender are still too low to indicate a sudden or rapid deterioration in the NVA's ability to fight. It seems likely that for the foreseeable future the North Vietnamese soldier will continue to follow the path of least resistance--that of obeying orders of his cadre, and of staying with his unit.

2. <u>Viet Cong Regulars</u>**

Like NVA formations, indigenous Southern Viet Cong regular units have good combat morale. Almost invariably, they fight well, and under skilled leadership. So far, no regular unit has given up <u>en masse</u>. Few Viet Cong officers have surrendered. Whatever the rank and file may feel off the battlefield, they are tightly disciplined in combat.

Yet the morale problems of Viet Cong regular units are more numerous and more concrete than those of NVA battalions. Exact statistics are unavailable, but it is estimated that approximately 1,400 regulars defected to the government last year. (That is, about 3% of the total mean regular strength.) Several hundred additional regulars surrendered last year. The overall yearly desertion rate of regulars, including defectors and those who go home, probably runs around 25%, somewhat higher than ARVN rates. The high desertion rate is a relatively recent development.

---

* An NVA document captured in Binh Dinh complained of the "relatively low political awareness of the newly-recruited southerners."

** There are two types of regulars:

1) Main Force units, directly subordinate to COSVN, or to a military region headquarters.

2) Local Force units, directly subordinate to a provincial or district headquarters.

The decline in off-battlefield morale has come about principally for two reasons. The first is the constant harassment and heavy losses inflicted on regular units by the Allies. Captured documents attest to the effect of the pounding. A report captured in Hau Nghia Province, issued in November 1965 by the "Unified Command Committee" (apparently a regional party organization) outlines some of the problems that Viet Cong regulars face:

> To cope with our mobility on the battlefield, the enemy increases his air and artillery activities day and night or conducts continuous sweep operations to wear down our armed forces or foil our plan of attack if he foresees our intentions... (Our) movements frequently take place at night. Troops must carry heavy loads and move great distances... (They) must frequently bivouac in the field, lie on the ground, endure bad weather, and are kept awake by enemy aircraft and arillery; therefore, their health is highly affected... (Consequently) the troops' morale and nerves are permanently high strung and many complications arise in case of alarm.*

The second reason for the decline in off-battlefield morale among regulars is the changing composition of the Viet Cong army. In 1964, regular units consisted largely of well-motivated volunteers. Since then, the Viet Cong have had to rely increasingly on unwilling conscripts. A study of Chieu Hoi records shows that recently-recruited conscripts make up a large portion of those who defect. They are also far more prone than volunteers to desert. As the proportion of poorly-motivated draftees among Viet Cong regulars increases, desertion and defection rates should rise.

It would be a mistake, however, to picture the morale of Viet Cong regular forces as completely gloomy. Neither the low-level cadre nor the rank and file are as

---

*Documents and prisoners captured in other parts of the country attest that such problems are widespread.

staunch as they used to be, but many noncoms and apparently most officers appear as determined as ever. Yet the trend in the quality of regular personnel seems inexorably downward. Eventually, the erosion in quality of regulars, accompanied by an increasingly high desertion rate, may limit the Viet Cong's ability to carry out their present strategy.

3. <u>Viet Cong Irregulars</u>*

Viet Cong irregular forces continue in large part to perform their tasks. In fact, the incidence of terrorism and sabotage--usually carried out by guerrillas --rose substantially in the last quarter of 1965, and except for a seasonal drop around Tet, has stayed at high levels ever since.

A considerable body of evidence suggests, however, that the morale of the irregulars has been dropping over the past year. Last year, about 7,000 defected to the government. Approximately 5,000 more surrendered. In 1964, about 1,500 defected and 3,500 surrendered. The overall frequency of defection and surrender has continued to increase this year. Desertions among guerrillas appear to be increasing, although hamlet militiamen who serve at home, apparently seldom desert.

When Allied activity is intense, irregulars in some areas have surrendered and defected in large numbers. Early this year in Binh Dinh Province, for example, while the six-week-long Operation WHITE WING was in progress, some 650 irregulars gave up and about 250 rallied. According to a US official involved in the Chieu Hoi program, "several 10-15-man groups" were among those who defected in Binh Dinh.

---

*Viet Cong irregular forces are those subordinate to the village and hamlet. They include:

1) Guerrillas, consisting of full-time squads and platoons, not always based in their village or hamlets.

2) People's Self-Defense Force (often called the militia), consisting of part-time paramilitary forces assigned to defend hamlets and villages.

The rise in defections among irregulars probably has occurred for the same reasons that an increase took place among the regulars. Allied operations have resulted in an increasing decline in guerrilla morale, and the quality of personnel has declined.* As Viet Cong casualties mount, both trends seem likely to continue.

4. Recruitment Problems

Until the middle of last year, the Viet Cong appeared to be able to fill its ranks with relative ease. Volunteers were still fairly plentiful, and draftees usually went willingly. Somewhere around mid-1965, however, the situation apparently began to sour. As Viet Cong demands for manpower soared, volunteers became scarcer, and conscripts joined the Viet Cong more reluctantly. The trend is illustrated by an undated document captured in late November 1965 in Long Khanh Province. The document stated that "the Youth's enlistment... in January, February and March 1965 increased over that in the last six months in 1964... However, the result of enlistment obtained in the first six months of 1965 failed to meet the requirements of the armed forces... The draft movement in May, June and July declined."** Some Viet Cong draftees interviewed by RAND have stated that "they wanted to avoid military service with either side, but that if they had to serve, they preferred to do so with ARVN, where they were paid and their families received death benefits."

The Viet Cong are using several expedients to relieve their manpower demands. They have resorted to kidnapings, are employing large numbers of women as irregulars,***

---

* A substantial number of documents indicate that one of the main reasons for the decline has been the Viet Cong policy of sending guerrillas and militiamen who show promise to serve with regular units. The "upgrading" process has been particularly intense in IV Corps, where Viet Cong fortunes are gradually deteriorating.

** Other documents and POW interrogations indicate that the problem is widespread.

*** A Viet Cong directive written in August 1965 stated that one-third of all "guerrillas" should be women.

and are increasing the use of ARVN defectors and POW's to fill regular ranks.*

Such measures probably provide some temporary alleviation of Viet Cong recruitment problems. They do not solve the problems however. In addition, as casualties mount, it is possible that the Communists will eventually be unable by any device to replace their losses from within South Vietnam, thereby placing an even greater demand on North Vietnam for troops.

D. Gauges of Military Morale

1. Defection

Since early 1963, according to the Chieu Hoi office in Saigon, about 20,000 Viet Cong regular and irregular soldiers have rallied to the government. Of these, about 2,900 defected in 1963. The number dropped to 1,900 in 1964. In 1965, largely as a result of the American intervention, Communist military defections increased to about 8,500. In the first half of this year, approximately 6,500 soldiers rallied.

Generally speaking, the low-level, poorly motivated Viet Cong soldier defects at a far higher rate than does the cadre.** Nonetheless, defectors tend to share certain characteristics. They are usually of short service, and they tend to rally near their homes.

---

* A directive issued by the Central Trung Bo Liberation Army, Unit 2B, dated 26 October 1965, stated that units were required "to select 50% of surrendered RVNAF soldiers to fill vacancies in our units." A number of documents indicate that the Viet Cong are wary of ex-government troops.

** The percentage of regular defectors appears to be rising, however. Monthly percentage of regulars to total military defectors: July 1965 - 15%; August - 13%; September - 18%; October - 17%; December - 19%; January 1966 - 23%; February - 26%; March - 23%; April - 23%. Although there have been 6,500 military defectors in the first half of this year (compared to about 8,500 all last year), regular defectors this year (about 1,450) already outnumber regular defectors last year (about 1,400).

2. Desertion

   a. Southern Viet Cong

Desertion is an extremely serious problem for the Viet Cong. Available evidence, direct and indirect, indicates that deserters who do not defect are far more numerous than those who do. A clandestinely obtained document, probably genuine, issued by the Central Office for South Vietnam (COSVN) late last year stated that "...desertion for the specific purpose of defecting to the enemy (is) rare in comparison with desertion from other motives..." COSVN undoubtedly is aware of how many of its soldiers desert, and also knows how many of these defect.

COSVN's assertion about the ratio of deserters to defectors is supported by other documents. A Viet Cong "Top Secret" Directive dated 20 October 1965, captured by the 173rd Airborne Brigade in early January 1966, stated that in one area "desertion is prevailing in various armed and paramilitary forces. According to incomplete statistics, there were 138 deserters from January to August 1965...five defected to the ARVN government." Another Viet Cong document mentioned that "during a one-month period in one unit, 47 men deserted to go home and two defected to the enemy." A check of 20 deserters listed in a Viet Cong roster captured in late December, 1965, against records of arrivals in local Chieu Hoi centers indicated that none of the deserters defected.

Although desertion is frequently mentioned in captured Viet Cong documents, only seven so far have included all the ingredients necessary for establishing rates: the size of the unit, the number of deserters who left it, and a time frame. If all seven units are added together, and their respective time frames stretched to a year, their overall projected annual desertion rate would be 32%. However, two of the seven documents imply that the units mentioned had unusually high rates. If these units are excluded from the total, the overall average annual rate of the sample drops to 27%. The seven-unit sample includes two battalions and five companies. The five-unit sample includes two battalions and three companies.

Twenty-seven percent--or rounded off, 25%-- seems plausible as an overall desertion rate for 1965 from regular Viet Cong units. A reading of most POW and rallier interrogations would suggest that the rate is substantially

VI-14

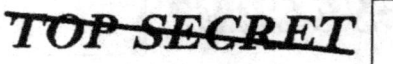

higher than 25%, but prisoners and defectors may be inclined to exaggerate. The interrogations appear to indicate that desertion is more common in local force units than in main force units, and likewise more common in main force units recruited locally than in like units serving away from home.

If the mean size of the regular Viet Cong army (excluding NVA soldiers) was 45,000 last year, and 25% is accepted as the regular desertion rate, then some 11,250 Viet Cong regulars deserted last year.* Since approximately 1,400 regulars defected last year, the ratio of deserters who go home to defectors among regular units would appear to be about seven to one. It should be noted that available documentary evidence suggests the ratio is a good deal higher.

In the first six months of 1966, an estimated 1,450 southern Viet Cong regulars defected (See Defection). If the ratio of deserter to defector is 7-1, and if defection/desertion rates continue at current rates during the rest of the year, then there will be a total of 23,200 defectors and deserters during 1966 from southern Viet Cong regular forces. (2,900x7=20,300 deserters + 2,900 defectors = 23,200). Assuming the mean size of the southern regular force will be about 60,000 for 1966, then the Viet Cong regular force desertion rate would be 38%. Many of these, of course, would be retrieved.

Little is known about desertion among Viet Cong irregular units. The rate of desertion, however, varies considerably by type with the highest rate found among the village guerrillas--the highest category of irregulars. Hamlet militia and guerrillas apparently do not desert in large numbers, but, since they never leave home, they may just refuse to fight.** Within each category of irregular

---

* What is not known is how many Viet Cong deserters return to the ranks, either voluntarily, or through being caught. US advisers estimate that from 15 to 20% of men listed as deserters by the RVNAF return to their own or some other unit. The rate of return among Viet Cong deserters may be comparable.

** Captured documents indicate that hamlet militiamen in several areas have refused to fight, or, as one report put it, "quit rank to live as civilians."

forces the highest desertion rate is probably among the fresh recruits.*

So far, the southern Viet Cong have been able to live with their desertion problem, probably because their manpower pool has been adequate to fill the gaps. If the pool begins to dry up, or if desertion rates increase, the desertion of southerners could become a crucial problem for the Viet Cong. Among the consequences of a higher desertion rate would be an increased reliance on fillers from North Vietnam.

b. The NVA

So far, NVA desertion rates have been relatively low. Captured documents, including diaries, indicate that NVA units moving south lose a few men to desertion in North Vietnam and more along the corridor.** Once in South Vietnam, the average NVA soldier seldom deserts, probably because he has no place to go. Captured documents indicate there are some exceptions. For example, a notebook containing strength figures of a 488-man North Vietnamese outfit shows that 9 were deserters and that 17 men were "lost." Some of the errant may have been South Vietnamese attached to the unit, however. On balance, desertion is not now a serious problem for the NVA, and seems unlikely to become one in the foreseeable future.

3. Surrender

While desertion and defection have been increasing, the rate of battlefield surrender has gone down. In 1963, according to MACV J-2 statistics, 4,771 Viet Cong surrendered. The number dropped to 4,187 in 1964, and rose

---

* A considerable body of evidence points to a high desertion rate among recruits. For example, in one group of 152 recruits being sent from the delta to a training depot in III Corps, 33 deserted enroute. Documents captured at the depot indicate that it had a special "stragglers' and deserters' barracks."

** Where deserters in Laos go is unclear. A diary of an NVA battalion commander suggests that at least some are eaten by tigers.

to 5,982 last year--an increase of 43%. The rise in captives failed to keep pace with the expansion of the Viet Cong, however, whose numbers increased by at least 50% during the year. Furthermore, since 1964, while the number of Viet Cong killed has been growing substantially, the number of captives has increased only slightly.* As one might expect, Viet Cong irregulars are far more prone to surrender than Viet Cong regulars.**

   Why Viet Cong surrenders have failed to keep pace with burgeoning defection and desertion rates is difficult to determine. One explanation lies in the Viet Cong's excellent battlefield discipline. Another may lie in the increasing use of air power by the allies. Many who might otherwise surrender are struck down by bombs before they can reach allied lines.

---

* Ratios of estimated killed to captured:

1964	1965	First 5 months 1966
$\dfrac{16{,}785}{4{,}187}$	$\dfrac{36{,}900}{5{,}982}$	$\dfrac{21{,}245}{2{,}837}$
	(or approximately)	
4:1	6:1	8:1

** In operation WHITE WING, conducted in Binh Dinh Province early this year, 718 Viet Cong reportedly surrendered. According to II Corps estimates, only about 60 of these were regulars.

ANNEX VII

MORALE AMONG THE PEOPLE IN VIET CONG AREAS

ANNEX VII

MORALE AMONG THE PEOPLE IN VIET CONG AREAS

The morale and support of the populace in the areas under Viet Cong control, (the "sea" in which the Communist "fish" must swim) are matters of prime long range importance to the Communists. There is a substantial body of evidence that morale, and therefore, support for the Communists, is dropping in the Viet Cong areas. The flow of refugees has increased dramatically. The desire for safety, of course, is the main motive for this exodus; increasing numbers of people now realize that no Viet Cong region is immune from attack. Among other reasons given by the refugees are high Viet Cong taxes, forced labor, and conscription.

Popular support for the Viet Cong probably will continue to dwindle as insurgent taxes rise and forced labor demands increase. Should the populace begin to think the Viet Cong are definitely losing, movement away from the Communists--if not always towards the government--will probably increase, and the Viet Cong will be faced with an eroding popular base.

Refugees

The principal evidence that the Viet Cong have lost the active support of many people in areas they control is the flow of refugees toward regions dominated by the government. Although there were some refugees during and before 1964, most have fled since the beginning of 1965. The rate of flow appears to have increased particularly since the summer of 1965, coincidental with the build-up of US forces in Vietnam and the large-scale increase in the number of airstrikes. Statistics compiled by the South Vietnamese government* illustrate the upward trend:

---

* These statistics must, of course, be taken with some reserve. There are omissions, duplications, and delays in reporting by provincial officials. Although required to report to Saigon on a weekly basis, some provinces are said to have a statistical backlog of from one to three months. To add to the confusion, many refugees register more than once, in order to pick up extra benefits.

	27 Jun 65	31 Jan 66	30 Jun 66
Refugees in Temporary Shelters	144,717	442,522	500,732
Resettled Refugees	106,435	269,794	360,574
Refugees Returning to Native Villages		72,035	140,502
	251,152	784,351	1,001,808

Moreover, many more flee the Viet Cong than are reflected in government statistics. The government records only those who register. Large numbers of refugees do not, many in order to circumvent local government policies which exclude them from certain areas. The largest number of such unregistered refugees is in Saigon, which has a law on the books forbidding refugees from settling in the city. Estimates of the number of refugees in one of Saigon's nine precincts run as high as 30,000 to 40,000, although the government lists only 1,518 in the entire city.

The principal reason for fleeing given by most refugees is a desire for safety, but a large proportion add that they are weary of Viet Cong taxes, conscription, and demands for forced labor. Whatever the motive, once the refugee has entered a government camp active support for the Communists generally stops. Most refugees cooperate to some extent with the South Vietnamese government.

At present, the Viet Cong do not appear to have a clear, overall policy on what to do about the exodus.* Their course seems to vary by time and place. In some areas, they have merely tried to make the refugees' lot unpleasant. Elsewhere, the Viet Cong have made direct attacks on refugee camps, for instance in Quang Tin Province where 30 refugees were killed and 60 wounded in an attack on a refugee center last January. The refugee flow continues despite such tactics, indicating the inability of the Viet Cong to stop it.

---

* It is abundantly clear from captured documents that the Viet Cong do not want refugees to leave Communist-controlled territory. There is no documentary evidence to support a frequently made assertion that the Viet Cong encourage the flow of refugees to overburden the South Vietnamese government's administrative apparatus.

Those Who Stay

For those who remain in Viet Cong territory, life is becoming increasingly unpleasant. As refugees flee, the pressure on those who remain grows more intense. Taxes are higher, demands for labor have increased, and controls are tighter. Although the Viet Cong have been losing favor in many of their areas in the last twelve months, they still maintain firm control in most of them and still are able to carry out their tasks adequately. By and large, the Saigon government has not been able to translate distaste for the Viet Cong into support for itself by the people in contested and VC-controlled areas, although there have been a few dividends for the government in the form of information provided about the Viet Cong.

1. Taxes

The Viet Cong tax burden--collected in money and goods--falls most heavily on the South Vietnamese peasant, and the Viet Cong effort is costly. According to the captured minutes of a COSVN-level conference held on 15 February 1966, the chief of the COSVN Rear Service Department disclosed that supply requirements for 1966 would be "three times higher" than those of 1965. The Viet Cong frequently set goals considerably in excess of what they expect to achieve, but the COSVN supply officer's disclosure still suggests that tax pressures on the inhabitants of Viet Cong areas will be much heavier this year than last.*

---

* The plight of the taxpayer in Viet Cong areas is illustrated by a document, captured in October in Binh Duong Province, outlining the Viet Cong plans for taxation in the province for the last six months of 1965. The document reviewed earlier tax revenues and estimates:

Estimated Revenue for 1964	: 16,920,000
Actual Revenue for 1964	: 20,531,612
Estimated Revenue for 1965	: 31,130,000
Actual Revenue for Six Months of 1965:	8,951,084

A comparison of the estimated revenues of 1964 and 1965 makes it apparent that the Viet Cong almost doubled tax goals in Binh Duong in 1965. Yet a comparison of actual revenues shows that the Viet Cong were having greater difficulties in collecting the 1965 taxes. Documents captured later in the province indicate that many Binh Duong taxpayers did "not enthusiastically contribute to the resistance," and that "generally speaking, residents in the liberated areas lived a destitute and miserable life."

Although complaints about Viet Cong taxes are amply documented, one must be careful to avoid reading too much into them. A "1965 Tax Collection Report," issued by COSVN's Financial and Economic Section, indicated that complaining was by no means universal in Viet Cong territory, and that in some areas taxes were collected without too much trouble. Yet Viet Cong taxes are much higher than those of the South Vietnamese government, as many refugees have pointedly remarked. High taxes probably will not by themselves cause people in Viet Cong areas to shift their allegiances. If combined with other burdens, however, the taxes may induce additional inhabitants of Viet Cong territory to flee, or, ultimately, to curtail their support of the Viet Cong.

2. Labor

The Viet Cong need large numbers of people to grow food, haul supplies, and move earth. The number of volunteers is inadequate. Forced labor has become increasingly prevalent as Viet Cong operations have expanded, and as the labor pool has shrunk--partly because of the draft, and partly because of the flight of refugees. Although the Viet Cong try to persuade laborers to work willingly, the number of volunteers is inadequate and often the Viet Cong must use harsh methods.

A document, dated 20 September 1965, illustrated some of the labor problems the Viet Cong face. The author, apparently a high-ranking provincial labor official, stated that "the people in areas where mobilization is still possible are not fully aware of our policies. Therefore, they do not work enthusiastically, lack a sense of responsibility, and waste manpower as well as equipment. Village and hamlet cadres, instead of persuading, tend to order the people to work. Front line Supply Commands in villages and hamlets do not have sufficient personnel for operations... The mission is burdensome and there are not enough laborers to move rice available from production."*

---

* The shortage of labor is a recurrent theme in Viet Cong documents. Furthermore, recruited laborers frequently desert. One document stated that of 600 short-term civilian laborers needed for evacuating casualties from a battle which had taken place a few days earlier, only 54 were gathered; these all went home after completing their first evacuation trip. The removal of wounded from the battlefield was thereafter improvised.

It would be a mistake to exaggerate Viet Cong labor problems, or the extent to which the enemy's forced labor policy alienates the people. Viet Cong performance in most areas still shows their ability to get things done; and the South Vietnamese peasant is used to being put upon. Yet if labor shortages increase--as seems likely--the Viet Cong will probably have to resort to still more draconian methods to make sure that work is accomplished. An increasingly severe labor policy would probably estrange still more Vietnamese peasants.

3. **Willingness of the People to Provide Information on the Viet Cong**

In the past year, the amount of information volunteered about the Viet Cong has increased greatly. Some of the increase is due to more efficient collection techniques, higher agent pay, and the presence in the field of large numbers of intelligence officers. However, most Allied intelligence officials--military and civilian--state that much of the increase has resulted from a greater willingness on the part of the populace to inform on the Viet Cong.

Some of the voluntary informants became available because they thought the Allies were beginning to win, some because they harbored grudges against the Viet Cong. Some had other reasons. A report, dated 7 March, written by the US G-2 adviser to the ARVN 1st Division, stated, for example, that "it is believed that the local population in the 1st Division area does not feel an identity with Viet Cong Main Force... probably because [Main Force units in the region] are composed primarily of North Vietnamese draftees and some regroupees." The people apparently were more willing to inform on northerners than on the local boys in the militia and guerrillas. The prevalence of such a reaction is not known. If it is generally true throughout Vietnam, the intelligence picture may improve still further as the proportion of North Vietnamese in Main Force units continues to rise.

ANNEX VIII

VIETNAMESE COMMUNIST VIEWS ON THE
LIKELY LENGTH OF THE WAR

ANNEX VIII

VIETNAMESE COMMUNIST VIEWS ON THE LIKELY LENGTH OF THE WAR

I. The Anticipated Timing of Victory in 1955 and 1956

During the first two years following the Geneva Conference, the Communists believed that they could attain a position of dominance in South Vietnam mainly through the medium of political, rather than military action. This was clearly indicated in their secret communications. One order, for example, from the top Communist echelon in South Vietnam to the provincial Communist leaders declared in September 1955 that "at present, the only way to unification of our country" is to hold the conference and elections called for under the Geneva Accords.

The Communists apparently believed that their candidates could win the elections and that it would not take long after the voting, which was scheduled under the Agreements for July 1956, to accomplish a Communist takeover. Furthermore, in 1954 South Vietnam's chances of political survival as a viable political entity appeared so slight that the Communists had every reason to anticipate an eventual collapse which would permit them to take over even if the elections were not held. A secret Communist party directive of late 1954 said that the "struggle" to assure that the "French imperialists and their puppets" leave the South was targeted for completion "within two years," and that "despite our impatience, we can accomplish this no sooner." Most of the other Communist assessments of their situation through mid-1955 were also highly optimistic and implied that victory was not far away.

From mid-1955 to mid-1956 the Communists gradually grew more pessimistic about their chances of a takeover under the terms of the Geneva Agreement, as the Diem government repeatedly refused to agree to an election which it realized the Communists would inevitably win. The Communists were never again so optimistic about their chances after their failure during this era. The evidence shows them in succeeding years to have been much more cautious and vague in their references to the time necessary to complete a takeover.

II. Victory Timing in the Period 1956-1959

Captured documents reveal that the failure to hold the elections agreed on at Geneva resulted in deep and widespread disillusionment in Communist ranks in the South. For the next few years, party leaders in the North and the South cast about for a new strategy to accomplish their objectives. Difficulties were increased by the success of Ngo Dinh Diem's regime in repressing the low-level terrorism which had been mounted by the Communists in the hope of weakening and undercutting the Saigon government's position before and during the elections. Communist documents speak of great damage inflicted on the underground cadre organization by Diem's operations.

This combination of difficulties, particularly the Diem government's military pressure, led many of the southern Communists to believe that only a turn from reliance primarily on political action to reliance primarily on military operations against the government would bring about a Communist victory in the South. Communist documents indicate that there were various strategies put forth by the cadres in the South for insuring the success of military action. One called for concentration on the construction of a large Communist base in the highlands from which the lowlands and the population centers could be threatened. Those who advocated this policy, according to the documents, suggested that the Communists focus almost all their assets on the highlands and delay the solidification and enlargement of their position in the delta until the highlands effort was completed. Others argued for a concentration of effort in the delta to the exclusion of the highlands.

It can readily be seen that debates over strategy as basic as this would have a strong influence on Communist estimates of the time needed to accomplish their goals, and that such estimates would thus be cast in only the haziest and most indefinite of terms.

Documents indicate that the Communists eventually decided on a country-wide effort which theoretically would put equal emphasis on military and political "struggle." The documents give much of the credit for the adoption of this strategy to Le Duan, the present first secretary of the Communist Party in Hanoi. Le Duan went to the North in 1956, apparently from the top leadership position in the South. He appears to have convinced the Communist hierarchy in the North that an all-out military effort should be started in the South. Communist records generally date the decision to mount an all-out struggle in the South as having been made in late 1958 or early 1959.

It was clear by 1959 that the Communists were already organizing for a full-scale military effort in the South. One captured document stated that "instructions from the political department of the party in about May of 1959" reminded the cadres in the South of the "necessity of making full use of the armed forces," and that the cadres then started to "lay out" the "necessary policies." Since "October of 1959," the document asserted, "the armed forces have been fighting powerfully."

III. The Time Frame and Goals in 1959

There are no specific references in any available Communist materials as to what amount of time the Communists believed in 1959 would be necessary to accomplish a takeover of South Vietnam, or even to achieve any significant proportion of their objectives. Language on the anticipation of victory in Communist materials of this period was cast in very general terms. A broadcast by the Communists in late 1959, for example, said that the "day of victory" would "depend mainly on the changing aspects of the struggle." Such statements suggest a desire to avoid raising false hopes among the cadre or to make predictions which might later prove wrong.

Analysis of Communist materials, however, does point rather firmly to a Communist belief in 1959 and 1960 that it would take at least five years of all-out military and political action to bring about Communist domination of the South. It does not appear that they expected at this time to be in power before 1966 at the earliest. This can be inferred from indications as to what the Communists believed they had to accomplish in order to achieve victory. They fully recognized that they were still a negligible factor in the urban areas, and that in the rural areas their position was still weak.* That the Communists planned to take their time and build carefully was reflected in a basic order on the insurgency sent south from Hanoi in August of 1960. According to this order, the revolutionary movement was recognized as "still weak this year," but "we have the time to prepare any aspect where we are weak."

IV. The Initial Deferral of Victory Anticipations

Until early 1962 the Communists appear to have believed that they were making satisfactory progress in the development of the insurgent movement as originally envisioned.** By the spring of 1962, however, the step-up in American military assistance to the Diem regime and the counterinsurgency programs put into effect by the government had begun

---

*One example of their appraisal of their situation was apparent in the interrogation of a VC battalion commander captured in 1960. He stated that the Communists were at the time devoting nearly all their efforts to the rural area. He implied that the establishment of a significant urban apparatus to take advantage of the "urban uprising" which the Communists expected would take several more years.

Another 1960 captive, the chairman of a VC district committee in Kien Giang province, indicated that the Communists would be satisfied if they could make significant strides in 1960 in the elimination of government influence in the southwestern part of South Vietnam.

In a 1961 radio message, the Viet Cong leadership offered the opinion that, "depending on how the situation develops" it is "possible" that we will be able in "two or three years" to build up our units so that they "will be able to destroy part of the enemy's forces." Accomplishment of this would necessarily have left them still several years away from an overpowering position throughout the rural sections of the country.

**In at least one instance, Communist cadres were told that the situation was moving as had been forecast by top Communist authorities in 1961.

to cause increasing difficulties for the Communists, and enemy materials indicate that their estimates of the time needed for achieving a victory were stretched out.*

It was at this point, Communist documents suggest, that the insurgents began to put more emphasis on the so-called "urban uprising," a key element in Communist guidelines for success in South Vietnam, but one that did not receive very heavy emphasis in their writings during the first few years of the insurgency. In the Communist view, victory could be anticipated as near at hand when the expansion of the Communist base among the rural populace was combined with a general uprising of the city populace against the government. This has gradually received more stress in Communist instructions to cadre in recent years.**

Communist documents indicated that, by early 1963, the Viet Cong felt they were successfully countering Diem's military push and the American effort. However, they also indicated a Viet Cong expectation that the fighting in South Vietnam still would last longer than the Communists had originally thought. One of the best summaries of Communist views on the war in early 1963 was contained in an article

---

*One document commenting on the period discloses that "at first we did not realize the harm and danger of the strategic hamlets," and "consequently the question of countering and destroying them was not properly examined." The same document notes that the "increase in direct aggression against us" resulted in "making the revolutionary war last longer and become more difficult." The revolution could no longer "go smoothly ahead," but would be "a long and fierce tug of war."

**An instruction document written in early 1963, for example, says that the Communists expected the "cities in the South, chiefly Saigon and Cholon, to stir up the revolution and cooperate with the rural zones when opportunity was available." According to the document, the revolution would succeed through a "combination of city and rural uprising." The Communists would be "unable to overthrow the enemy through a general offensive" by itself, if mounted mainly from the rural areas.

by the North Vietnamese historian Minh Thuan who had often sized up the progress of the revolution since the era of the war against the French.

Thuan took the position that the insurgency had suffered "many ups and downs and many failures." The initiation of a large US advisory/support effort meant that the rebels "had to face the enemy under new circumstances" and could no longer "expect a rapid and easy victory." Thuan stressed the importance of the appearance of a "general uprising" as an omen that success was around the corner. According to Thuan, the Communists should "keep in mind the appearance of a pre-revolutionary situation" which would come about "only when the broad masses" are ready to "rise up and fight" against the regime. "Decisive victory," he declared, can be achieved "only when this pre-revolutionary situation appears."

Another Communist document of this period indicated that the Communists realized they could do little to hasten the fulfillment of their objectives. In "time to come," it said, help from the "North" and from the rest of the bloc would give the Communist armed forces the "capability to grow relatively fast." But "that is a question of time and we just cannot do it in a hurry. All our efforts up to now are just the first steps." Such statements imply that the Communists probably believed they were still at least five years away from victory.*

V. The Growth of Communist Optimism in 1964 and Early 1965

Enemy materials discussing the war situation grew progressively more optimistic during 1964, as the Communists assessed the political disarray in Saigon and the provinces following Diem's overthrow and the success of their efforts

---

*They were also, however, still very flexible and opportunistic, perhaps even more so than in 1959. One document, in discussing the future, said it would be necessary "to play seesaw with the enemy for a certain period." If, however, "enemy strength begins to sag significantly in the process, we will fight against the clock to overcome our weaknesses and rapidly develop our power, especially our military power, hoping to win victories of a decisive nature."

to counter the increases in US aid to the Saigon government's anti-insurgency programs. A February 1964 article in the North Vietnamese party journal, for example, declared that the fighting, "although protracted, will not last forever," and "final victory" could be achieved "in the near future."* There were a number of Communist moves which suggested that they were trying to get in a position to take maximum and rapid advantage of the government disintegration which they expected. One such move was an effort to speedily build up Communist main force strength in the area of the III Corps north of Saigon by levying very heavy manpower quotas on the guerrilla units in the delta.

Communist optimism appeared to reach its height in early 1965. Although they still carefully refrained from fixing a definite timetable, they do appear to have believed at the time that they were possibly within a year or two of victory. This, for example, was the implication of an important article by the chairman of Hanoi's "Reunification" committees, Nguyen Van Vinh. Vinh's views have long appeared to reflect some of the inner thoughts of the top Communist leadership. Writing in the January 1965 issue of the party journal, he argued that the Republic of Vietnam forces had been forced to disperse widely and to use about half of their strength to protect the capital region. The government reserves, according to Vinh, were only about one third as great as the French reserves had been, and thus Saigon would "soon" have to abandon large areas of the countryside to the Viet Cong.

Vinh pointed to the period in 1953 and early 1954 in the war against the French as a similar one, a time in which the Viet Minh inflicted the most "decisive" defeats on the French. Vinh seemed to be implying that a similar development might take place in this war, a development which could mean a Communist military victory in 1965

---

*At the June 1964 congress of the National Liberation Front, the Front's president claimed a "new" period of the insurgency had arrived and the "situation has never been so bright." In July 1964, North Vietnamese Defense Minister Vo Nguyen Giap also saw the war as "entering a new phase," with the Communist forces in "an offensive position."

or 1966. The insurgents, according to Vinh, were "advancing to the fulfillment" of their mission "in the coming year."*

Among the lower-level Viet Cong leaders, it appears that the idea was being promoted at this time that the "general uprising" was near. A defector from a district Communist committee in Kien Hoa Province, for example, claimed that Communist plans called for the "general uprising and complete overthrow of the government in 1966." It does not appear that the initiation of sustained US air attacks against the DRV in February 1965 or the landing of US Marine combat units in northern South Vietnam in March served initially to dampen Communist optimism.

VI. The Communist Reassessment in Mid-1965

By mid-summer 1965, the weight of the direct US combat effort in South Vietnam had thoroughly disabused the Communists of any hopes of an early victory. Both in public and in private, the probability of a protracted conflict again became a major theme in Communist statements. Nguyen Van Vinh, for example, who had spoken so optimistically in January, talked in July only of "eventual" victory. General Giap was also more sober in his assessment of the situation in July 1965 than he had been in July 1964. The entry of the US, Giap said, had created a "serious situation" throughout Vietnam.** Giap spoke only about "ultimate victory" over the US.

**Giap no longer focused his main attention on the prospects for the Viet Cong, as he had in his previous assessments, but now stressed the necessity of defending the DRV against US "aggression." This in itself seemed an implicit admission of the major setback dealt to Communist hopes in Vietnam by the direct US involvement.

In May of 1965, the top leaders of the military affairs committee of the Communist party in the South met to "assess the enemy and friendly situation." A report of that conference has been captured. It indicates that the meeting was dominated by discussions of the growing American involvement in the war. Analysis of the nature of the Communist military and political weaknesses set against those of the allies, as discussed at the session, suggests that the party hierarchy must have believed at the time that the Communist position was such that the war could easily last another three and possibly five more years.

During 1966, Communist materials have continued to reflect an expectation that the war will be indefinitely long and protracted. A January 1966 editorial in the North Vietnamese party paper, for example, claimed that the Communists still had confidence in their "final" victory, but admitted that the "enemy has not budged as yet" and his "intention" to crush the "insurgency" "had not weakened." In March, a DRV diplomat in Laos who had just returned from briefings in Hanoi said that the Communists now realized that the US war potential meant "there would be no quick and easy victory" in South Vietnam. Ho Chi Minh reaffirmed this as late as mid-July when he promised that the Vietnamese people would fight until final victory if it took "five, ten, twenty-five years, or even longer."

ANNEX IX

THE COMMUNIST VIEW AND APPLICATION
OF LESSONS LEARNED IN
FIGHTING THE FRENCH

ANNEX IX

THE COMMUNIST VIEW AND APPLICATION OF LESSONS LEARNED IN FIGHTING THE FRENCH

The attitude of the North Vietnamese leadership toward the current military situation in South Vietnam is shaped to a considerable extent both strategically and tactically by their experience in fighting the French. Drawing heavily upon this experience, they have carefully plotted their actions in the current war to duplicate as far as possible their successes against the French and to avoid mistakes committed in the earlier war.

I. The Three Phased War

Their experiences in the Franco-Viet Minh war doubtless convinced the Communists that the predictions on the course of this conflict made in 1947 by the then Party Secretary General Truong Chinh had proved valid, and could probably be applied in the planned takeover of South Vietnam. In essence, Truong Chinh's blueprint for victory called for a protracted struggle through three stages which would enable the small and weak forces of the Viet Minh to defeat the more numerous and better-equipped French forces.

According to Truong Chinh, the first phase of the war would see the French in control of the cities using primarily "conventional" tactics. In this period the French would be on the "offensive." The Viet Minh, on the other hand, were small, poorly armed forces and therefore had to fight a "defensive" type of war. The chief strategy for the Viet Minh during this period, argued Truong Chinh, should be to attack the enemy using guerrilla tactics, i.e., ambushes, sabotage, and small-scale attacks on French units of smaller size than the local Viet Minh unit. The Viet Minh during this period, he said must avoid pitched battles with the enemy and must build its strength.

Truong Chinh took the position that, although the Viet Minh would be strategically on the defensive, tactically they should always be on the offensive. Since the French would be strategically on the offensive, they would overextend themselves, thus giving the Viet Minh opportunities for attacking isolated and small units. During this first stage of the "people's war," he said, the Viet Minh must also concentrate on gaining the support of the peasants. Political efforts, Chinh held, were in some respects even more important than military efforts, because without the support of the people there could be no military effort.

At some point, Truong Chinh asserted, the enemy would extend his position as far as he could. At that time, the harassing action of the guerrillas would combine with the enemy's inherent weaknesses to create an equilibrium. During this stage of the war, the enemy would concentrate on consolidating his overextended positions with particular emphasis on his lines of communications and supply. He would continue to launch attacks on the Viet Minh strongholds. In the political sphere, the enemy would concentrate on setting up "puppet" local adminstrations, infiltrating the Communist zones with spies, and repressing the Viet Minh political movement.

The Viet Minh, during this period, should employ to the maximum the tactic of guerrilla warfare to harass the enemy day and night. This would be designed to force the enemy to disperse his forces, to overextend his area of operations further, and to use up his manpower and resources. The key tactic during this period would be a combination of guerrilla and mobile warfare, with the guerrilla taking the lead at first, followed by later and stronger efforts at mobile warfare. The tactic of positional war was given only a limited role at this stage, since the enemy would still be able to bring superior force to bear on static defensive positions.

During the second phase of the struggle, the Viet Minh forces would swing from a defensive strategy to an offensive one. This stage should see not only military defeat of the enemy but also a collapse of morale on his home front, i.e., in metropolitan France. Economic and morale problems at home would have a decisive effect on France's will to fight. On the battle front, the French would be forced to withdraw from their advanced positions in order to defend their major bases. The Viet Minh would depend primarily on mobile warfare tactics supported by guerrilla activities. Finally, in the third phase near the end, mobile warfare would often be transformed into positional warfare for the decisive battles.

Truong Chinh's analysis proved an amazingly accurate prediction of the actual course of the war with the French. Chinh's assessment of the weaknesses of the French was unerring and his program for the development of both tactics and strategy for the Viet Minh proved effective. His views permeated the outlook of the Viet Minh leadership and particularly that of General Vo Nguyen Giap. It was largely Giap's responsibility as commander of the Viet Minh army to put into practice Truong Chinh's military concepts. He did just that and led the Viet Minh to final victory at the famous battle of Dien Bien Phu.

The extent to which the Vietnamese Communists still rely on this basic design for victory is evidenced in the writings of their leaders. On several occasions in the last two years Giap, in his articles, has applied Truong Chinh's concepts of military analysis to the situation in the South. In remarkably similar terms, Giap has stressed the need for a prolonged war, emphasized that the US would become overextended in its ability to supply its troops in the field, and predicted that popular dissatisfaction with the war in the United States would undermine the determination of the administration to continue the war. Giap has claimed that the tendency of both French and US strategists to fix short deadlines for accomplishing major goals is proof of their inability to outlast the Communists.

According to Truong Chinh's criteria, the Viet Cong presumably would have reached the point of equilibrium with the ARVN in 1964 or early 1965 and would have gone over to the offensive relying more and more on mobile rather than guerrilla tactics. However, the use of US forces in a combat role has since then probably removed any notion from the Communists' minds that they have managed to move into an advanced part of Truong Chinh's second phase, one in which the opponent is forced to withdraw from his advanced positions to defend his bases. This is evidenced in their discussions of the large and successful US/ARVN offensive raids into Viet Cong base areas this year.

Apparently the Hanoi high command believes that its forces in the South, at least in the northern half of South Vietnam, are in the first part of Truong Chinh's phase two, that is to say, that the US and ARVN are now overextended and are concentrating on keeping open lines of communication to their exposed outer posts. To some extent, of course, this is true. What is new in the situation, however, is the fact that with its improved intelligence, extreme mobility, heavy firepower, and tremendous air-support capability, the US can also attack Viet Cong strongholds and thus by spoiling actions throw Communist tactical planning and movements off balance.

Moreover, there has now developed a serious challenge to what the Communists regard as one of the keys to their ultimate victory, their own rear base. In the war with France, this safe rear was first in China, then in the highlands of North Vietnam. In the current war, the Communists have made it clear that they regard North Vietnam as the rear area for the war. Since February 1965, however, this base for the movement of men and supplies to the Viet Cong has come under heavy aerial attack by the US. While these air strikes have as yet not prevented North Vietnam from continuing to send men and material to the South, they have made the process much more costly and time consuming.

II. Tactical Military Lessons

The lessons learned in fighting the French are being applied in a myriad of practical steps by the Vietnamese Communists in the current war. The reliance on the tactic of ambush, for example, results in large measure from the successful development of this technique against the French. The Viet Cong have frequently set up ambushes against the South Vietnamese and US forces on almost exactly the same spots where French elements were ambushed nearly twenty years ago.

Another lesson, learned the hard way against the French, is the need to avoid precipitous military action against superior forces. In 1951 and 1952, Vo Nguyen Giap launched several major attacks on French forces only to have his units shattered by superior French firepower. Giap drew back, reformed, re-equipped, and retrained his units, and from then on faithfully followed the advice of Truong Chinh who urged that such actions be undertaken only when the Communists positively enjoyed the superior position. Giap's dedication to this formula led ultimately to Dien Bien Phu, where his forces had the superior position. That the Vietnamese Communist High Command learned its lesson is evident in Communist tactics in the present war. The Viet Cong/PAVN forces rarely venture out on an attack now unless they are virtually certain that they will have the advantage. The Communists instead, attempt to draw friendly forces into remote areas where terrain, transportation, and weather tend to neutralize the superior firepower and mobility of the allied side.

The success of the North Vietnamese in keeping their transportation routes open is also due in some measure to their experience in the Franco - Viet Minh war. In addition, they appear to have drawn heavily upon Chinese and North Korean experiences in the Korean War. The extensive use of coolie labor for bomb-damage repair is not something uniquely Vietnamese, but the Hanoi leadership has had great experience, due to the war with France, in forming and operating coolie labor units. The mobilization of rudimentary forms of transportation is also a technique learned well in the war against France.

III. Political Lessons

Experiences gained in the political sphere in the war against the French are also being used by the Communists in the present conflict. They continue to put heavy emphasis on the "political struggle" and to express confidence that enemy military superiority cannot in the long run prevail in a "people's war." To the extent that it is more than propaganda, this line partly reflects adherence to Marxist dialectic principles that "contradictions" in the opposing forces (referring here to "contradictions" between the Americans and their "puppets" as well as to conflicts among the South Vietnamese themselves as evidenced by the recent succession of internal coups) will inevitably work in the Communists' favor. The Communists are mindful of the fact that in the earlier war the lack of positive support by the majority of non-Communist Vietnamese for the French was a major factor contributing to the ultimate defeat of France.

On the practical level, the Communists have in their current "struggle" sought to apply their political view of the war through methods which parallel those used earlier by the Viet Minh. In addition to propaganda which seeks to foster South Vietnamese hatred for the Americans as the true "aggressors," the Communists set out to repeat the combined tactics of terror and benevolence used successfully by the Viet Minh. Thus they have revived the terrorist bombings in Saigon and conducted terrorist reprisals against supporters of the Saigon government at all levels throughout the countryside, while at the same time they have tried to ingratiate themselves with the general populace by various good works--helping with the harvest, improving sanitation, conducting educational programs, etc. Land reform, a technique used with some success by the Viet Minh through simply granting ownership outside the colonial administration, became a platform of Viet Cong's Liberation Front.

The Hanoi leadership also learned in part from the Franco-Viet Minh war to proceed cautiously on the matter of negotiations, even while not rejecting the idea of talks at an appropriate point. Premier Pham Van Dong was the primary agent for the Vietnamese Communists in the series of negotiations with the French between 1945 and 1954. He stated in 1965 that the Vietnamese Communists had learned from their negotiations with the French that the "imperialists" merely use discussions as a technique to gain a pause in the shooting so that they can prepare for further fighting. Dong went on to state that they do not intend to make the same mistake with the Americans. Instead, they intend to wear the US down to the point of accepting the bulk of their terms for a settlement through the tactic of protracted war.

The Vietnamese Communists do have some reason to feel that the various negotiated agreements reached with the French were used to the disadvantage of the Viet Minh. The French moved against Ho's self-proclaimed Democratic Republic of Vietnam in 1946 despite an agreement signed with representatives of his government recognizing its autonomy. The aftermath of the Fountainbleau conference in 1946 at which a cease-fire agreement was reached, showed the French moving to escalate the war. The final proof of Western perfidy, in the eyes of the Vietnamese Communists, was the failure of the Western powers to implement the 1954 Geneva Agreements on Indochina, agreements which the Hanoi leaders felt would assure their peaceful takeover of all Vietnam.

Although chary of actually entering into negotiations with the US from a position of relative weakness, the Vietnamese Communists also realize that the tactic of "talk, fight, talk," was in some respects used effectively by both sides in the Franco - Viet Minh war. Thus they have been reluctant to close the door completely to possible negotiations with the US; a talk stage in the "struggle" could prove attractive to Hanoi itself at some point to gain a respite from allied military pressure.

This is probably in part why the North Vietnamese have continued to receive a fairly steady flow of visitors from Western and nonaligned countries with various ideas for getting talks started between Hanoi and Washington. North Vietnam probably has at least two aims in accepting these visitors. One aim is to encourage the notion that the Communists are reasonable, although firm, in their attitude toward what it would take to reach a settlement of the war. The second, and probably more important purpose, has been to put increased pressure on the US to cease its bombings of the North. A number of foreign visitors have come away from Hanoi believing that they had received intimations that if the bombings ceased, talks could begin.

~~SECRET~~

ANNEX X

THE EFFECT OF THE INTERNATIONAL POLITICAL CLIMATE ON
VIETNAMESE COMMUNIST PLANS AND CAPABILITIES

ANNEX X

THE EFFECT OF THE INTERNATIONAL POLITICAL CLIMATE ON VIETNAMESE COMMUNIST PLANS AND CAPABILITIES

I. World Public Opinion

The evidence shows that the Vietnamese Communists believe popular opposition throughout the Western world to US policy in Vietnam can be an important factor in restraining the allied hand against the insurgents. Virtually every significant Vietnamese Communist statement on war strategy has stressed the necessity of mustering the maximum amount of world opposition against allied--principally US--action in the conflict.*

Also significant in the eyes of the Vietnamese Communists are the "liberation movements" and other outbreaks of civil unrest and rebellion which occur elsewhere in the world against Western authorities. Hanoi and the Viet Cong see these, in part, as developments which hopefully will draw a direct American military or economic reaction which will distract and weaken the US war effort in Vietnam.** Such "people's action" is also regarded as encouraging the morale

---

*In an important speech setting forth the DRV's terms for settling the war in April 1965, for example, Premier Pham Van Dong devoted nearly a quarter of his address to this theme. "Strong and unrelenting opposition" from the "world's people," Dong said, "has the effect of checking and repelling" the "aggressive and warmongering plots" of the enemy. In the face of this opposition, he claimed, "the rear" of the enemy is "disintegrating" and "contradictions" in his ranks are increasing.

**According to the DRV chief of staff, Van Tien Dung, the US cannot put "all its economic and military potential" into action in Vietnam if it has to "cope with the situation in many other countries and in many fields...to repress other peoples."

of the Communist rank and file in Vietnam by demonstrating that they are not alone in their opposition to Western "imperialism and colonialism." Largely for these reasons, Hanoi has frequently urged greater cooperation and unified action by the Soviet Union and China during the last two years in support of the world "liberation movements." The North Vietnamese apparently consider such action a matter of great significance to Vietnamese Communist interests, since North Vietnamese usually refrain from offering advice to the rest of the bloc.

If the situation in Vietnam develops to the point where the Vietnamese Communists are forced to make a decision on whether to continue to support large-scale insurgency in the South, it is probable that their estimate on the extent of world popular opposition to allied policy in Vietnam and of the strength of the various "liberation movements" would be a significant factor in influencing their decision. It would, however, almost certainly not be a critical factor.

II. Domestic Opposition in the United States

A more important issue in any Vietnamese decision on continuing the war would be the extent and effect of opposition to American policy from within the United States. It is clear that the Vietnamese realize general Western agitation against the allies will never be particularly effective unless accompanied by important opposition in the US.*

The Vietnamese Communists do not view this opposition as simply a manifestation of moral reticence among American intellectuals and leftists over Washington's war policy, but also believe that important opposition may develop as a result of the economic pinch of the war on the American public and business, and that such opposition may be further fanned by the continuing American casualties in Viet nam. It is clear that the Vietnamese believe the US will

---

*This has repeatedly been a theme of Vietnamese propaganda in such assertions as "the struggle of the American people plays an important role in the common struggle of the peoples to check the acts of the US Government in Vietnam."

be forced to go on an extensive wartime footing eventually and that this will greatly increase domestic opposition.*

There have been other indications in private that the Vietnamese believe domestic opposition in the US, if developed strongly, would seriously inhibit US war options. Vietnamese Communist cadres have been told by their leaders that the "increase in anger in world opinion over US activities in Vietnam" could be "among the more important factors," in addition to "casualties and economic costs," which would cause the "American government to desist and decide to give up and get out."**

It is hard, however, to assess just how far the Vietnamese Communist inner councils really believe domestic opposition to US war policy has developed to date. In their view of the American situation, the Vietnamese are doubtless influenced to some extent by their overall lack of sophistication on American politics and by their earlier successful experience in bringing significant pressure from French public opinion to bear on French war policy in 1953-1954. In private conversations with visitors to Hanoi, the North Vietnamese have sometimes compared the present war with their own experiences against the French.

Their lack of sophistication and eagerness to seize on evidence of mounting US domestic opposition can perhaps

---

*We have the word of North Vietnamese party first secretary, Le Duan, on this. Late last year, he told a visiting Western Communist that he was sure the US would have to mobilize a reserve force of 1,200,000 men in order to support a force of 400,000 men in Vietnam. The US, he said, could not maintain that kind of war effort without being forced eventually by opinion in the US to re-examine and change its policy.

**Western statesmen have been told by Vietnamese Communist spokesmen that they believed the opposition to US policy shown by some congressional leaders and by well-known American journalists indicated a basic "lack of confidence" in the administration's policy. According to the Vietnamese, the "US is suffering from a lack of a clear objective which would unify American public opinion" behind the American policy on Vietnam.

best be seen in their reaction to the American student protests over Vietnam policy which reached at least an initial peak in the fall of 1965. There was an increasing air of optimism over the strength of the student agitation in Vietnamese Communist propaganda at that time, capped by an announcement from Hanoi on 24 October that a "united front of the Vietnamese and American people has de facto taken shape." The propaganda strongly suggested that the Vietnamese were overreading the extent and depth of the protests in the US.* It is possible that the optimistic tone of the propaganda was intended in part to give a boost to the Vietnamese rank and file by demonstrating the sympathy which allegedly exists for their position in the enemy's own camp.

There has been some evidence in Vietnamese Communist materials during 1966 of substantial realism regarding the potential for domestic opposition in the US. This could be seen, for example, in General Vo Nguyen Giap's assessment of the war situation in the DRV party journal in January 1966. Giap placed US domestic opposition last when reviewing American weaknesses in the war. He indicated that the opposition would exercise a restraining effect on American options in Vietnam, but implied that it would not be decisive in determining US staying power in the conflict. Giap placed more emphasis on US limitations in maintaining strong economic and military positions throughout the world while pursuing a large-scale commitment in Vietnam. He did not, however, assess even this latter problem as critical in determining the outcome of the conflict.**

---

*Communist misjudgment of American opinion was also evident in Hanoi's threats recently to take punitive action against US flyers, and in its public abuse of the pilots. When Hanoi realized the depth of feeling in the US over the issue, it hastily stopped its propaganda regarding trials. Its willingness to do so is indicative of the importance it assigns to influencing US opinion.

**In private, visiting Western officials in Hanoi have been given much the same line during the past few months. One official was told that the DRV was "not counting" on US opinion to win the war. The same theme has been reflected
(continued on next page)

It would appear that the Vietnamese Communist leadership does not expect any important difficulties for Washington in the near future, at least, as a result of popular opposition to the war or because of economic/military stresses caused by the conflict in the United States. Thus, in any basic decision taken on the war by the Vietnamese Communists over the next few months, the status of domestic American opposition would probably not be regarded as critical. If over the longer pull, however, the US was not forced into extensive wartime mobilization measures and strong domestic opposition was not triggered as Hanoi appears to expect, the situation could possibly become a very important factor in any basic Vietnamese Communist decision on prolonging the fighting.

III. Cambodian Attitudes

Phnom Penh's attitude toward the Vietnam war is of importance to Hanoi's own plans chiefly on two counts: (1) Cambodia's ties to the 1954 Geneva agreements and, (2) its contiguity with Viet Cong operational bases in South Vietnam. By appealing to the nationalistic proclivities of Cambodia's leader, Prince Sihanouk, the Asian Communists have been able to gain a substantial amount of political support for the Vietnamese insurgents during the past several years. This has included Cambodian condemnation of the US role in South Vietnam as well as accusations that the US presence there is, as Hanoi claims, in violation of the Geneva agreements. Both of these themes are regarded by the Vietnamese as important foundation stones in their own political policy on the war.

On the physical side, Cambodia has served as a source and a transit channel for limited amounts of both food and other supplies for the Viet Cong. The Cambodians have also taken a primarily neutral stance in permitting limited use of their territory as a refuge and a secure base for the Vietnamese Communist forces.

---

in the remarks of DRV diplomats abroad. In May, a French newsman was told by the DRV representative in Paris that Hanoi was greatly interested in encouraging the efforts of students and intellectuals in the US in their opposition to US policy, but realized that they represented only a minority.

The Communists, nevertheless, do not have an ally or even a constant sideline supporter in the Cambodians. Cambodia's ambivalent foreign policy has frequently been at odds with Hanoi's stand on such issues as Indo-Chinese neutrality and the exact terms for settlement of the Vietnam war. The Communists have thus had to adopt a basically cautious policy in exploiting Cambodia for their war effort. They are probably reluctant to make any really large scale or far reaching plans for the use of Cambodian territory by the Viet Cong, and they cannot automatically count on receiving consistent and favorable political support from Phnom Penh.

On balance, the situation probably tends to exert a restraining influence on Vietnamese Communist policy options in the sense that it forces the Vietnamese to focus primarily on better strategic use of South Vietnamese and Laotian territory in their efforts to cope with the growing allied military pressure on their operational bases.

IV. The Effect of Links With Western Leaders

The Vietnamese Communists also regard the establishment and preservation of adequate links to leaders and key officials of Western countries as an important element in their war strategy. There are a number of reasons for this apart from a natural inclination to enhance Vietnamese Communist prestige at the international level. Such contacts, for one thing, offer the Vietnamese an opening to promote opposition to allied policy on Vietnam among influential individuals in the free world.

This can be seen in Hanoi's treatment of the Indian Government. Although Indian proposals for settling the war have consistently been rejected by the Vietnamese as unacceptably generous to the allies, Hanoi has been very careful to avoid direct attacks on the Indian Leaders in its propaganda. It has assiduously cultivated its diplomatic relations with New Dehli and treated Indian representatives visiting North Vietnam with considerable courtesy and friendship. The Vietnamese doubtless believe the Indian outlook has an important influence on over-all Afro-Asian opinion about the war. Hanoi apparently also regards some Indian leaders as potential channels for floating Vietnamese views about the war to the allies.

During 1966, the Vietnamese seem to have given special attention to the use of Western statesmen as third party channels to the allied leadership. This development has been most evident in Hanoi's treatment of the Canadian representatives who have visited or have been stationed with the ICC in Hanoi. The North Vietnamese have frankly told them that they wish to preserve the channel which the Canadians provide to the US, and have suggested that Canadian visitors be empowered to discuss more than just ICC business while in Hanoi.

From what has been learned of third party contacts with the North Vietnamese, it does not appear that the greater Hanoi interest in talking to prominent Westerners during 1966 represents any softening as yet in Vietnamese resolve to continue the war. It probably does mean, however, that the Communist leaders realize it might become necessary at some point to change their tactics and actively consider a political settlement of the conflict. At such a time, third party contacts could prove especially valuable, in part because they would provide a channel to the allies that did not first filter through the bloc. At such a critical point, the Vietnamese might not see eye to eye on strategy with bloc leaders.

V. The Public Posture of the National Liberation Front (NFLSV)

Since the creation of the NFLSV in 1960, the Vietnamese have made a continuous effort to demonstrate that the Front enjoys broad political support and control throughout South Vietnam and that its "growing strength" is supplemented by mounting recognition of Front claims and position in international circles. The results of this have been disappointing at best for the Communists. Front influence in South Vietnam is limited chiefly to the rural areas under Communist control; even in those areas, the Front is widely regarded as a facade to cover the operations of the hard core Viet Cong (see ANNEX III for a discussion of the numerical strength and influence of the Front in South Vietnam).

On the international side, although there is a substantial body of opinion in the free world which holds that the insurgency in the South is an indigenous, patriotic and legitimate revolutionary movement, the Front's own activities have contributed relatively little to the spread of this belief.

The Front is widely regarded in the West as more or less a voice for the Communist view on Vietnam. Efforts to achieve quasi-diplomatic status for the Front have not been very successful. Even some of the bloc countries where the Front has opened "permanent representations," have made it clear that the NFLSV is accredited only to local national front organizations and not to the bloc government itself.

The best evidence, perhaps, of the weak position of the Front lies in its failure to establish a provisional national government in South Vietnam. While both North Vietnamese and Front officials have hinted on several occasions in the past year that such a move was in process, it will probably not take place in the predictable future. Such an action would pose formidable problems for the Communists and actually further expose the lack of public support for the Front. It would almost certainly alienate politically active groups in the South, such as the Buddhists, who do not entirely support the Saigon government and have political ambitions themselves. The Front would also find it difficult to establish a satisfactory seat of government in South Vietnam.*

Despite the weaknesses of the Front, however, there are compelling reasons for the Vietnamese Communists to continue to operate under its banner. It provides, for example, a formal medium under which all facets of the insurgent political and military activity in South Vietnam can be organized. Although it does not yet pretend to formal government on a national scale, it does establish for the Communists a needed organizational alternative to the Saigon regime. It is also useful as a platform for advertising the broad program of political and economic objectives which the Communists have set forth as their alleged goals in South Vietnam.

---

*The leadership of any provisional NFLSV government would have little attraction among politically conscious elements of the population in South Vietnam not allied with the Communists. Movement toward the opening of negotiations on the war, should the Vietnamese Communists decide to do so, might also be complicated by the establishment of a Front government.

ANNEX XI

THE PROBABLE NEAR TERM MILITARY AND POLITICAL
STRATEGY OF THE VIETNAMESE COMMUNISTS

ANNEX XI

THE PROBABLE NEAR TERM MILITARY AND POLITICAL
STRATEGY OF THE VIETNAMESE COMMUNISTS

I. General Concepts

The near-term military strategy of the Communists will probably revolve around two major efforts: (1) to keep intact, as far as possible, their main force units in the South, and (2) to build up this main force strength, both in quantity and quality, so as to be able to counter the allied power when US forces in Vietnam have built up to the level of 400,000 expected by the Communists at the end of 1966. The North Vietnamese leaders probably hope that if they can go into 1967 with an ability to field a main force strength of what we estimate to be about 125,000 as compared to a US strength of 400,000, they will be able to continue the war. Hanoi probably estimates that a four-to-one manpower advantage in favor of the US will not be enough for the US to decisively defeat the Communists. Of particular importance to the Communists is the fielding of sufficient combat units to counter the expected US strength in combat maneuver battalions. (See ANNEX IV for a discussion of ratios in US and Communist combat strength)

One of the best recent Communist assessments of the military situation was contained in a lengthy article carried in the June issue of the North Vietnamese army journal. This article, as well as a discussion of tactics in a document captured in Binh Dinh Province in June 1966, indicate that the Communist plan for the rest of this year is largely a continuation of their 1964-1965 concept. According to the article, by mid-1965, Communists attacks in the highlands were coordinated with those in the "delta"--a clear reference to what in fact was an almost simultaneous launching of operations in the Kontum-Pleiku-Phu Bon provincial area of the highlands together with large operations nearer the central coast in Quang Ngai Province and in the provinces around Saigon. The result was, as the article declared, a spreading of ARVN's forces, particularly its reserves, so thin that the South Vietnamese army's ability to keep going was in question.

The article indicated that the Communists will concentrate again this year on opening simultaneous campaigns in the highlands and in the area northeast and northwest of Saigon. The frequency of other actions in the northern coastal provinces may accelerate toward the end of the year as the northeast monsoons begin there.* The primary aim will again be to stretch the enemy's forces "thin," and to inflict as many casualties as possible. This time, however, the primary opponent will be US rather than South Vietnamese units. Although the latter continue to be struck as attractive targets of opportunity, captured documents and recent Communist propaganda identify US troops as the principal threat and dismiss the South Vietnamese "puppet army" as "no longer a force which can deal on equal terms with us."

The article also covered specific military concepts which appear to constitute advice from the High Command on how to battle the US in South Vietnam during the rest of 1966. It suggested that the Communists believe they can be relatively effective in limiting the mobility of US forces. It referred, for example, to the creation of what it termed an "extermination belt" around Da Nang. This belt was not explained in detail, but the positioning and activity of Communist forces in the Da Nang area suggest that the Communists believe they can create a type of flexible cordon around Da Nang and other US base regions which can restrict many US forces largely to their general base and confine them primarily to static defense tasks.

One major tactical adjustment the Communists will have to undertake is better concealment of the locations of their

---

*The document captured in Binh Dinh stressed that the enemy must be attacked on successive days both in the highlands and in the lowlands. It declared, however, that our capabilities for this area are still low and far from being able to completely annihilate an enemy unit." Thus, "it will be difficult to attack the enemy continuously," and "if the enemy reacts with great strength, with high mobility, we can hardly avoid being pushed into a negative situation and suffering losses." To cope with this problem, it stresses the need for superior morale and discipline to offset the superior US firepower, for a continued build-up of forces, and for the devising of new plans to "keep up with the situation and mission."

main force units. US forces are now gathering more and better intelligence on the tactical disposition of Communist forces than was ever available to the ARVN alone. The ability of the US to conduct "spoiling operations" on the basis of this intelligence appears to be keeping the Communists off balance and inflicting heavy losses which require two to three months for a unit's recovery. These "spoiling operations," moreover, are playing havoc with the practical application of one of North Vietnam's cardinal military tenets--that main force units must avoid pitched battles during the period in which they are still building up.

As a result, it seems likely that during the rest of 1966, the Communists will stick primarily to ambushes, hit-and-run strikes at isolated posts, terrorist bombings, and guerrilla harassment, although they will almost certainly attempt to conduct operations in regimental strength and greater should favorable conditions arise. Their recent military conduct suggests that they may frequently try to devolve large-scale battles into a series of skirmishes in which Communist units hit piecemeal at smaller US or allied units.

II. <u>Probable Areas of Communist Operations</u>

Although it is difficult to predict precisely what the Communist forces will attempt to do during the next six months to one year, there is considerable intelligence, gathered from captured documents, prisoner interrogations, and agent reports, and derived from known deployments of Communist main force units and from their operations this year, to indicate certain priority areas and targets. The totality of this information reinforces the belief that the Communists hope to repeat their operational patterns of 1965.

    A. <u>The Highlands</u>

The continued reinforcement this year of the central highlands area bordering Laos and Cambodia with regular PAVN regiments suggests that this area is envisaged as a major base and staging area, first for operations to lure and attack US units under favorable conditions, and secondly for gradual encroachment on the "delta" or lowland areas. There have been numerous indications--in prisoner statements, in agent reports, in Communist propaganda, and in the pattern of increased guerrilla harassment--that the

Communists hoped this year to renew their 1965 monsoon effort in the highlands.*

These Communist plans apparently have been disrupted by the series of US "spoiling" operations conducted, some in conjunction with ARVN troops, in the highlands areas since early 1966. The Communists may nevertheless continue their efforts to apply "mobile warfare" principles in the highlands, although these may be preceded or accompanied by smaller action designed to disperse friendly forces and to permit the Viet Cong to regain the initiative. One document captured in the spring of 1966 contained battle plans for an attack against the US 1st Cavalry Division (Airmobile) base at An Khe.** Attacks on such US strong points, however, will probably be limited to mortar attacks or attempted sabotage and be designed largely to tie down US troops and achieve a psychological impact.

B. Coastal Areas of II Corps

Elsewhere in the II Corps area, the principal Communist interest continues to focus on Binh Dinh Province on the coast. There is some recent evidence, however, that at least one PAVN Regiment--the 18B--has moved eastward from the Cambodian border area of the highlands, possibly to fill out a divisional structure under the Communist Southern Front

---

*Reportedly singled out for attack were Special Forces camps such as those at Duc Co, Plei Me, Plei Mrong, and Plei Djereng in Pleiku Province, and other targets extending as far as Toumorong district in Kontum Province to the north and into Darlac Province to the south. Coupled with road interdiction efforts, these attacks presumably would have the dual purpose of providing traps for the ambush of reinforcing units, and of eliminating some allied outposts in strategic territory.

**The Communists could find this a tempting target for many reasons--the frequent fog there which limits air response, the vulnerability of Route 19 to interdiction or ambush, and the previous Viet Minh success in trapping the French in this area. The Communists' recognition of their own vulnerability in positional warfare, however, makes it unlikely that they will attempt a major assault on An Khe.

headquarters in the Phu Yen-Khanh Hoa Province area on the coast. Long-term allied military operations to protect rice-harvesting activities in this area appear to be successfully denying the Communists access to their primary targets in this part of II Corps--food and manpower.

The heavy Communist troop concentrations in the Phu Yen-Khanh Hoa area and in the Binh Dinh-Quang Ngai area, where another division operates on both sides of the provincial border across ARVN corps boundaries, may foreshadow renewed attacks toward the coast. The latter months of 1966 and the early months of 1967 would appear to be the most favorable period for larger scale Communist operations in this area, although hit-and-run raids coordinated with actions in the highlands could occur here at any time.

C. <u>I Corps</u>

One of the provinces consistently suffering the greatest number of Communist-initiated actions has been Quang Ngai, in the southern part of I Corps. Extensive operational plans for extending the already considerable Communist control over this province have been captured this year, but the Communist main force units have not yet proved sufficiently strong to carry out such plans in full or to threaten the province capital itself. At present the Communists in this area also appear to be seeking to avoid sustained, large-scale engagements in favor of rapid hit-and-run attacks and continued erosive tactics. They may, however, resume efforts to grab off isolated district towns as weather conditions become more favorable.

There is little hard evidence available on Communist intentions in the northern Quang Ngai-Quang Tin-Quang Nam part of I Corps. The presence of sizeable forces in this area appears primarily designed to protect their Military Region 5 headquarters area from US operations and to tie down substantial US forces in the vicinity of the US bases at Chu Lai and Da Nang. More immediately significant may be the presence of two Communist divisional structures in northernmost I Corps --the Northern Front headquarters area in Thua Thien Province and the recently infiltrated PAVN 324B division near the Demilitarized Zone (DMZ) in Quang Tri Province. One mission of these forces probably is to draw US units into the area and spread them "thin."*

COMUSMACV has for some time anticipated an increased Communist thrust in the Quang Tri-Thua Thien area. This would not only divert attention from Communist efforts to develop a base in the highlands and permit some respite there, but would facilitate support from or sanctuary in the Communist "rear base" in North Vietnam. The presence of the 324th, which infiltrated across the DMZ, may portend increased use of this shorter, more direct route in addition to routes via the Laotian corridor. The Communists may also hope to exploit the inactivity and possible lowered effectiveness of South Vietnam's 1st Division in this area. The immediate offensive plans of the 324th Division now appear to have been disrupted or delayed by early US detection and counteroperations, but increased Communist activity in this northernmost part of South Vietnam remains probable.**

D. III Corps

There is strong evidence from the deployment of Viet Cong forces, [redacted] that the Communists intended

---

*One recently captured PAVN prisoner claims that there are two other PAVN divisions--one just above the DMZ in North Vietnam and one near Route 9 opposite western Quang Tri in Laos--prepared to cooperate in just this effort. The presence of additional PAVN divisions around Quang Tri could also reflect further infiltration in process, or possibly plans to seize territory in Quang Tri. Such plans have been reported by some 324th Divison prisoners.

**An entrenched Communist position in northernmost I Corps could provide them an alternate, although less effective, base area for ultimately moving against the lowlands. The Communists appear to have been trying for some time to forge a secure area stretching from their zone C stronghold in Tay Ninh Province northwest of Saigon across the highlands to North Vietnam at the 17th parallel. This appears to have been one aim of the coordinated drives in mid-1965 in the central highlands and in the Phuoc Long-Binh Duong area near Saigon.

to resume an effort to link up the southern portions of their base complex in III Corps during the 1966 summer monsoon period. The primary targets appear to have been a district town and a Special Forces camp in Binh Long Province which separates Zone C and Zone D, northwest and northeast of Saigon, respectively. Possibly related efforts to improve their position in III Corps include the presence of an understrength division or Front headquarters southeast of Saigon in coastal Phuoc Tuy Province, and efforts to build up main force units in previously neglected areas east of Saigon, presaged in part by intensified guerrilla harassment throughout early 1966.

US operations targeted against both the Viet Cong Central Office for South Vietnam (COSVN), headquartered in Zone C, and against Communist regiments in the Binh Long-Binh Duong area appear to have thwarted or delayed Communist plans in the III Crops area.* Nevertheless, the heavy concentration of both main force units and guerrillas in much of the III Corps area gives the Communists the capability to place a variety of military, economic, and psychological pressures on the area around Saigon. This pressure is reinforced through road interdiction, shipping harassment, and terrorism within the capital itself.

E. IV Corps

In the delta areas south and west of Saigon the number of large-scale Viet Cong operations have been dropping for some time. This probably reflects some reduction in capability because of both heavy casualties and heavy troop levies for other areas especially III Corps. Sporadic attacks against ARVN and paramilitary outposts and Special Forces camps have occurred in recent months, however, and probably will continue. The delta area is of vital importance to the Communists as a source of rice and manpower, and in substantial portions they remain solidly entrenched. Except when

---

*US operations in this northern part of the III Corps area are being sustained on a long-term basis to drive a secure wedge between Zones C and D, apply increasing pressure on the Communist military and political headquarters in the area--COSVN, Military Region 7 (now known as MR1), and Saigon/Gia Dinh--and gradually weaken the Viet Cong hold on their traditional base areas.

engaged in strength by ARVN operations, the Communists in IV Corps will probably continue to give primary emphasis to maintaining their lines of communication between the delta and Zone C--as stressed in captured documents--and to retaining base areas and secure zones for training and for the smuggling of supplies. They will probably also attempt to harass road and water communications between Saigon and the delta in order to put an economic squeeze on Saigon and on the provinces served by the capital.*

III. <u>Prospects and Problems</u>

Although there is as yet no hard evidence available on Communist planning beyond 1966, we anticipate no significant change in present Communist military strategy through at least the spring of 1967. The primary objective of the Communists, if they can succeed in maintaining their main force basically intact through this year, will probably be to inflict enough heavy casualties on the US forces--particularly in the highlands--to cause the US to pull in its horns and stop its "spoiling" operations.

The Communists, however, will be under severe pressure to come up with some new ideas or modifications of their present tactics. Although they will almost certainly maintain their reliance on the ambush, recent failures in this tactic, resulting from US anticipatory moves and rapid counteraction, have caused them setbacks. They will probably also work to improve their "close-in" battle tactic which is designed to inhibit US use of artillery and air support. The increasing emphasis noted in captured Communist documents on the need for a superior human element--improved cadres and improved troop discipline and morale--points up the Communists' awareness that, under continued pressure from US troops and air bombardment, the coming year will be a highly signficant one for them.

IV. <u>The Near Term Political Strategy of the Vietnamese Communists</u>

Within South Vietnam, Communist political goals for the remainder of 1966 and early 1967 will have to take account

---

*Harassment of district towns, outposts, and US and ARVN airfields, primarily by mortar fire, will probably continue, along with small-scale actions to disrupt and undermine the government's Revolutionary Development (pacification) program.

of recent Communist setbacks. Captured documents indicate that the Communists will give priority to strengthening and improving their political apparatus, notably by trying to improve the quality of political cadres down to the village level, and by continued emphasis on the recruitment of party members and sympathizers in both rural and urban areas.

With regard to particular target groups for penetration, concentration will probably continue to be on the South Vietnamese army and civil service. Laboring class elements may attract increasing attention, not only in the hope of fostering new wage-price spirals and further economic discontent, but because of the access of construction workers to US base facilities and of porters and other supporting workers to US logistical supply lines. The Communists will probably continue their efforts to exploit communal tensions--between the Buddhists and Catholics, between the Chinese and ethnic Vietnamese, between the Vietnamese and the ethnic tribes, and among other rival political factions. The failure of the Buddhists in confronting the military in Saigon may well give the Communists second thoughts about expending too many assets on trying to gain a handle on the Buddhist organization. There is little question that the Communists will continue to focus their proselyting efforts on the ARVN in an attempt to encourage desertions and defections. They will also try to sow distrust and dissension among the Vietnamese over the US presence, role, and intentions.

The Communist policy with regard to South Vietnam's coming constitutional assembly election in September is still unclear. It seems doubtful at this time that the Communists have any significant number of followers among the candidates who have filed, though many of the candidates are relative unknowns even to local government officials. There are scattered reports that the Communists will make serious efforts to disrupt the election. Similar such reports preceded past elections, but Communist interference turned out to be relatively ineffective. Communist propaganda statements have, however, vigorously denounced the coming election as a farce and a trick. They may thus feel impelled to try to take a more active position through covert campaigning against candidates, or through terrorism and other direct sabotage efforts.

In areas under their control, the Communists are likely to continue their efforts to consolidate their hold. There has been evidence over the past year of some quasi-governmental reorganization at the local level through the establishment of village "Liberation Committees." Documents indicate that these committees are Party-controlled administrative bodies rather than a part of the Liberation Front structure. This local government endeavor may receive increased emphasis, possibly in concert with local plebiscites with which the Communists might hope to challenge and undercut the impact of elected institutions created by Saigon.

~~TOP SECRET~~

ANNEX XII

AN HISTORICAL ANALYSIS OF ASIAN COMMUNIST
EMPLOYMENT OF THE POLITICAL TACTIC OF NEGOTIATIONS

~~TOP SECRET~~

ANNEX XII

AN HISTORICAL ANALYSIS
OF ASIAN COMMUNIST EMPLOYMENT
OF THE POLITICAL TACTIC OF NEGOTIATIONS

Summary

This Annex discusses the Asian (particularly Chinese) Communist practice of negotiating, focusing on the motives which, in the past, have impelled Asian Communists to negotiate and the signs they have given when they were prepared to talk. It includes an analysis of the fight-talk tactic used in the Chinese civil war in the 1930s and 1940s as well as a detailed examination of the Korean experience of 1950-53 and the Vietnamese experience of 1953-54. Finally, there is a short discussion of implications for Vietnam today.

a. General Findings

On the two occasions when the Chinese Communists have initiated negotiations during military conflicts, their forces were either
    (a) weak and in danger of annihilation, as in the Chinese civil war, or
    (b) badly hurt in the field, as in the Korean war.
As they negotiated, they continued to fight. This fight-and-talk tactic was formulated by Mao Tse-tung in 1940 as a means to preserve his weak forces from being destroyed by Chiang Kai-shek's militarily superior armies. Subsequently, it was used in Korea by the Chinese and North Koreans, at first as a expedient to shield their badly hurt armies in 1951, and then, from 1951 to 1953, as a holding tactic until they could extract terms enabling them to disengage from a costly limited war.

In Indochina, however, the decision to begin negotiations was imposed by the Soviet and Chinese leaders on Ho Chi Minh when they feared American involvement and escalation of the war more than he did in 1953. They urged Ho to close out the war, which he was by no means losing in the field, and persuaded him to make concessions to the French after talks started and to try to seize Vietnam by a process

of low-risk political subversion. Even after Ho had been induced to begin negotiations, his desire to use Mao's original fight-and-talk tactic for a protracted period was subordinated to the larger interests of Soviet policy (to split the Western alliance in Europe) and Chinese policy (to prevent the US from establishing alliances in Asia). The Soviets and Chinese viewed these interests as being best served by a "peace" offensive and hindered by continuation of the Indochina war. Ho made concessions, particularly on the matter of partition, which were later viewed by him and his lieutenants as a mistake not to be repeated.

b. The CCP-KMT Civil War (1937 to 1949)

Constantly maneuvering to preserve the badly depleted ranks of his Red Army from complete destruction by Chiang Kai-shek's militarily superior forces, Mao in September 1937 finally induced Chiang to establish, on paper, a CCP-KMT united front against Japan. But within the context of this paper alliance, Mao expanded his military and political forces in the northwest and even directed quick-decision thrusts to be made against isolated KMT units. As a pattern of limited armed conflict and political struggle emerged in 1940, Mao avoided major military operations which would provoke a major counterattack and developed a tactic of limited-fight, limited talk: "After we have repulsed the attack of the [KMT forces] and before they launch a new one, we should stop at the proper moment and bring that particular fight to a close. In the period that follows, we should make a truce with them." (Mao's statement of 11 March 1940). In this way, Mao gained a series of small victories without running the risk of a general civil war, while expanding his territorial holdings behind the Japanese lines.

While fighting continued on the local level, CCP-KMT negotiations went forward on the national level intermittently from 1940 to 1946. Represented in Chungking by his brilliant negotiator, Chou En-lai, Mao used various lulls in the civil war to increase his regular forces, and in 1944, he permitted the American Army Observer Mission to operate in Yenan because its very presence had a political restraining effect on Chiang. Recognizing the strengthened military and political position of Chiang after the surrender of Japan in August 1945, Mao tried to settle for a half-way station--legalization of the CCP--on the road to an eventual seizure of national power. Chiang refused to facilitate this eventual takeover. On 19 August 1946, shortly after KMT planes bombed Yenan, Mao dropped the talking half of his dual tactic

XII-2

and began to fight the all-out civil war, which his forces decisively won in mid-1949.

c. The Korean War (1950 to 1953)

Initial Chinese Communist military successes from November through December 1950 increased Mao's confidence that the UN forces could be driven from Korea if military pressure was sustained, and Chou En-lai rejected a cease-fire as "a breathing spell" for the UN. But a series of manpower-killing advances by UN and ROK units in March and early April 1951 followed by the blunting of the Communists' big April and May offensives, which cost them an estimated 221,000 men, left the ranks of Mao's best armies decimated by 1 June 1951. Of the 21 Chinese Communist divisions which had initiated the April and May offensives, 16 had suffered about 50 percent casualties.

These disastrous defeats impelled Mao to begin negotiations, but there were no prior indications that he was prepared to drop his previous political conditions for a cease-fire. When, on 23 June 1951, Soviet UN delegate Malik for the first time called for talks for a cease-fire, he merely avoided raising the preconditions that the US must withdraw from Taiwan and that Peking should be admitted to the UN. Mao seized upon the military breathing-spell to improve the badly impaired combat capabilities of his forces in the field.

Mao's strategy at the armistice negotiations (July 1951 to July 1953) was to wage a "protracted struggle," combining tactics of political attrition with limited military pressure. But this strategy did not break the determination of the US negotiators to defend the principle of voluntary repatriation of war prisoners. The death of Stalin (5 March 1953) permitted the development of a new Soviet attitude toward East-West tensions in general and concluding an armistice in particular. Their pressure on Mao and his own recognition that further resistance was purposeless, and even harmful to his economic program, inpelled him to retreat and accept voluntary repatriation--a move which opened the way for the armistice agreement of 27 July 1953.

d. Vietnam (1953 to 1954)

The same considerations that led the Soviets and the Chinese to negotiate an end to the Korean war in mid-1953 made them look with favor upon a negotiated settlement of the Indochina war. At the time, however, the fortunes of the Vietnamese Communists in their eight-year fight with the French were steadily improving and Ho Chi Minh gave no indication that he would be willing to accept less in a negotiated settlement than his forces could seize on the battlefield.

The first indication that the Communists might consider negotiations came from the Soviets, who began in August 1953 to quote with approval demands in the French press for a "Panmunjom" in Indochina. By September, the Chinese had also indicated a willingness to discuss Indochina at the conference table. But Vietnamese Communist propaganda made it clear that these Soviet and Chinese initiatives were being made at a time when Ho was still resisting the concept of negotiations. The attitude of the Viet Minh leaders at this time is illustrative of the generalization that Asian Communists have been unwilling to begin negotiations when they have been in an advantageous position militarily, or have not been badly hurt in the field.

As the French Government was being subjected to increasing pressure from many members of the National Assembly and from the French public for an end to the costly war, Moscow and Peking acted to convince Ho that he could make major gains through negotiations. On 29 November 1953, he finally took the initiative in proposing negotiations, but it was a hedged proposal that, in effect, demanded a complete French surrender.

Premier Laniel was able to resist the strong domestic pressure for immediate bilateral negotiations with the Viet Minh by agreeing to discuss Indochina at the Geneva conference in May 1954. Although Ho clearly preferred bilaterals, (in which he would have been in a much stronger position vis-a-vis the French than he was at Geneva), he was again pressured by the Soviets to agree to international negotiations.

At Geneva, Molotov and Chou En-lai moved adroitly to avoid any impasse that could be used by the US as an excuse for intervention in the fighting. Ho, whose delegate, Pham Van Dong, started with maximum demands after the fall of Dien Bien Phu (7 May 1954), apparently calculated that negotiations could continue for some time without leading to American involvement. His tactics of protracted negotiations, which would afford him more time to solidify his military position, were similar to those of Mao in Korea. But again and again, the Soviets and Chinese acted to undercut his delegate's maximum demands at Geneva for French political concessions in exchange for a ceasefire.

The Viet Minh certainly had not expected to have to make as many political concessions as they finally agreed to at Geneva. Ho was in a position to negotiate from strength and to do so for a long time, but he found himself caught in a Sino-Soviet political web and was persuaded not to use his growing military capability to force major concessions. It was clear at the time that the North Vietnamese were far from completely satisfied with the Geneva compromises. As time has gone on, they have probably become even more convinced that the political concessions they made there were a mistake. The clear awareness that they were impelled, primarily by Moscow and Peking, to stop at a half-way station on the road to total military victory has made them all the more determined to fight on in the present situation.

e. Implications for Vietnam Today

North Vietnamese and Chinese Communist officials have indicated privately that the compromises made in 1954, providing the Viet Minh with something less than a total takeover of Vietnam, were a mistake. Ho's determination not to stop half-way again, even in the face of increased US airstrikes, is bolstered by Mao's special need to keep him fighting. Mao's special need, which stems largely from an image of himself as "leader" of the international Communist movement, is to prove Soviet and other doubters wrong regarding the ability of revolutionaries to defeat the US in a protracted small war.

Discussion

A. The CCP-KMT Civil War (1937 to 1949)

The badly depleted ranks of Mao's Red Army, which straggled into the sanctuary of northwest China in November 1935 after the punishing attacks of Chiang Kai-shek's forces during the Long March, were incapable of resisting an all-out KMT offensive. Aware of this basic fact, Mao repeatedly appealed to Chiang to end the civil war and establish a CCP-KMT united front to expel Japanese forces from north China. Chiang was unwilling to comply primarily because Mao insisted on preserving his military units for use in the revolution: "It goes without saying that we shall never allow Chiang to lay a finger on the Red Army." (Mao's statement of 14 March 1936). But Japan's large-scale attack on China in July 1937 provided Mao with a new opportunity to move Chiang into a united front against Japan. Mao took the first formal step; on 22 September 1937 the CCP declared that its armed forces would be under the "direct control" of Chiang. Actually, three days after this paper statement, Mao made it clear that "direct control" was only an anti-Japanese political facade and that units and their weapons would remain under Communist control:

> It is necessary to maintain the CCP's absolutely independent leadership in what originally was the Red Army as well as in all guerrila units. Communists are not permitted to vacillate on this principle. (CCP resolution of 25 September 1937)

Mao used the mythical anti-Japanese united front to deter the KMT forces from attacking his new sanctuary in the northwest and to expand his military, territorial, and political holdings. Most of the CCP effort was directed toward extending its assets, some was directed toward guarding against a KMT attack, and only a little was directed toward engaging Japanese armed forces. Negotiations for the reorganization of the former "Red Army" units moved very slowly in 1937 and 1938, and clashes continued on the local level between some Nationalist and Communist forces. As friction increased, Mao began to formulate his political-military tactic. On 6 November 1938, he directed that the CCP's main field work should be in the relatively secure rear areas of the Japanese forces, calculating that the political-military vacuum behind the Japanese lines would shield the CCP from superior KMT forces until the foothold in the northwest could be expanded. Mao enlarged his armed forces as quickly and efficiently as possible. but he always stopped just short of provoking an open break with Chiang and the retribution of a major KMT offensive.

Calculated restraint, intended to provide Chiang with no pretext for an offensive, was designed by Mao to be a temporary tactic to gain vitally needed breathing spells prior to the opening of a revolutionary advance in the future. Mao indicated the "positive" role of reduced military aggressiveness as a tactic in advancing the revolution:

> Our concession, withdrawal, turning to the defensive or suspending action, whether in dealing with allies or enemies, should always be regarded as part of the entire revolutionary policy, as an indispensable link in the general revolutionary line, as a segment in the curvilinear movement. In short they are positive.
> (Mao's statement of 5 November 1938)

That is, defensive or suspended action was part of Mao's policy to expand his armies and the CCP membership behind Japanese lines with the aim of seizing more territory at the expense of the KMT. But quick-decision thrusts were never abandoned. For example, in the spring of 1939, Communist forces moved quickly into Shantung Province, and in the winter of 1939-1940, they decimated KMT forces in Hopei Province. These clashes were fully concordant with Mao's policy of expanding holdings by armed struggle within the context of the CCP-KMT paper united front.

A pattern of limited armed conflict and political struggle emerged in CCP-KMT relations in the spring of 1940. Mao began to refine his fighting-and-talking tactic. Militarily, he limited the offensive operations of the Communist armies, which were still considerably inferior to KMT armies; politically, he worked vigorously to indoctrinate workers, peasants, and intellectuals. In this fashion, he groped his way, seeking out and exploiting the soft spots in Chiang's military and political armor.

Mao systematized his tactic. On 11 March 1940, he set forth the unique position that there was no incongruity between waging a political-military struggle against Chiang while maintaining a united front with him. The struggle half of this dialectical policy was intended to demonstrate to Chiang that Mao's forces could not be destroyed--that they would fight back against any KMT offensives. The unity half was intended to deter KMT attacks and to "avert the outbreak of large-scale civil war." Mao depicted the partial struggle against Chiang as "the most important means for strengthening KMT-CCP cooperation," his calculation having been, as he pointed out on 4 May 1940 in a directive to Communist field commanders operating in east China, that clashes with the KMT forces were necessary —

> so as to make the KMT afraid to oppress us...and compel them to recognize our legal status, and make them hesitate to engineer a split.

That is, Mao, on occasion, used military action in certain areas rather than direct political concessions to sustain the united front on paper.

He correctly estimated that small CCP military thrusts would not provoke Chiang to move beyond limited counter-attacks because Chiang did not have the military capability in 1940 to open a nation-wide offensive against CCP forces so long as the war against Japan was being waged. Mao's estimate of 4 May 1940 was that

> The present military conflicts are local and not nation-wide. They are merely acts of strategic reconnaissance on the part of our opponents and are as yet not large-scale actions intended to annihilate the Communists.

In this way, he defended the general plan for limited civil war which he had enunciated on 11 March 1940 as a limited-fight, limited-talk tactic. Mao had set forth the important tactic in considerable detail:

> First, we will never [sic] attack unless attacked; if attacked, we will certainly counterattack.... Second, we do not fight unless we are sure of victory; we must on no account fight without preparation and without certainty of the outcome....Third, the principle of truce. After we have repulsed the attack of the die-hards [i.e., the KMT forces] and before they launch a new one, we should stop at the proper moment and bring that particular fight to a close. In the period that follows, we should make a truce with them. We must on no account fight on daily and hourly without stopping, nor become dizzy with success. Herein lies the temporary nature of every particular struggle. Only when the die-hards launch a new offensive should we retaliate with a new struggle.

This became the basic tactical principle of Mao. His practice indicated that his forces were directed to fight, close off the particular battle with a defeat of KMT forces, and then seek a truce and be prepared to negotiate in the hope that Chiang would not take a local and limited defeat as the reason for a large-scale offensive against all Communist armies. This is the tactical principle designed to advance Mao's protracted war waged with initially weak forces, limiting their actions to safe proportions.

In this way, Mao gained a series of local victories without running a great risk of general civil war. At the same time, he seized territory by expanding the base areas behind the Japanese lines and by controlling the actions of his field commanders, whose forces sporadically chopped away at small KMT units. For example, the First Contingent of the Communist New Fourth Army commanded by General Chen Yi decimated KMT forces in northern Kiangsu in July 1940 and, in the second half of 1940, several Communist victories were won in the lower Yangtze valley. Mao had directed that the New Fourth must be expanded to 100,000 men; by the end of 1940, his generals were successful in expanding this army to approximately that number of combat regulars.

While fighting continued on the local level, CCP-KMT negotiations took place on the national level in the second half of 1940 as Mao implemented his fighting-and-talking tactic. Even when vastly superior KMT forces unexpectedly surrounded and destroyed 9,000 men attached to the New Fourth's headquarters as they were withdrawing to the north of the Yangtze River, Mao refused to consider this setback as invalidating his principle of waging a limited war. In June 1943, the intermittent negotiations between the KMT and CCP reached another major impasse in Chungking, just as they had in late 1939 and in January 1941. Chiang asked Mao to give a conclusive reply to his demands to relinquish the independent CCP government and to incorporate CCP forces into Nationalist armies. Chou En-lai, the brilliant Communist representative in Chungking, deflected these demands and charged the KMT with increasing their forces along the northwest border base areas. Chou attained some success in his political effort to depict Chiang as the obdurate element in the united front.

The failure of Chiang to launch large-scale attacks against Communist forces in 1943 was attributed by Mao at the time to the political success in arousing domestic and international opinion against Chiang's policies. (<u>Liberation Daily</u>, 5 October 1943). Two additional factors were Japan's east China offensive against KMT forces and US efforts to stop Chiang's attempts to suppress the Communists. That is, Mao adroitly used political pressures to compensate for military weakness: "The Communists are not capable of much, if any, offensive action." (Report of Colonel Depass, 16 November 1943)

Expediently, from 1943 to 1945, Mao used the lull in the CCP-KMT protracted war to further expand his armed forces, which increased to 475,000 regulars by October 1944. The Wallace mission to China in June 1944 resulted in the dispatch of the American Army Observer Mission to Yenan, which Mao favored because of "its political effect upon the KMT":

> Any contact you Americans may have with us Communists is gold. Of course, we are glad to have the Observer Mission here because it will help to beat Japan. But there is no use in pretending that--up to now at least --the chief importance of your coming is not its political effect on the KMT. (Mao's remarks to John S. Service, interview of 27 August 1944)

That is, Mao exploited the US desire to end the civil war and get on with the war against Japan, adroitly using it as a political shield against the potential offensive-power of Chiang's superior military forces. He was capable then of considerably more tactical flexibility than he has been in recent years.

By insisting on policies which made the KMT appear unreasonable, Mao deflected Chiang's demand that, to become a legal party, the CCP should disband its armed forces. In a carefully worded proposal, which Mao maneuvered Ambassador Hurley to sign with him in Yenan on 10 November 1944, Mao agreed only "to work for" the unification of all military forces while insisting on the formation of a "coalition national government and a united national military council." His intention was to exploit the generally held view that the CCP was justified in refusing to disband its armies before the formation of a coalition government. However, in order to keep the negotiations alive, he directed Chou En-lai in Chungking to join Ambassador Hurley in pressing Chiang to accept the proposal. Chiang insisted on disbanding the Communist armies, and Mao was then able to "expose" Chiang as recalcitrant in rejecting a "reasonable" negotiations compromise--i.e., a coalition. The widespread domestic and international appeal of the Maoist program for a settlement, the rapidly expanding military-political power of the CCP, and US anxiety to bring about unity put Chiang at a considerable disadvantage in the talks. Mao's success with dilatory tactics--that is, his substituting of talks about "working for" unified armed forces in the place of action taken to disband CCP armies--further isolated Chiang in China and internationally.

All along, Mao had continued to expand his forces, and by 24 April 1945, he claimed that they totalled 910,000 regulars and more than 2,200,000 militia. Mao made a major move shortly before Japan's surrender, ordering CCP troops to link up with Soviet troops driving southward in Manchuria (10 August 1945). As CCP and KMT armies raced for control of various Japanese-vacated areas and as Chiang prepared to strike at Mao's forces, the Communist leader accepted Chiang's invitation to accompany Ambassador Hurley to Chungking, arriving on 28 August 1945. Mao was still anxious to gain a series of breathing spells. Two days before flying to Chungking, Mao drafted an inner-party policy line on negotiations, in which he indicated that the CCP should be prepared to make some concessions--namely, some reduction in the size of those base areas which were indefensible and in the strength of CCP armed forces:

> Without such concessions, we cannot explode the KMT's civil war plot, cannot gain the political initiative, cannot win the sympathy of world public opinion and the middle-of-the-roaders in China and cannot gain in exchange legal status for our party and a state of peace.
>
> But there are limits to such concessions: the principle is that they must not damage the fundamental interests of the people [i.e., CCP control of the base areas and the armed forces].
> (Mao's statement of 26 August 1945)

Mao in Chungking recognized the strengthened military and diplomatic position of Chiang after the surrender of Japan and the signing in Moscow of the Sino-Soviet treaty. In private talks, he dropped his demand (to which he later returned) for a coalition government and high command, but insisted on retaining not less than 20 divisions as well as exclusive control of the base areas in north China. He wanted to obtain a settlement, a half-way station of legalization on the road to an eventual seizure of national power, inasmuch as his armies were still smaller and more badly-equipped than Chiang's. "The Communist armies do not possess sufficient strength to directly oppose the KMT armies in positional warfare; but over a long period of time as an occupying force, the KMT cannot hold out even with US help." (August 1945 report of Colonel Yeaton from Yenan) Chiang accurately summarized Mao's position as equivalent to allowing the CCP to carry on its political revolution without opposition or hindrance while professing to end the KMT-CCP military clashes by negotiating. Actually, while Mao was talking, CCP forces were consolidating their control over newly taken territory in the north, and when Mao returned on 11 October 1945, after refusing to disband his forces, he justified in the context of protracted revolution, his willingness to negotiate.

Mao made it clear to cadres in Yenan on 17 October that reducing CCP forces to 20 divisions would not mean handing over weapons. "The arms of the people, every gun and every bullet, must all be kept, must not be handed over." He then reminded cadres that his strategy was to wage a long revolutionary war:

> Was our party right or wrong in deciding at its 7th Congress [in April 1945] that we were willing to negotiate with the KMT provided that they changed their policy? It was absolutely right. The Chinese revolution is a long one and victory can only be won step by step.

As both sides raced to seize Japanese arms and fill the territorial vacuum, Mao directed the Northeast Bureau of the CCP to expand its holdings and use the newly-arrived 100,000 Communist troops to hold the rural areas remote from the existing centers of KMT control. Between the truce of January and June 1946, both sides took territory in Manchuria. During the whole period of the Marshall mission in late 1945 and 1946, Mao tried to disgrace Chiang politically by advocating a moderate program of "peace, democracy, and unity" while his armed forces expanded. He relied heavily on their ability to avoid decisive engagements, to prolong the stop-start fighting, and to counter-attack against small KMT units.

In the final series of negotiations of Mao's long revolutionary war, he gave priority to the goal of attaining a ceasefire and an extension of the Manchurian truce. He was also concerned in June 1946 about US aid to Chiang's forces. On the one hand, he relied on General Marshall's mediation to gain an immediate cease-fire, to ameliorate Chiang's demands, and to state his own settlement terms. Chou En-lai, urbane and persuasive, ably discharged his task by appearing conciliatory, moderate, and reasonable. On the other hand, Mao's press and radio in Yenan criticized US policy with increasing vehemency in an effort to deter Washington from giving further aid to the KMT. By 26 June 1946, Mao demanded that the US stop all military assistance to Chiang and withdraw all US troops from the mainland; his concern with the modern equipment sent to KMT forces had been deepened. "Let them know that whatever happens, if we are faced with mechanized war, we shall fight on if necessary with our hands and feet." (Mao's statement to Robert Payne in June 1946)

Although his armies were still numerically inferior to Chiang's Mao issued an inner-party directive on 20 July warning his forces to prepare to smash Chiang's offensive by an all-out "war of self-defense," which required the temporary abandonment of indefensible cities and the opening of mobile warfare. Mao had no alternative but to fight against superior forces and on 19 August 1946, shortly after KMT planes bombed Yenan, Mao was impelled to drop the talking half of his dual tactic and prepare for all-out civil war, which his forces won in the straightforward contest of military strength waged between late 1946 and mid-1949.

In drawing an analogy between the Chinese civil war and the Vietnam war today, CCP propagandists emphasize the protracted nature of both conflicts and the evolution of weak into strong Communist forces. But they deliberately de-emphasize, or avoid any reference to, the talking-half of Mao's tactic and the temporary half-way station he tried to obtain. Unlike the Soviet propagandists, they insist that talking should take place only _after_ the US withdraws its forces from South Vietnam.

B. The Korean War (1950 to 1953)

Military developments in Korea in the spring of 1951 provide a clear-cut example of the Asian Communists having been impelled to switch to the talking phase after they had been hurt in the field. That is, they viewed the large losses of Chinese Communist Forces (CCF) combat regulars as the sufficient cause for drastically reducing the fighting phase. The military struggle was subordinated to a political "protracted struggle," the intention being to wear down Western negotiators.

When, in late November 1950, the CCF entered the war in force, North Korean Peoples Army (NKPA) combat casualties were already very high, estimated by the United Nations Command (UNC) at 200,000 in addition to 135,000 prisoners. The NKPA had been virtually destroyed and never fought again above corps strength in the Korean war. The initial CCF successes against UNC forces from November through December 1950 increased the confidence of the Chinese Communist leaders that they could drive UNC forces from Korea if CCF pressure was sustained. On 22 December 1950 and again on 19 January 1951, Chou En-lai rejected a cease-fire, describing it as a means to gain "a breathing spell" for UNC forces, and demanded that prior to any halt in the fighting all foreign troops must be withdrawn from Korea, US armed forces must be withdrawn from Taiwan, and Peking's representatives must be admitted to the United Nations. As UNC forces retreated from the Yalu River, however, they took a heavy toll of CCF combat units. For example, between 27 November and 11 December, the 60,000 men of the eight divisions committed by the 9th Army Group, Third CCF Field Army, were estimated by the Marine Corps to have suffered 37,500 combat casualties, a little over half of them inflicted by ground forces and the rest by air attack. The 9th Army Group was so damaged by firepower that it disappeared from the Korean battlefield for three months. By mid-January 1951, UNC forces had stopped the CCF all along the front.

General Ridgway directed UNC forces to comply with his dictum of "inflicting maximum casualties on the enemy" rather than gaining ground. The dictum was put into practice in the months following the UNC offensive which started in late January 1951. By 9 February, OPERATION PUNCH had annihilated at least 4,200 CCF (body count) and when, on 14 February, CCF infantry for the first time in Korea attacked in mass waves, UNC forces killed thousands of Chinese at Chipyong-ni. CCF mass infantry assaults resulted in further heavy Chinese casualties on the 20th and again on the 21st with the start of OPERATION KILLER. By 1 March, the entire Chinese front south of the Han River had collapsed and UNC

XII-14

units moved to within 30 miles of the 38th parallel. CCF manpower and equipment losses continued to be "heavy" after the start of OPERATION RIPPER on 7 March, and on 14 March, Seoul was retaken as CCF and small NKPA forces fell back. A series of manpower-killing advances launched by UNC and ROK units in late March and early April moved the allied forces across the 38th parallel. The ranks of the best armies--Lin Piao's 4th Field Army and Chen Yi's 3rd Field Army--which the Chinese leaders used in the first massive assault against the UNC forces had been seriously depleted. "Now the best troops are annihilated; this forced the CCF to send replacements from the 1st and 2nd field armies.... The CCF suffered high casualties and its faith in victory had been reduced." (From interrogation report of Assistant Battalion Commander, 40th Army, 4th CCF Field Army)*

General Van Fleet met the first Communist spring offensive, launched on 22 April 1951, with the manpower-killing tactics of General Ridgway, and directed his corps commanders on 30 April

> Expend steel and fire, not men.... I want so many artillery holes that a man can step from one to the other.

Because they used massed infantry assaults against concentrated US artillery, automatic-weapons, and air firepower, units of six CCF armies suffered a total of 70,000 casualties between 21 and 29 April and were forced to end their first spring offensive. Their second spring offensive was even more destructive to CCF men and materiel.

On 16 May, 21 CCF divisions, flanked by a total of 9 NKPA divisions, opened the second spring offensive along a 105-mile front using human wave tactics against strongly fortified UNC positions. Although gains of 10 to 15 miles were made along most of the front, the Communist offensive was completely spent by 21 May, and UNC forces, which had recoiled only slightly, lashed back in a major counter-offensive, depriving the Communists of the opportunity to place screening forces between their main armies and the

---

*The prisoner reports that are referred to in this Annex are, in almost every case, the reports of prisoners captured and interrogated in March and April 1951--that is, after the collapse of the January 1951 CCF offensive and before the even more costly defeats of the spring of 1951.

UNC units. UNC counterattacks quickly carried into CCF and NKPA former assembly areas, where large quantities of supplies were captured as many dumps were overrun. By 1 June, the CCF and NKPA lost more than 102,000 men, and of the 21 CCF divisions which had initiated the offensive, 16 had suffered about 50 percent casualties. The following table, which is based on US Far East Command estimates, indicates the magnitude of the Communist losses:

Unit	Strength 16 May	Strength 22 May	Strength 1 June	% Losses
East Central Front (Main attack)				
12th CCF Army	30,000	17,000	10,000	67%
27th CCF Army	31,000	25,000	21,000	32%
39th CCF Army	20,000	20,000	19,000	5%
40th CCF Army	17,000 (?)	27,000 (?)	27,000 (?)	0
II NK Corps	18,000	18,000	17,000	5%
V NK Corps	19,000	18,000	16,000	16%
Central Front				
10th CCF Army	24,000	24,000	23,000	4%
15th CCF Army	32,000	23,000	14,000	56%
20th CCF Army	32,000	32,000	31,000	3%
26th CCF Army	21,000	17,000	19,000	9%
60th CCF Army	31,000	27,000	14,000	55%
63rd CCF Army	29,000	22,000	15,000	48%
Western Front				
64th CCF Army	28,000	22,000	20,000	29%
65th CCF Army	29,000	22,000	18,000	38%
I NK Corps	17,000	11,000	12,000	29%
VI NK Corps	28,000	28,000	28,000	0
TOTALS:	406,000	353,000	304,000	25%

The table indicates that as of 1 June 1951, the Communists had sustained a loss of 25 percent of their <u>total</u> 16 May strength in Korea. From 1 to 14 June, they suffered an additional 49,000 casualties (not included in the table above).

Most of the CCF prisoners were taken during the last week of May in frantic efforts to escape, indicating that the political-control fabric of many CCF units had been shattered, primarily because large numbers of political officers and non-coms had been killed. UNC ground pursuit ended on 2 June after all of South Korea except for a small part on the Western flank had been cleared of Communist forces, enabling fortification of the UNC line in depth to begin in the vicinity of the 38th parallel.

The combined heavy losses to the first wave field armies--i.e., the CCF 3rd and 4th--and the second wave armies--i.e., the CCF 1st and 2nd--had significantly reduced the quality of the forces which the Chinese leaders could put in the field in June 1951. Many of their best combat officers and political cadres had been killed or captured, partly because of the Maoist practice which required that they take front-line positions to lead their troops. Many political officers were killed in combat "because they spent much of their time with the men in the front line to lead the battle themselves" (from interrogation report of a private in the 125th Division, 4th CCF Field Army), and in some companies all officers including the company commander had been ordered to the front line to raise the men's "fighting spirit" (from interrogation report of the Company Political Officer in the 118th Division, 4th CCF Field Army). "The casualties among the commanders were high...because they took the lead at the front" (from interrogation report of Battalion Commander, 64th Army, 1st CCF Field Army). The massed infantry attacks--used for the first time by the CCF in Korea in mid-February 1951--facilitated the destruction: "We fought only with human wave tactics; great numbers of men have been sacrificed; it was indescribably miserable" (from interrogation report of Private, 42nd Army, 4th CCF Field Army). The Maoist doctrine of "defeating the enemy's firepower with a superiority in manpower...is a military idea which is no good.... These views of mine were shared by most lower-level leaders and the men in the CCF, though they could not dare to make them public" (from interrogation of Assistant Battalion Political Officer, 40th Army, 4th CCF Field Army). "'Human wave' tactics are supposed to overwhelm the enemy's firepower with predominance of manpower and thus win the victory. From my first experience in this war, I found that this tactic had no sense and no value.... In actual combat, it was nothing but a mass loss of lives and defeat" (from interrogation report of Squad Leader and CCP member, 40th Army, 4th CCF Field Army). The quality and number of CCF cadres who were lost to the four CCF field armies probably was the sufficient cause for the Chinese Communist leaders, whose forces comprised about 95 percent of the Communist combat units in Korea, to switch to the talking phase. Heavy losses of NKPA officers of the I, II, and III Corps were also indicated by intercepted messages in June 1951.

In the disastrous offensives of spring 1951, the CCF and NKPA sustained an estimated 221,000 casualties from 21 April to 16 June. By 16 June, the Chinese casualties since the CCF entered the Korean war were approximately 577,000, including roughly 73,000 non-battle casualties--mostly due to various epidemics--and 16,500 prisoners. (NKPA casualties as early as November 1950 had already been very high, estimated at 200,000 in addition to 135,000 prisoners. No data is reported here on NKPA _total_ casualties since November 1950.)

The war was increasingly costly for the Chinese in other ways. It forced the regime to modify its program of long-range economic development and to place the economy on a war footing. The war also subjected the regime to economic sanctions imposed by the West, increased inflationary pressures, and strained economic relations between urban and rural areas. The Chinese Communists became increasingly dependent on the USSR, partly because the Chinese were unable to replace from their own resources the stocks of material being expended in Korea.

The first step toward ending the commitment in Korea was to begin negotiations for a cease-fire, the calculation apparently having been that political concessions could be gained by combining protracted talks with propaganda accusations, while the fighting was kept limited.

Following a series of statements made by American and United Nations' officials in late May and early June 1951 regarding the UNC's willingness to end the fighting without demanding a surrender of Communist forces, the Chinese Communists and the Soviets apparently decided to gain a breathing-spell. Prior to the 23 June radio speech of Soviet United Nations' delegate Jacob Malik, there apparently were no indications that the Chinese were willing to accept these Western proposals. On the contrary, the indications continued to point to Chinese intransigence. (For example, early in June 1951,

Vice Foreign Minister Chang Han-fu had been completely negative in a talk with Indian Ambassador Panikkar in Peking and insisted that the war must be settled only "in a military way.") Unexpectedly, in his radio speech, Malik indicated a change in the Communist position when he avoided linking the Communists' proposal for a cease-fire to their earlier demands that the US must withdraw from Taiwan and that Peking must be admitted to the United Nations. "The Soviet peoples believe that as a first step, discussions should be started between the belligerents for a cease-fire and an armistice providing for the mutual withdrawal of forces from the 38th parallel."

The Chinese, too, were careful not to admit they had dropped preconditions. On 25 June, the Peking People's Daily frontpaged Malik's proposal without acceding to truce talks. The Chinese did not accede to truce talks publicly until 1 July, and on 2 July they rationalized the change in their basic position without acknowledging explicitly that it had changed. That the Chinese were anxious to deny that they were operating from a position of weakness is suggested by their statements to Burmese embassy officials in Peking shortly after Malik's speech. They insisted that "China and the USSR are confident of their joint strength, as none is equal to them." The Chinese also indicated to the Burmese that they had moved into the war's political phase in order to attack--that is, "to brand" the US and its allies as "warmongers" and to create dissension in the Western camp, their strategy having been to wage a low-risk, high-volume propaganda war in order to gain concessions at the truce talks. The Chinese later formulated their switch to the talking phase as follows:

> After the five great campaigns [i.e., offensives from November 1950 to May 1951], the Volunteers switched over in good time to the strategic line of "engaging in protracted warfare while conducting positive defense" and strictly subordinated the military struggle to the political struggle. (NCNA commentary of 28 November 1958)

The Chinese used the military breathing-spell to improve their impaired over-all combat capabilities. By the time the armistice negotiations started on 8 July 1951, the Chinese had improved their artillery and small-arm stores and had replaced their manpower losses while the NKPA divisions were rebuilt. Politically, they had already exploited the theme of seeking peace and of opposing American "warmongering" with considerable success, gaining face internationally and placing themselves in a favorable propaganda position as the initiators of the truce talks. They were unwilling to move the talks along to a mutually acceptable conclusion within any short period. On the contrary, they used Mao's tactic of wearing down UNC negotiators in a "protracted struggle" (Peking's phrase of 3 September 1951) in order to extract major concessions.

This tactic of political attrition succeded in frustrating UNC negotiators, but it did not gain the Communists major concessions. Small-scale but sustained UNC military pressure on Communist forces in Korea in October 1951 was reflected in the talks. On 26 October, the Communists in effect dropped their demand that the demarcation line be moved down to correspond with the 38th parallel. On the other hand, they gained a 30-day de facto cease-fire from 27 November to 27 December, enabling them to further strengthen front-line defenses and to augment unit strength.

The Chinese desired a political victory together with a military truce, and as the talks centered on the prisoner issue, they adamantly refused to accept a political setback. The major deadlock on the matter of voluntary repatriation of prisoners prolonged the talks from April 1952 to July 1953, inasmuch as the Chinese insisted on the forcible return of all CCF (and NKPA) prisoners in order to avoid a major propaganda defeat if large numbers were to opt for the West. The Communists would not recognize the UNC stand on voluntary repatriation as a valid principle and argued that it was in conflict with the Geneva Convention which required a compulsory, all-for-all exchange. As an alternative, they calculated that if a relatively small number would resist repatriation--that is, about 16,000 of a total of 132,000 CCF and NKPA prisoners--they could tacitly agree to the UNC screening process.

Both the Communists and the UNC were shocked by the results of the screening process after about only half had been questioned. Over 40,000 of about 65,000 prisoners screened indicated that they would resist repatriation to China and North Korea, but the UNC had given the Communist negotiators an estimate of 116,000 willing to return of the total 132,000 prisoners. When, on 19 April, the Communists were informed that only 70,000 would return without the use of force, the CCF Colonel Tsai was speechless, asked for a recess, and on the following day--apparently on instructions from Peking--

XII-20

said that the UNC's earlier estimate of 116,000 was a far cry from 70,000. It was "completely impossible for us to consider" and "you flagrantly repudiated what you said before." Because the Communists had been stung once by the screening procedure, they indicated they would have nothing more to do with it.

Small, division-scale battles continued in the field, but the Communists were still unwilling to change the nature of the war into that of major offensive actions. They tried to deflect politically damaging charges of inhumanity on the prisoner issue by launching a concerted propaganda campaign, accusing the US--starting in late February 1952--of waging "bacteriological warfare" in North Korea and Manchuria. More importantly, Communist-instigated riots in the POW camps were intended to undercut the UNC position on voluntary repatriation by discrediting the entire screening process. In the POW camps, the Communist soldiers shifted their responsibilities from military to political goals. Close coordination was established between the POW camps and the Panmunjom truce talks. On 20 May 1952, after forcing a contrived confession of "compulsory screening" from General Dodd, who had been held prisoner by the prisoners of the Koje-do camp, chief negotiator Nam Il charged that

> The commandant of your prisoner-of-war camp could not but confess before the whole world your inhuman treatment and murderous violence against our captured personnel, and the criminal and unlawful acts committed by your side in <u>screening</u> and re-arming war prisoners by force. (emphasis supplied)

The Communist negotiators adroitly used the Koje-do incident to discredit the UNC figures and insisted that they obtain 132,000 prisoners in exchange for 12,000 prisoners held by them on the principle of an all-for-all exchange and forcible repatriation. Neither side conceded, and at the recess of talks on 26 July 1952, a year of negotiation had produced an estimated 2,000,000 words of discussion and nearly 800 hours of formal meetings. The prisoner issue was the only remaining agenda item.

On the battlefield, a military stalemate continued. Mao had confronted the US with his limited-risk protracted war. He apparently believed that Washington would continue to avoid pressing for an all-out military victory because of the potential manpower losses such a victory would require. By July 1952, CCF and NKPA ground forces strength had almost doubled since the start of the talks in July 1951 --from 502,000 to 947,000. He also apparently believed that he could deter the US from initiating airstrikes against the China mainland because of Washington's uncertainty regarding Stalin's reaction to such strikes. As part of his deterrent effort, Chou En-lai and the Soviet ambassador in Peking told Indian Ambassador Panikkar that the USSR would retaliate with air attacks against Japan if Manchuria was bombed by the US.

　　　　While Stalin lived, Communist negotiators at Panmunjom refused to retreat from their demand for forcible repatriation. New Dehli's efforts to smooth the way for a compromise were rejected when Foreign Minister Vishinsky on 24 November 1952 and Chou En-lai on 28 November 1952 attacked the Indian resolution on repatriation as unacceptable. As late as 17 February 1953, in an interview with Indian Ambassador Krishna Menon, Stalin avoided advancing new proposals on Korea and showed no real interest in the Indian compromise effort. Mao, too, remained adamant into 1953, declaring that "however many years American imperialism prefers to fight, we are ready to fight it..." (speech of 7 February 1953). Stalin had raised East-West tensions to a high level, and Mao was prepared to sustain those tensions.

　　　　On the battlefield, small-unit actions continued in localized struggles for hill positions and, although the Communists had taken losses in October 1952 that had cut their estimated total strength from 1,008,900 to 972,000 at the end of the month, their total began to climb slowly again in November as fighting tapered off. Both sides made the same calculation, namely, that a major offensive would lead to a very high casualty rate but not a military breakthrough.

The death of Stalin (5 March 1953) permitted the development of an entirely new attitude among the Soviet leaders toward East-West tensions in general and toward concluding an armistice in particular.* Moscow now appeared to be more anxious to negotiate a quick end to the war than did Peking. Soviet statements in March following Stalin's death were more conciliatory toward the West than those of the Chinese. Chairman of the Council of Ministers Malenkov stated on 15 March that "there is no disputed or unresolved question that cannot be settled peacefully by mutual agreement of the interested countries." For the first time since the end of World War II, Moscow Radio on 21 March admitted that the US and Britain had played a role in winning a "common victory" over the Axis powers. This followed Foreign Minister Molotov's unexpected agreement on 18 March to intercede with the North Korean leaders to obtain the release of 10 British diplomats and missionaries interned in North Korea since the start of the war. A further indication of the change in the Soviet attitude was Malenkov's depiction of the Korean war as a "defensive" operation in his 17 March message to Kim Il-sung on the anniversary of a Soviet-Korean agreement. Significantly, it differed from a similar message to Kim in 1951, when Stalin had described the war as a "struggle for liberation of the fatherland," in which any cease-fire would be conditioned on the withdrawal of US forces from Korea.

Three days after Chou's return from talks with the post-Stalin leadership in Moscow, the Communists unexpectedly agreed to a routine UNC offer for an exchange of sick and wounded prisoners which General Clark had reiterated in his letter of 26 February. In suggesting that the exchange of the sick and wounded might be the first step leading to the "smooth settlement of the entire question of prisoners of war, thereby achieving an armistice in Korea for which people throughout the world are longing," the Communists indicated

---

*The death of Stalin provided the Soviet leaders with the opportunity to jettison Stalin's more senseless and unproductive positions and to use methods of flexibility in diplomacy--such as a variety of goodwill gestures and a diminution of doctrinal hostility to Western governments. Stalin was concerned about the international situation leading to a general war, but for reasons of doctrinal obsessions and personal prestige, he refused to moderate the Soviet attitude toward the West and toward neutrals, and refused to make concessions on important international issues dividing the West and the Communist bloc.

on 28 March a new and real interest in solving the last crucial problem blocking a cease-fire agreement. This was the first indication that the Chinese might be willing to make a concession on repatriation.

But Mao waged a protracted political struggle as he prepared to make his retreat on forcible repatriation as small as possible. The Chinese used ambiguous and face-saving language in an effort to hold a series of fallback positions, which they surrendered only after it was clear the UNC would insist on the voluntary principle. An ambiguous proposal by Chou En-lai on 30 March--that both sides

> should undertake to repatriate immediately after the cessation of hostilities all those prisoners of war in their custody who insist upon repatriation and hand over the remaining prisoners of war to a neutral state so as to ensure a just solution to the question of their repatriation (emphasis supplied)--

left unclear the matter of final disposition of prisoners who were unwilling to return to China and North Korea. The Chinese propagandists described Chou's proposal as a "procedural concession," which it was, as the point that prisoners who were unwilling to be repatriated should be handed over to a neutral country represented a Chinese retreat. Chou had been deliberately vague in not stating Chinese demands for forcible repatriation, but Chinese propaganda returned to the demands by insisting on the principle of total repatriation by way of a neutral state. That the Chinese had made a concession in fact while insisting on the principle to cover their retreat is indicated by the statement of the senior Soviet member of the UN Secretariat, Kassaniev, who told a member of the Norwegian delegation on 30 March that Chou's declaration on prisoners was "the real thing" and that only "technicalities" remain to be worked out.

The UNC appraised this concession as indicating no change on the substantive matter of voluntary repatriation, and they pressed the Communists to clarify their position on where screening would take place, on its duration, and on whether the voluntary principle would be part of a cease-fire agreement. After manipulating the language of their counter-proposals throughout April, on 7 May the Communists

XII-24

made two more key concessions. They dropped the requirement that no repatriates should be sent physically to a neutral state and reduced the explaining period from six to four months. Finally, on 4 June, the Communists' chief negotiator, Nam Il, using language designed to conceal the Chinese capitulation on forcible repatriation, stated that "according to the application of each individual, those who elect to go to the neutral nations shall be assisted by the Neutral Nations Repatriation Commission and the Red Cross Society of India." That is, men who refused to return to the Communist countries could reach non-Communist countries through the channel of a neutral-nations commission stationed in Korea, if explanations failed to persuade them to return home. In this way, Mao accepted voluntary repatriation in a disguised form. His propagandists stated that ex-prisoners may go to "neutral states," without making it clear that they were in fact free to go wherever they chose.

Mao was anxious to still extract a degree of political prestige before the cease-fire agreement was signed. Face-saving offensives were launched in June and July by the Communists to achieve several objectives: (a) to move the line farther south, (b) to give ROK forces a bloody-nose in order to convince Rhee that his forces could not "March North," and (c) to convince international opinion that the CCF and NKPA were not weaker than UNC forces and that the Communist motive in seeking an armistice was not that of avoiding military defeat. Although suffering heavy losses between April and July 1953--an estimated total of 134,412--there were over one million CCF and NKPA forces in Korea, well-fed adequately clothed, and effectively supported by massed artillery by the time of the signing of the armistice on 27 July.

Mao's capitulation on the principle of forcible repatriation--a capitulation which provided the West with a major propaganda victory--apparently stemmed from several major considerations.

1. One was pressure from the post-Stalin leadership. The Soviet leaders were clearly anxious to consolidate their internal position and to relax international tension. They were alert to the harder policy taken toward the China mainland by the new administration of President Eisenhower. Neither the Soviet nor the Chinese leaders could be certain that the new administration would keep the war limited in the event that truce talks remained deadlocked. Chinese apprehension over the possibility of an attack, or at least a series of substantial raids, from Taiwan was reflected in

the resumption of recruiting in Shanghai in February and March 1953 and in defense activity along the south China coast. Implicit warnings from U.S. officials that Washington would not accept an indefinite deadlock and Secretary of State Dulles' explicit statement to Nehru on 22 May--viz., if a truce could not be arranged, the U.S. could not be expected to continue to refrain from using atomic weapons--further increased Communist apprehensions. They were also aware that in the spring of 1953, the U.S. had moved atomic missiles to Okinawa. The post-Stalin leadership desired to move a greater distance from the brink of involvement in the Korean war than Stalin had believed necessary; they were unwilling to risk an escalation on the battlefield which might well have provoked extension of U.S. airstrikes to the China mainland.

  2. Mao could perceive no further advantage in continuing the limited war. He was aware that the talking phase--i.e., the war of political attrition, intended to reduce the staying power of the UNC on the voluntary repatriation issue--had failed. The blackmail accusations--that is, American "warmongering" and "bacteriological warfare," which were components of the talking phase--had not forced a UNC concession. His plan of attrition, requiring policy critics in non-Communist countries to soften up the leaders of enemy governments (while policy critics in the Communist countries were effectively eliminated), did not provide him with the advantage he calculated would be decisive in inducing a major retreat. Despite his efforts during the talking phase, the UNC prevailed on the issue of repatriation, announcing on 21 July that 69,000 Koreans and 5,000 Chinese would return to Communist control, but 7,800 Koreans and 14,500 Chinese would be non-repatriates. (Earlier, on 18 June, Rhee had released 25,000 Korean prisoners.) Obviously, these figures represented a political embarrassment to his regime which the new Soviet leaders had to convince him to accept.

  3. Mao wanted to get on with the job of industrialization. Although political and economic conditions in China and North Korea probably were not exerting compelling pressure on the Communists to conclude an armistice in the summer of 1953, the war was probably viewed as injurious to long-term economic development programs. Political controls had been increased in China during the war and the

economic strains on the Chinese were probably less severe in the spring of 1953 than they had been in 1950 and 1951. But Mao was anxious to begin China's First Five-Year Plan of economic development, and the North Koreans were aware that they would have to start virtually from scratch to rebuild.

To sum up, Mao moved into the talking phase in Korea because his best field armies had suffered very heavy losses and were retreating under UNC military pressure. He apparently viewed the enormous loss of human lives with revolutionary callousness, but was forced to draw back because the military capability of his armies had been greatly reduced. When confronted with the UNC's demand that no prisoners should be forced to return to Communist control, he engaged in a "protracted struggle" in the hope of forcing a major concession from the Western powers by combining division-level battlefield pressure with political wearing-down tactics. But he decided to end the Chinese commitment when UNC presistence and Soviet pressure convinced him that further intransigence was purposeless and even harmful to the mainland's economic construction.

C. Vietnam (1953 to 1954)

Near the end of the Korean war, Viet Minh prestige was steadily increasing, and its military successes and organizational effectiveness bolstered Ho Chi Minh's confidence that he could attain a decisive military victory. He was determined therefore, to prosecute the revolutionary guerrilla war more actively and felt under no real compulsion to move toward the talking phase of his long-term effort against the French. On the other hand, lack of French military success and increasing domestic political pressure to reduce or close out the commitment in Indochina made a succession of French premiers and cabinets pessimistic about ever attaining a military decision over Ho's forces.

Even after General Navarre assumed command in Indochina on 8 May 1953, the French were unable to revise their losing strategy in the field despite a much touted (but never implemented) plan for mobile warfare drawn on paper. The force of 150,000 Vietnamese regulars, 50,000 Vietnamese auxiliaries, 15,000 Laotians, and 10,000 Cambodians that Navarre commanded proved unable to take over effectively the job of static defense, so Navarre was impelled to fall back on the old losing policy of tying down and dispersing French and French Union regulars to defend a series of key strongpoints. Out of a total of 175,000 regulars and about 55,000 auxiliaries, there were only seven mobile groups and eight parachute battalions--the equivalent of three divisions--that were not assigned to immobile, defensive duties.

In contrast, the Viet Minh was not tied down to static defense and with about 125,000 regulars, 75,000 full-time regional and provincial troops, about 150,000 part-time guerrillas--in short, the operating equivalent of nine regular divisions--moved freely through the countryside and chose the place to attack the enemy forces. For example, strong Viet Minh guerrilla elements together with two Viet Minh divisions sufficed to contain the 114,000 regular French Union forces in the Tonkin Delta. The Viet Minh skill in guerrilla warfare and in infiltrating into areas under French control seriously reduced Navarre's ability to take the offensive.

While the French were cursed with the necessity of defending a number of politically important but militarily unimportant points, Navarre was also under political restraint from Paris. Because of domestic criticism of the war in Indochina, the French government had directed its commander in the field to incur the fewest possible number of French casualties. The Viet Minh, on the other hand, was receiving strong support, both military and political, from its allies. The armistice in Korea had enabled Mao to increase significantly his aid across the southern China border to Ho's forces, strengthening their unit firepower and overall military capability. All along, Viet Minh regular forces in northern Indochina continued their gradual evolution from lightly armed guerrilla bands to a regularly organized military force with Chinese and Soviet equipment.

For all these reasons, Ho clearly preferred a complete military victory and gave no indication that he would be willing to attain less in a negotiated settlement than his forces could seize on the battlefield.

The post-Stalin Soviet leadership, however, viewed a softer policy toward East-West military conflicts as a necessary element in their long-range effort to dissolve the Western alliance in Europe. They tried to temporize on every major East-West difference in order to increase pressure against the US by its allies for a relaxation of trade controls, for great power negotiations, and for delays in rearmament and in European integration. The Soviet leaders calculated that such pressures and frictions would progressively reduce the West's capability for united action, as witness Malenkov's statement of the Soviet strategy in his speech of 8 August 1953:

> If today, in conditions of tension in international relations, the North Atlantic bloc is rent by internal strife and contradictions, the lessening of this tension may lead to its disintegration.

This strategy formed the basis of the Soviet campaign of negotiations, the pivotal slogan of which had been set forth by Malenkov in his statement that "there is not a single controversial or unsettled question which could not be solved by peaceful means on the basis of mutual agreement of the interested countries." (Speech of 15 March 1953) But Ho apparently was unwilling to end the war for Soviet political interests, and Moscow was impelled to make a distinction between the need to settle the Korean war and the need to continue the Indochina war.

Shortly after Stalin's death (5 March 1953), the Soviet leaders had made a distinction between the Korean war, which should be settled, and the Indochinese fight for "national independence," which should continue. (Pravda article of 11 April 1953) They insisted that the Soviet Union cannot be expected to "retard the Liberation movement" of colonial peoples. (Pravda editorial of 25 April 1953) But the Soviet leaders also tried desperately to deny that their position on Indochina cut across their "peace policy and seized upon and quoted with approval Churchill's remark that the Viet Minh offensive into Laos was not necessarily a Soviet-inspired move "inconsistent" with the attitude of the Soviet government," and suggested that the chances for mutual understanding between East and West would be improved if other Western leaders would recognize the real causes of the "liberation movements." (Pravda editorial of 24 May 1953) Ho made it clear to the Soviet leaders, who did not have the influence with him that they had had with Kim Il-sung, that the distinction between the peace movement and the Indochina war must be maintained. A Viet Minh message of 13 June relayed through Peking to the Viet Minh ambassador in Moscow informed the latter that the war in Laos should not be treated

XII-29

as contributing to the defense of "world peace," but as a "liberation movement." The message clearly indicated that Ho refused to have his effort subordinated to the needs of Moscow's European policy, particularly at a time when Chinese aid deliveries were averaging as much as 1,000 tons a month and Viet Minh forces were moving closer to the desired objective of a complete military victory.

Ho was also aware of the demoralizing effect that French political disputes were having on French troops in Indochina and almost certainly viewed this development as improving Viet Minh chances in the field. The French military initiative in Indochina was constantly being tempered by political considerations in Paris, and on 9 June 1953, a senior French official in Saigon stated privately that the confused state of French politics and the political issues involved in handling the Indochina war were complicating General Navarre's task of restoring morale and confidence in the French officer corps. The Viet Minh continued to insist inflexibly on their hard-line demand that the basic condition for negotiations was the complete withdrawal of French troops. By late July 1953, they had gained effective control over more than half of the Tonkin population and were believed to have the military capability of occupying the entire delta.

The signing of the Korean armistice in late July 1953 provided the Soviet leaders with the opportunity to maneuver actively for a negotiated settlement of the Indochina war. During the first two weeks after the armistice, Moscow's statements directed in large part to the French, established the line that the Korean truce demonstrated the "victory of negotiations over force" and that this has given a "new stimulus" to the struggle for a peaceful solution to the "dirty war" in Indochina. Whereas prior to the truce, Moscow had attacked suggestions for East-West negotiations concerning Indochina, by mid-August 1953 it was quoting with approval demands in the French press for a "Panmunjom" in Indochina. By contrast, Viet Minh broadcasts in mid-August 1953 warned that the armistice must not affect the continuation of the war against the French, who will not seek an armistice "in a short time," and that "we must wage a protracted struggle...intensify our fighting so as to annihilate more enemy troops; this is the only way to compel the enemy to accept peace in Vietnam."

As the Soviet leaders began to maneuver for a negotiated settlement, they acted to impress the Chinese leaders with the political benefits which would accrue to China in the event of high-level talks. They gave increasing prominence to the big-power status of the Peking regime and declared that "serious current problems" in Asia could not be resolved without Chinese Communist participation. (Soviet note to the Western powers of 4 August 1953)

The Chinese, who had been working for several years to gain wider recognition as the only legitimate government of China, welcomed this Soviet line. Indicating that Chinese Communist position was closer to the Soviet position, their delegate to the World Peace Council called for "step by step negotiations" of East-West issues. (Speech of 15 June 1953 by Kuo Mo-jo) On 2 September, Peking specifically cited the Indochina issue as one which could be solved "only by applying the principle of negotiated settlement," and Chou En-lai in mid-September privately informed the Swedish ambassador in Peking that a big-power conference on Korea could also discuss Indochina--a significant change in Chou's previous position that Indochina could not be discussed at such a conference.

By late summer, the Soviets had begun to contact important French officials privately; in early August, Ambassador Vinogradov indicated to Foreign Minister Bidault Moscow's desire to begin "general discussions" and openly hinted that the Indochina issue could be included. By early September, the Soviet leaders had indicated to the French ambassador in Moscow that a Soviet mission was to go to Viet Minh territory "to study conditions under which the Viet Minh can undertake peace negotiations." These Soviet initiatives were made at a time when Ho was <u>still resisting the concept of negotiations</u>: the "French...and American propaganda campaign, which has the "semblance of peace," is advanced in the "vain hope of weakening the will of our people, who ask only to fight...however painful and long." (Ho Chi Minh speech on 2 September 1953) Ho continued to insist on a "protracted struggle," inasmuch as his forces had not been hurt in the field. On the contrary, in the fall of 1953, Viet Minh military capabilities were at a new high point as a result of the marked increase in Chinese aid, the relatively light casualties suffered during the previous campaign season, and the excellent state of its intelligence regarding French troops dispositions and tactical plans.

The attitude of the Viet Minh leaders at the time is further confirmation of the generalization that the Asian Communists have been unwilling to begin the talking-phase of their dual tactics at a time when they are militarily in an advantageous position and have not suffered high casualties in the field.

French operations to counter expanded Viet Minh guerrilla warfare in the southern Tonkin Delta area had met with very limited success in October 1953 and at the cost of heavy casualties. After an area was "cleared" by the French, the Viet Minh reappeared quickly and Navarre's men, like those of Stalin, his defensive-minded predecessor, were tied down and dispersed in a static defense of provincial crossroads waiting for the Viet Minh to come at them again in the night. As the French waited for the Viet Minh fall offensive, reliable reports indicated that they had only four battalions in their mobile reserves in Tonkin and that their military position was "grave." The Viet Minh was aware of this French weakness through a Viet Minh source which was believed by American officials to have penetrated the French high command; Viet Minh messages indicated knowledge of the complete order of battle of the Vietnamese national army, detailed reports of French briefings, and information on the deployment and plans of the French-Vietnamese forces.

As certain French cabinet officials and many members of the National Assembly increased their demands that Premier Laniel and Foreign Minister Bidault move to end the costly war by negotiations, Ho apparently was brought under increasing pressure from Moscow and Peking to agree to enter the talking-phase of the Viet Minh effort in Indochina. Quoting Izvestiya in its Vietnamese-language broadcast of 24 September, Moscow Radio declared that there exists no international misunderstanding which could not be settled peaceably.

In April 1953, a senior French official had indicated to American State and Defense Department officers that the French were fighting in Indochina to maintain a position of strength from which they could negotiate an "honorable" settlement and that the French government was convinced that France could not win the war in Indochina any more than the US could win the Korean war. In early October 1953, this theme was taken up again by a French Foreign Ministry spokesman who indicated to American officials that the only way France saw of ending the war lay through a negotiated settlement with the Viet Minh.

According to a reliable source on 7 October, French cabinet ministers agreed to ask Foreign Minister Bidault to suggest to Washington that a five-power meeting, including Communist China, should take up the matter on how to end the war as soon as possible. On 10 October, Chou En-lai accepted the US proposals for a meeting to discuss the time and place for the Korean political conference, and Peking's propaganda continued to point to the need to settle international problems through peaceful means.

Ho was clearly reluctant to switch to the talking-phase, but because of Soviet and Chinese pressure as well as domestic pressure on the French government to agree to bilaterals, he apparently believed that even a hedged offer to talk would improve his international prestige without hindering Viet Minh military initiatives. In their note of 26 November to the Western powers, the Soviet leaders had indicated their desire to prepare the way for a five-power East-West foreign ministers' conference at which Communist China would be present, and they apparently insisted that Ho should at least appear to be less adamantly against talks with the French than he had been. (Politburo member Truong Chinh had declared on 25 September 1951 that peace negotiations would be "illusory" and that the French would have to be expelled as a necessary condition of peace, and Ho personally stated on 2 September 1953 that "We know that only the resistance, however painful and long it may be, can give us victory and restore peace to us.")

When, in late October 1953, Ho began to bring his position a step closer to that of Peking and Moscow, he accepted the principle of negotiations but insisted on the practice of continuing military methods to gain a settlement satisfactory to the Viet Minh. He conceded through his spokesmen that "every international problem can be settled by negotiations" (28 October) and that "to stop the Vietnam war through negotiations is completely necessary and also possible" (23 November). But in his reply to questions posed by the Stockholm paper, Expressen, Ho on 29 November in effect demanded a complete French surrender. He asked the French to begin bilateral negotiations by making a peace proposal--which Ho was only prepared to discuss--to stop fighting, to recognize the Viet Minh regime, and, by implication, to withdraw from Vietnam. Ho implied that, in return, he might not continue his war until the Viet Minh gained a complete military victory.* Actually, he continued to fight, and despite some displays of French aggressiveness, the military initiative was with the Viet Minh, whose forces in late November 1953 included divisions in Tonkin so disposed as to permit attacks against northwest Tonkin, against the northwest corner of the delta, or against Laos.

Ho's hedged proposal of 29 November was a three-pronged exercise of considerable political skill. It (1) advanced the Soviet and Chinese "peace offensive, (2) further isolated the Laniel government from the National Assembly and the French press, and (3) revived and deepened Vietnamese distrust of the French, who were viewed as being at the brink of a "pacifist trap" and who might decide against a greater military effort in the field. At the same time, Ho had his own paramount interest to protect, namely, winning a complete military victory, and in the first Viet Minh comment on his proposal, it was made clear to Moscow and Peking that peace could be attained only through "prolonged" military struggle and that the Viet Minh had no illusion that peace could be easily won. (Viet Minh news agency broadcast of 7 December 1953)

In France, Premier Laniel, supported by Foreign Minister Bidault, rejected immediate negotiations with the Viet Minh in the illusory hope that future negotiations could be attained on more favorable terms after military successes in the field.

Ho's generals continued their highly successful strategy of dispersing French forces in static defense positions while moving into areas of their own choosing. When, in early December 1953, General Navarre made the recently captured Dien Bien Phu a strongpoint to prevent moves into northern Laos, some Viet Minh forces began to move artillery into the surrounding area and, in late December, other Viet Minh forces swept southward into central Laos.

---
*Ho stated that "if the French government wishes to have an armistice and settle the question through negotiations, we will be ready to meet the French proposal."

This invasion of Laos by the Viet Minh was treated cautiously by Moscow and Peking, who muted reports of the new development in their commentaries and stressed the demand for an end to the war. The Soviet leaders, who were searching desperately for "proof" that Ho really intended to negotiate, centered their commentaries on this proposal of 29 November. "The recent statement by President Ho Chi Minh on his preparedness to examine a French proposal on an armistice, should such a proposal be made, constituted striking proof of the peaceful intentions of the Democratic Republic of Vietnam." (Moscow Radio commentary of 10 January 1954) While initiating little independent comment, Peking continued to rebroadcast foreign statements alleging that only US pressure prevented Paris from seeking an end to the Indochina war.

By contrast, the Viet Minh generally avoided the matter of a negotiated settlement and reminded its forces that real peace could be won "only by pushing forward the armed struggle and by dealing deadly blows at the enemy until he is compelled to demand negotiations." (Viet Minh radio broadcast of 24 December 1953) By mid-January 1954, when at least six battalions of Viet Minh were maintaining pressure on French forces in central Laos and more than 18 battalions were blocking all avenues of exit from Dien Bien Phu and bringing in artillery for the siege, the divergence between Ho, on the one hand, and the Soviet and Chinese leaders, on the other, remained clear-cut and reflected his reluctance to enter the talking-phase when his forces were consolidating portions of northwest Tonkin. By insisting that Paris submit a formal proposal for talks to the Viet Minh, Ho had placed the onus for avoiding negotiations on the French government, which continued to equivocate on the issue.

His forces held the initiative throughout Indochina as the result of widespread simultaneous offensive actions by the time the four-power Berlin conference convened on 25 January 1954. The drive into northern Laos of an estimated 12,000 Viet Minh troops, continued encirclement of Dien Bien Phu, the capture of small French posts in southern and central Laos, and extensive harassing operations in the Tonkin delta forced a further overall dispersal of French regular forces. On 3 February, the American army attache in Saigon reported that staff thinking and procedures at French headquarters were of the "1935-39 vintage" and that Navarre's strategy was identical to that of the defense-minded Salan. Navarre tied up 12 battalions of regular troops at Dien Bien Phu, only to be by-passed by the Viet Minh, who had moved into portions of Laos but had not been engaged even where the French had a three-to-one advantage. French patrolling from strongpoints was "the exception rather than the rule," reflecting apparent instructions from Paris to Navarre that he must conduct a "minimum-casualty holding action" with a view to eventual big-power negotiations.

As domestic pressure to end the war increased on the French government in the absence of victories in the field, two alternatives to bilateral negotiations with the Viet Minh were considered: (1) an international negotiated settlement or (2) "internationalization" of the war through UN--i.e., American--involvement.

Regarding (1), Foreign Minister Bidault reported from the Berlin conference on 31 January his intention to work for "joint discussion of the Indochina question by those principally concerned," and suggested an approach to Foreign Minister Molotov to try to end the war. Bidault expressed the hope that he had convinced Secretary Dulles earlier that the reasoning behind American acceptance of an armistice in Korea was even more valid for Indochina. Military prospects were dismal. A French officer in Saigon, responsible for estimates of the over-all situation in Indochina, told the American military attache on 8 February that the situation in the Tonkin delta was "rotten," that a French military victory there was impossible, and that the population was turning increasingly to the Viet Minh. According to Ambassador Heath, who spoke with General Navarre on the same day, the General's main concern was the effect any losses he might incur would have in Paris, and when the visiting French air force chief of staff said that France could take its officer losses for only one year more, Navarre replied that if that was the spirit in France, it had better pull out now. General Le Blanc, chief of staff of the French army, also stated in Saigon that France should use its officers and troops for NATO and appeared to catalogue the reasons why the war could never be won.

In short, well before the fall of Dien Bien Phu, French government officials and army staff officers regarded a negotiated peace as the inevitable solution to the war. In a message to Saigon on 20 February, Bidault indicated that at the forthcoming Geneva conference

> The time and the conditions of the negotiation, or, negotiations, which are likely to be necessary to to end the Indochina war are left in large measure to our initiative. The Americans have committed themselves to sit by our side at the time of the examination of the problem in Geneva with the Chinese, but it will be our responsibility to say how we desire to orient the continuation of the talks.

Despite Bidault's 17 February promise to Secretary Dulles at Berlin to push for a strong military offensive to counteract the Viet Minh drive, it was clearly impossible for the dispersed French forces to concentrate in the spring for a maximum effort.

Regarding (2), almost all French spokesmen had vigorously opposed internationalization of the conflict. Speaking for himself, Pierre de Chevigne, French secretary of state for the army, told the American consul in Hanoi on 18 February that he would not be averse to "internationalization." He said that American equipment alone could not alter the situation, implicitly rejected the build-up of the Vietnamese army as a substitute for American participation, and said that nothing was to be gained by seeking a political arrangement with the Viet Minh. His opinion, however, was atypical. By contrast, French officials in Paris, largely for fear of giving a pretext for Chinese intervention, continued to rebuff firmly any suggestion that American troops would be necessary.

The Communists hit hard at the possibility of American involvement in responding to speculation in the Western press, reflecting their own calculation that the increasing Viet Minh initiatives in the field might impel "direct intervention" by Washington. One of Molotov's chief aims at the Berlin meeting in agreeing to the Geneva conference was to block any possible increase in American military assistance to the French. The Chinese Communists, satisfied with the Berlin agreement as a first step in gaining general acceptance by the international community, warned that increased American involvement in Indochina was making the issue of Geneva more complicated. Ho Chi Minh expressed his concern when, on 3 March, he accused the US of "another step" toward direct intervention in "allowing the American air force to participate" in the Indochina war.

Soviet plans to end the war by a negotiated settlement at Geneva included a move to convince Ho that important international prestige could be derived from entering the talking-phase of his military effort in Indochina. According to an intercepted French message, Molotov was quoted as saying at the Berlin meeting that "all parties concerned" should participate in the Geneva conference on Indochina, just as both Koreas should take part in discussions on Korea. Pravda on 8 March attacked Foreign Minister Bidault's public statement that it was not necessary to invite Ho's representative to Geneva and insisted that "it is impossible to solve the Indochina problem without considering the lawful right of her people." As Soviet propaganda continued to press for Viet Minh participation at Geneva, Ho was provided a clear insight into his prospective political gains: unprecedented international prestige, intensification of French-Vietnamese frictions, demoralization of French forces in the field, and reduction of the risk of direct American involvement in the war. Nevertheless, he clearly preferred bilaterals with the French (in order to prevent US pressure on Laniel to remain intransigent) and considered the attendance at a multilateral conference would reduce his position of strength. He finally agreed, however, to multilaterals.

Moscow and Paris began to set forth their positions before the Geneva conference was convened. On 4 March, a Soviet embassy official in London told American officials that if the US and France object to an amalgamation of the Vietnam and Viet Minh administrations, "they can agree to a division along the 16th parallel." This first Soviet comment on Geneva suggested that Moscow was the most active advocate of partition which would deprive the French of the heavily populated, strategic Tonkin Delta and open the way for Viet Minh control of the whole country. Premier Laniel set forth the French position publicly on 5 March by calling for the complete withdrawal of all rebel troops from Laos and Cambodia, establishment of a neutral zone around the Red River delta, and withdrawal of all Viet Minh troops from that area. He was aware that these terms would be unacceptable to Ho, as was later conceded by the Foreign Ministry official who formulated them in order to forestall any Viet Minh offers for bilateral negotiations before Geneva. Rumors in Paris of direct French-Viet Minh contacts were not confirmed, and on 9 March, the Geneva alternative enabled Laniel to resist pressure for immediate bilateral talks with the Viet Minh.

All the while, Viet Minh tactical capabilities were continuing to improve, particularly with respect to anti-aircraft artillery and heavier infantry weapons acquired from China. Each succeeding campaigning season left the French occupying fewer outposts and the Viet Minh spread over larger areas of the intervening countryside.

Before entering the talking-phase of the Indochina effort, Ho apparently decided to demonstrate Viet Minh strength in the field. He made a major military move for political reasons; on 12 March, Viet Minh battalions hit strongpoints at Dien Bien Phu. He was willing to accept high losses--from 4,000 to 5,000 killed and wounded out of a total of 40,000 troops by 15 March. He was also willing to depart from Viet Minh military tactics by hitting a major strongpoint without the element of surprise (a French message of 11 March from Hanoi to Saigon revealed that the French were aware of the time the attack was to occur, the units involved, and the logistic build-up in the area.) Though the size and timing of the attack were anticipated, however, the Communist assault did incorporate one major factor for which the French were not prepared; the massive and extensive use of artillery. Communist possession and employment of artillery in itself provided a major element of surprise and rendered invalid the French tactical assumption, on which planning for the defense of Dien Bien Phu had been based.

In early April during the siege, Ho indicated to Communist newsman Wilfred Burchett that the French situation at Dien Bien Phu was hopeless. Ho placed a helmet upside down on a table, and compared the helmet's rim to the hills around Dien Bien Phu, saying: "They shoot up and we shoot in." He apparently calculated that loss of Dien Bien Phu would reduce Vietnamese army morale, already lowered by talk of an imminent truce; seriously discredit the "new" strategy of Navarre; give the Viet Minh a tremendous boost in prestige immediately prior to the Geneva conference, thus increasing the incentive for defection by Vietnamese nationalists; and increase French domestic pressure for direct negotiations with his representatives.

As Laniel and Bidault parried domestic demands for direct French - Viet Minh negotiations, they were also subjected to increasing Soviet pressure before the Geneva conference began. Soviet officials in Washington insisted to French officials on 30 March that direct talks between French and Viet Minh representatives should be held "in order to achieve a cease-fire prior to Geneva." The Soviets returned to the matter of bilaterals even after the conference began, and on 5 May, Molotov told Foreign Secretary Eden that the French and "Indochinese" should work out an armistice "themselves."

Moscow and Peking were anxious to disparage American foot-dragging and used Secretary Dulles' speech on 29 March, in which he suggested that the West should take "united action" to prevent a Communist seizure of Indochina, to spur Paris into bilaterals. They were particularly fearful that the American preference for the French to fight would stiffen Bidault further at Geneva and make French concessions more difficult to extract from him there, flanked by Secretary Dulles. They were also concerned about American statements regarding eventual if not immediate involvement: Pravda on 11 April claimed that the real target of US threats was China, and the Peking People's Daily declared on 21 April that "faced with armed aggression, the Chinese people will certainly not refrain from doing something about it." On

XII-40

28 April, Chou En-lai made another noncommittal deterrent statement: the Chinese "most emphatically will not tolerate aggression against us by any country" and the US is looking toward a "new world war." At the same time, the Chinese stepped up their already large military and medical aid shipments to the Viet Minh for the Dien Bien Phu siege.

The series of assaults on Dien Bien Phu throughout April indicated that Ho intended to take the strongpoint even at a very high cost. Despite murderous losses, which in late April and early May were variously estimated at about two divisions (about 18,000 men), Ho's forces continued to attack in intermittent phases. Their estimated strength was about 20,000 infantry plus some 9,000 supporting troops, as compared with less than 10,000 French Union Troops. There were 134,000 French and Vietnamese regulars in the Tonkin Delta, but the greater part of this number was still tied down in static defense, leaving the relatively few mobile units to counter the increased Viet Minh activity.

By the start of the Geneva conference on 27 April 1954, the overall military situation in Indochina and the particularly serious situation at Dien Bien Phu had provided Ho, and his Soviet and Chinese partners, with a position of considerable strength to use to offset American warnings about possible internationalization of the war. Soviet officials privately made various suggestions for a settlement —such as partition, nation-wide elections, and an immediate cease-fire. Calculating that the French would be more amenable to some sort of partition than to a coalition government, Soviet diplomats on the opening day of the conference privately suggested to American officials that the idea of partition would meet China's requirement that its southern border should be buffered by a Communist regime.

The Soviet-Chinese effort to soften up the French on the issue of partition was made in the face of the opposition of Ho, who like Bao Dai, claimed sovereignty over all Vietnam. As early as 4 March 1954, a Soviet official had suggested privately to American officials that partition along the "16th parallel" would be agreeable to Moscow.

XII-41

At the Geneva conference, the Viet Minh delegate, Pham Van Dong, tried to use military developments in Indochina as a backdrop in demanding major French concessions. Dien Bien Phu fell on 7 May, with Viet Minh losses estimated at about 21,000, of which about one-half were killed and French Union losses of about 18,000 men. On 10 May, Pham Van Dong set for maximum conditions in the form of an eight-point resolution, the main points of which were political which were linked with military provisions for a cease-fire: French recognition of the independence of the three Indochinese Communist-sponsored states, withdrawal of "foreign troops," elections in each state, and a total cease-fire involving occupation by each side of unspecified areas, no reinforcements, and a mixed control commission. Partition was not mentioned. By tying the French-desired cease-fire to political concessions, the Viet Minh put themselves in the position of using the military weapon to extract a French political retreat.

When a conference deadlock was threatened by French determination to deal with military matters first (i.e. to effect a cease-fire) and Viet Minh insistence that political and military questions be dealt with together, Chou En-lai and Molotov, playing major negotiating roles, moved adroitly to avoid any impasse that could be used by the US as an excuse for intervention in the fighting. In his major speech of 14 May, Molotov had explicitly rejected the French terms for an armistice because Bidault's formula did not deal with political questions. However, at the secret session on the 17th, he conceded that military questions could be discussed first. Chou En-lai also retreated; in a private conversation with Eden on 20 May, he stated that the military and political aspects of any Indochina settlement must be dealt with <u>separately</u>, with priority for a cease-fire. These concessions strongly suggested that neither Moscow nor Peking desired protracted talks; they undercut Viet Minh intransigence and policy to prolong the talks.

Ho calculated that negotiations could continue together with the fighting for some time without leading to American

XII-42

involvement. A Viet Minh commentary of mid-May seemed to be directed at reminding the Chinese and Soviets that there was no pressing need to end the war:

> We still remember the Korean lesson which taught us that one could negotiate and fight at the same time ...for two years.

Ho was clearly determined to protract the talking-phase to gain as much territory of Vietnam, Laos, and Cambodia as the French were willing to concede. As the Viet Minh augmented its forces in the Tonkin Delta with units from the Dien Bien Phu operations, helping to compress French-controlled areas there, Ho's delegate at Geneva apparently was instructed to insist again on political concessions in exchange for a cease-fire. He hardened the Communist position, which Molotov and Chou En-lai had been making increasingly more flexible.

Pham Van Dong on 25 May insisted on French political concessions before agreeing to end the fighting. He linked any cease-fire prospect with arrangements for "Khmer Isserak and Pathet Lao," the Communist-contrived regimes in Cambodia and Laos, and in effect denied that military and political questions could be separated. Dong also took a hard line on the Soviet-Chinese concept of partition, proposing the "readjusting of areas under control of each state...taking into account the actual areas controlled, including population, and strategic interests." Inasmuch as Chinese Communist maps showed the Viet Minh as holding most of Vietnam, about half of Laos, and parts of Cambodia, the Viet Minh proposal was a demand for considerable territory--more than its units held on the ground.

On 29 May, however, an agreement was reached to have representatives of both commands meet at Geneva to study the disposition of forces prior to a cease-fire. Molotov and Chou apparently were the prime movers on the Communist side in making this concession. Moscow and Peking, whose policy was centered on splitting the Americans from the French and preventing a system of alliances from forming in Asia, were apprehensive regarding the demands of most French military leaders and some Laniel cabinet members that the US enter the war. Accordingly, Molotov and Chou worked hard to attain some kind of agreement at Geneva and to prevent an abortive conference from leading to internationalization of the war. Militarily, Ho was keeping up the pressure:

XII-43

a captured Viet Minh document of late May 1954 directed Viet Minh commanders in the Tonkin Delta area to continue their harassing and guerrilla activities for an unspecified period "pending commitment of the battle corps."

Opposition of the French to the idea of partition began to weaken as they pressed for a cease-fire with controls, and on 5 June, the French minister for the Associated States told Ambassador Heath in Geneva that he favored partition as a solution at about the 16th parallel--i.e., at about the line suggested by the Soviets earlier.

The negotiations took a new turn as the Laniel government tried to survive the National Assembly debate on Indochina which began on 9 June. On the preceding day, the Communists indicated that they would use the weakened government position to gain their maximum demands; Molotov returned to a hard line, similar to that of Pham Van Dong as set forth on 10 May. Molotov demanded independence for Vietnam, Laos, and Cambodia, free elections in these states, and withdrawal of all foreign troops. He seemed to believe that the Laniel government would either move toward the maximum Communist position or be replaced by a government pledged to negotiate an immediate end to the war, and on 9 June, a Soviet Pravda writer told an American journalist in Geneva that no progress on Indochina was possible until after the French government crisis was resolved. On 11 June, a French official in Saigon told the American charge there that all members of the endangered Laniel cabinet except the Premier, Bidault, and Schumann had "written off the war" and were anxious to end it. On 12 June, the Laniel government fell, losing the vote of confidence in the National Assembly after the debate on the war; on 18 June, Pierre Mendes-France took over as the new Premier, and he promised to close out the fighting by 20 July.

In the military conversations between the French and the Viet Minh in Geneva, the latter asked for direct control of about three-fourths of Vietnam, half of Laos, and much of Cambodia. In the field, General Ely stated privately on 15 June that the military situation in the Tonkin Delta was precarious and that French and Vietnamese troops were "very, very tired." The Viet Minh maintained a capability for a full-scale attack on the delta.

The ever-present prospect of American involvement again impelled Molotov and Chou to keep the conference alive with small concessions. On 16 June, Molotov tried to break the deadlock over the composition of the international truce supervisory commission, and on the same day, Chou made a settlement proposal which implied withdrawal of Viet Minh forces from Laos and Cambodia. Under pressure, Pham Van Dong also suggested postponement of a political settlement for those two states. Thus by the time the Geneva conference terminated its Korea phase and temporarily adjourned, the Soviets and Chinese seemed to have moved back in effect to a position envisaging a partition of Vietnam and a neutral Laos and Cambodia. When Pierre Mendes-France took over as the new Premier pledged to seek an end to the war before 20 July, the road was opened to a final settlement.

In a conversation at Bern on 23 June, Chou told Mendes-France that an armistice should be reached in Vietnam as soon as possible, and that a final political settlement should be reached thereafter. This broke the link established by the Viet Minh between a military truce and political solution. Regarding Laos and Cambodia, Chou said that all foreign forces, including the Viet Minh, should be withdrawn and that there must be no American bases in either state. When the new French Premier complained that the military staff talks between the French and Viet Minh at Geneva had been stalled for several days because of Viet Minh intransigence, Chou agreed to intervene to speed the talks. During the conference recess, Chou, in discussions with Nehru in late June in New Delhi, apparently set forth a partition plan.

Chou then moved to apply pressure on Ho to drop his demands for retaining troops in Laos and Cambodia and for a partition line as far south as the 14th parallel. He met with Ho at Nanning on the China-Vietnam border in early July, on his return from India and Burma, to discuss with him the terms for a final settlement. A clear sign that Chou had insisted that Ho give some ground in the intransigent Viet Minh position appeared in the remark made by the Chinese deputy foreign minister to the French delegate on 8 July: Chou had had a "very good meeting" with Ho, the results of which "would be helpful to the French." When the Viet Minh tried again at the reconvened conference to gain permission to retain their troops in Laos and Cambodia and to settle on the 14th parallel, Mendes-France complained to

Chou that this was unacceptable and out of accord with Chou's position. Chou replied that both sides must make concessions, with the Viet Minh making the larger. On 13 July, following Chou's statement to the French Premier, Pham Van Dong changed his position and told Mendes-France that he was prepared to compromise on the 16th parallel. The French still preferred a line between the 17th and 18th parallels, and rejected Viet Minh demands for control of some part of Laos and elections in all three Associated States.

The final settlement on 20 July indicated that the Viet Minh had retreated on three points. They accepted the partition of Vietnam (they had insisted on "unity" of Vietnam) and with the line at the 17th parallel (they had wanted the 14th); they agreed to withdraw from areas south of that line in Vietnam and from all of Laos and Cambodia; and they accepted July 1956 as the date for national elections--a two-year delay contrasting with their demand for only a six-month delay.

Pham Van Dong had come to Geneva with the apparent expectation that the Viet Minh's increasingly strong military position in the field would enable him to extract considerable concessions from the French to open the way for Communist forces to further penetrate Laos and Cambodia and consolidate everything above the 14th parallel in Vietnam. But Soviet and Chinese pressures, stemming from larger policy considerations and fear of American intervention, frustrated this hope for maximum French concessions. Although Ho perceived certain advantages in ending the military phase--that is, his forces could take territory by political subversion and, therefore, his effort would be less costly in terms of manpower and safer in terms of non-involvement by the US-- he had not expected to have to make so many political concessions. These concessions were later viewed by him and his lieutenants as a major mistake. His forces had not been decimated in the field, as the Chinese armies had been in Korea in the spring of 1951 when Mao moved to the talking-phase of the Korean war. He probably was concerned about the prospect of US intervention, but Moscow and Peking were clearly more concerned about the consequences to their policy of internationalization of the war. He was in a position to negotiate from strength and to do so for a long time--"two years" as his radio declared in mid-May 1954--but he found himself caught in a Sino-Soviet political web and was persuaded not to use his growing military capability to force major concessions.

French military and intelligence officials agreed that Viet Minh forces in the delta following the fall of Dien Bien Phu were capable of launching a damaging full-scale offensive, but it never took place. In mid-July, one Communist journalist stated that he assumed Chou had pressed Ho to keep the fighting at a low boil when the Geneva conference was in its last phase. The Chinese indicated their national interest in settling the fighting-phase when, on 23 July, one of their journalists at Geneva declared privately: "We have won the first campaign for the neutralization of all Southeast Asia," the implication being that only Thailand was a probable area for the establishment of an American base. Chou in late July, after the Geneva agreements were concluded, stated on two occasions that Asian states must work out their "own" security arrangements, and Pravda on 22 July emphasized that the area will not be permitted to join any "aggressive groupings."

By contrast, the North Vietnamese leaders were far less categorical in priasing the Geneva conference agreements. Pham Van Dong declared at the closing session on 21 July that the problem of Vietnamese unification remained: "We shall achieve this unity, and we shall achieve it just as we have won the war." This contradicted the Pravda statement of 22 July that Vietnamese independence had been "won." On 22 July, Ho renewed his exhortations for a "long and arduous struggle" and declared that the division of Vietnam was only a temporary and transitional arrangement: "Central, South and North Vietnam are all our land, and our country undoubtedly will be unified, the compatriots throughout our country will certainly be liberated." The Viet Minh ambassador in Peking, Hoang Van Hoan acknowledged to Indian correspondents on 22 July that despite the strong military position of the Viet Minh, it had to compromise on several vital points, notably the timing of elections (put off for two years), the question of French troop withdrawal, and the location of the temporary demarcation line at the 17th parallel, in order to secure peace in Vietnam. The leaders of the "Resistance Government Khmer and Pathet Lao," repeated Ho's view that the agreements are but a "first step" and called for a long, hard struggle.

XII-47

Neither Moscow nor Peking revived propaganda support for these resistance phantom-governments. Moscow made little effort to describe the agreement on Vietnam as "temporary" or to stress that portion of the conference declaration disclaiming any intent to permanently partition Vietnam; that is, the Soviet leaders were satisfied with partition. Peking stressed its own new international prestige and the boost to the cause of "collective peace in Asia" provided by the agreements, which were a manifestation of Chou's five principles as declared jointly with Nehru, U Nu, and Ho.

To sum up, the Soviet and Chinese leaders induced Ho to enter the talking-phase of the Indochina war because:

1. It was a major problem which stimulated Western defense efforts and threatened to make a mockery of the "peace offensive" designed to impede these efforts. Soviet policy in Europe, devised to produce schisms and paralysis in France and to split Britain from the US, required that an end be brought to this war, just as the Korean war had been removed as a defense-stimulating conflict.

2. Peking as well as Moscow feared that any further military advances in Indochina by the Viet Minh might have led to the formation of a strong anti-Communist alliance including some of the previously uncommitted Asian states. Chou En-lai informed Indian, Pakistani, Indonesian, and Burmese leaders in his talks with them that their security could be guaranteed by his "five principles." At the same time, Peking insisted that the Geneva agreements barred all three Indochina states from any military alliance.

3. With the example of Korea before them, the Chinese and Soviet leaders could not ignore the possibility that a continued offensive in Indochina would greatly increase the risk of American intervention and a global war. They preferred a far lower level of risk, namely, political subversion carried out by the Viet Minh. They "paid off" Ho by continuing (in violation of the Geneva agreements) to supply military equipment to make his army a modernized fighting force.

The developments in 1953 and 1954 have influenced the attitude of Ho and his lieutenants toward the current war. The clear awareness that they had been impelled, primarily

XII-48

by Moscow and Peking, to stop at a half-way station on the road to total military victory in Vietnam, apparently has made them very reluctant to stop half way again.

D. Implications for Vietnam Today

It is impossible to exaggerate the importance of this historical lesson for Ho. It sustains his hostility toward any suggestion that he again stop at a half-way station on the road to control of all Vietnam. An official of the DRV embassy in Havana told a leftist journalist on 3 May 1966 that

> We thought we had achieved something with the French by compromising (in 1954) and it turned out to be shaky. Only through full and unconditional independence can we achieve stability....We are determined to continue to fight until we achieve total victory, that is, military and political, and the Americans leave and accept our four points. (emphasis supplied)

The Chinese leaders, too, apparently believe that they had made a mistake in pressuring Ho to stop at a half-way station in 1954. Chou En-lai told a visiting youth delegation on 1 January 1966 that

> China will continue her absolute support of Vietnam. To tell the truth, I personally signed the Geneva agreement and I regret that my having done so is causing trouble for our comrades in Vietnam. I am not going to be deceived by the American peace campaign this time.

Actually, it was the Soviet-Chinese (not the "American") peace offensive that required an end to the war, and Molotov was Chou's partner in persuading Ho to make concessions to the French.

Ho is now in a stronger position to reject any Soviet suggestions that he should close out the fighting, and Soviet influence on him is as strong or as weak as Moscow's positive support for the war. That is, when Moscow avoided involvement (i.e., when Khrushchev decided to stand clear

XII-49

of providing important political and military aid to Hanoi), Soviet influence was at an all-time low. On the other hand, when Moscow incurred a degree of commitment (i.e., when the post-Khrushchev leadership decided to supply Hanoi with military aid and political support against the US), Soviet influence increased. However, it will never be as great as it had been in 1954.

The Chinese leaders have helped to make this impossible. In contrast to 1954, they are now the opponents, not the partners, of the Soviets. Ho's militancy is bolstered by Mao's support, which itself stems from special personal requirements. That is, Mao is personally far more pretentious than Ho--as witness the current irrationalities of the Mao cult in China--and with increasing neuroticism insists that his unique doctrine of "people's war" should legitimatize his claim to be the successor of Lenin and Stalin as the "leader of the international Communist movement." Unlike Ho, whose sights are centered on his own national war, Mao has a larger anti-Soviet doctrinal point to make: protracted small wars are effective in all under-developed areas and must be the main strategy against the US.

Mao has a considerable personal stake in proving to active doubters--namely, the Soviets, the East Europeans, the neutrals, and even men in his own party and military establishment--that his principle of protracted small war will work against the superior American military capability anywhere. Vietnam is the main proving ground for this thesis. Chou En-lai told Japanese Diet members on 7 January 1966 that if the Vietnamese Communists continue their military operations

> they will make the Americans admit their defeat and drive them out....The most important thing ...is to prove this by actual deed. Unless we defeat the enemy, we will not be believed. (emphasis supplied)

Any sign, therefore, from Hanoi that Ho is willing even to consider the matter of negotiating a cease-fire or a cessation of US air strikes against the North before a total withdrawal of American troops occurs is criticized by Peking. For example, using a double-edged statement, intended for neutrals and for the North Vietnamese, Chou En-lai on 2 September 1965 warned that: "As long as the US does not withdraw its troops, it can carry on endless talks with you so that it may hang on there indefinitely." (emphasis supplied) That this was a clear warning to Hanoi is suggested by the fact that Chou made the statement to the DRV ambassador at the North Vietnamese embassy in Peking.

Despite the constant concern of the Chinese leaders that Ho might agree to negotiations <u>before</u> US troops are withdrawn from the South, Ho continues to assign a high priority to prolonging his reactivated war. He and his lieutenants have absorbed Mao's own view on protracted civil war. When, in December 1936, Mao said that "to wage a revolutionary war for ten years, as we have done, might be surprising in other countries," he was rejecting modern Western and Soviet military doctrine on quick-decision ("impatient") war. He made his point emphatic in June 1946, noting that the Spanish civil war was "fought for three years, but we have fought for twenty years." Ho declared on 17 July 1966 that

> The war may still last 10, 20 years, or longer. Hanoi, Haiphong, and other cities and enterprises may be destroyed, but the Vietnamese people will not be intimidated.

A similar statement of North Vietnamese determination to persevere in the event of air strikes against cities in the North was made by a DRV embassy official in Havana on 3 May 1966: "The imperialists may well do so (i.e., bomb Hanoi and Haiphong), but we are ready to accept this sacrifice as we have accepted the others and it will not change our position or determination one iota."

Ho apparently believes that he can continue the war primarily because, despite losses in the North and South, he is still able to put forces <u>into the South</u> and to supply them for operations. On the other hand, the Maoist doctrine he has absorbed has a strong ingredient of opportunism. That is, there is no fixed principle that determines when and in what situation negotiations or a cease-fire should be accepted. The deciding factor is a very practical consideration--namely, inability to keep fighting. In the event that US air strikes were to continue to increase his problems, his willingness to negotiate a cessation of the strikes would not be blocked by any doctrinal consideration. The Chinese leaders apparently are aware of the ever-present prospect that Ho might view negotiations as a means to gain a breathing-spell from US pressure and are attacking not only the matter of talks before a total American withdrawal but also the matter of talks to attain a suspension of air strikes against the North.

Unpopular Pessimism

Why CIA Analysts Were So Doubtful About Vietnam

Harold P. Ford

> " It is well documented and well known that for decades CIA analysts were skeptical of official pronouncements about the Vietnam war and consistently fairly pessimistic about the outlook for light at the end of the tunnel. "

Harold P. Ford held senior positions in both the National Intelligence Council and the Directorate of Operations.

In traveling through Tonkin, every village flew the Viet Minh flag, and had armed soldiers, many with Japanese weapons taken in raids. The women and children were also organized, and all were enthusiastic in their support. The important thing is that all were cognizant of the fact that independence was not to be gained in a day, and were prepared to continue their struggle for years. In the rural areas, I found not one instance of opposition to the Viet Minh, even among former government officials.

OSS report, October 1945[2]

It is well documented and well known that for decades CIA analysts were skeptical of official pronouncements about the Vietnam war and consistently fairly pessimistic about the outlook for "light at the end of the tunnel." Less well known is why the Agency's analysts were so doubtful, especially because CIA was all the while a central player in US operational efforts to create and strengthen South Vietnam. Thus, it is important to examine the sources of CIA analysts' doubts about successive administrations' repeated assurances and claims.

Not all CIA analysts thought alike, and at times there were substantial differences of view. Skepticism and pessimism about Vietnam were present chiefly among those officers who produced finished intelligence in the form of National Intelligence Estimates and in Intelligence Directorate (then the DDI) publications: that is, analysts in the Office of National Estimates (ONE), the Office of [Economic] Research and Reports, and the South Vietnam Branch of the Office of Current Intelligence (OCI). Such views were generally a bit less evident among officers of the North Vietnam Branch of OCI, many of whom had been transferred there from previous Soviet and North Korean assignments. The situation among the Agency's operational offices at home and abroad was mixed: some enthusiastically shared official White House views, while others were remarkably caustic. In more than a few cases, the Intelligence Community's (IC) coordination processes and top CIA officers muted doubts about Vietnam expressed in CIA's analytic ranks, yet the finished intelligence produced by the DDI and ONE maintained definitely pessimistic, skeptical tones over the years.

The danger always existed that individual CIA analysts could get locked into constant dark points of view, reluctant to accept new evidence to the contrary. Also, at times some CIA analysts overreacted to certain assertive personalities from other offices who happened to be arguing wholly unsupportable optimism. And there were a few occasions where CIA judgments on Vietnam badly missed the boat, or where Agency judgments were too wishy-washy to serve the needs of policymaking or, in a handful of cases, where analytic officers caved in to pressures from above and produced mistakenly rosy judgments. Despite these hazards, and, as Robert McNamara's recent book *In Retrospect* maintains, the war's outcome justified many of the CIA analysts' doubts and warnings.

Officials in other entities, especially in the Department of State's Bureau of Intelligence and Research, often came up with similar doubting judgments. At times, their doubts also were shared by certain officers in DIA and elsewhere in the Department of Defense and by certain junior and field grade intelligence officers in Vietnam. CIA's analysts had no special sources of data not available to other US Government offices, no unique analytic methodologies, no precomputer-age Window 95s. The Agency's analysts simply, if unscientifically, distilled their many sources of doubt into judgments that often did not square with official pronouncements—a record which the authors of *The Pentagon Papers* and numerous other historians have documented.

The following principal factors and forces are among the many reasons for the doubts exhibited by so many of CIA's Vietnam analysts:

CIA's cultural advantages. The fact that CIA judgments often were more candid than those of most other offices was due in important measure to the bureaucratic advantage the Agency's culture and purpose afforded. The job of CIA analysts was to tell it like it is, freer from the policy pressures with which their colleagues in Defense, the military intelligence agencies, and, to a lesser extent, the Department of State had to contend.[3] Many CIA Vietnam analysts had been working on Indochina problems for some time, often longer than most military intelligence officers. Those Agency officers were familiar with how intelligence reporting had been distorted during

> **" The fact that CIA judgments were often more candid than those of most other offices was due in important measure to the bureaucratic advantage the Agency's culture and purpose afforded. "**

France's fight against the Communist-led Viet Minh (VM) and how such unfounded optimism had contributed to the French defeat. CIA analysts subsequently witnessed near-identical patterns in much of the US military and diplomatic reporting from Saigon. In addition, they were at times told confidentially by middle-grade US military and Mission officers of such practices. A few CIA analysts served in Vietnam and experienced firsthand such distortion by some senior US officials there. The resulting candor of CIA judgments flowed also from the fact that the reports Headquarters analysts received from CIA's Saigon station were much more factual and exacting in their demanded authenticity than was much of the other reporting from Vietnam.

Recognition of the Vietnamese Communists' (VC) enormous advantages. CIA's analysts were aware that the basic stimulus among the politically conscious Vietnamese was nationalism and that, following World War II, the VM had largely captured the nationalist movement. Ho Chi Minh's apparatus came to be better led, better organized, and more united than any other of the competing, divided nationalist Vietnamese parties. Through a combination of some reforms and ruthless elimination of political rivals, the VM/VC dominated the countryside. Local populations seldom volunteered intelligence to the French, the South Vietnamese, or the Americans about Communist-led forces in their midst.

Then, too, the VM's 1954 victory over the French at Dien Bien Phu and the end of French rule had been tremendous boosts to nationalist sentiment and Ho Chi Minh's status and popularity. At that time, most observers of Indochina affairs, including US intelligence agencies, judged that if nationwide elections were held, the VM would win by a large margin.

A similar view was even shared by DCI Allen Dulles, who, according to the record of a 1954 NSC meeting, told that senior group that "The most disheartening feature of the news from Indochina . . . was the evidence that the majority of the people in Vietnam supported the Vietminh rebels."[4] South Vietnam's Ngo Dinh Diem (with subtle US backing) subsequently proceeded to frustrate the holding of elections, and this strengthened the determination of VM forces to continue subverting all Vietnam in order to redress their grievance at being robbed of what they felt had been their victory in the field and at Geneva.

And one of the greatest advantages Ho's movement enjoyed, at times indicated in reporting from the field, were the subversive assets the VM and the VC had throughout South Vietnam. Thousands of their agents and sleepers existed throughout South Vietnam's Government, armed forces, and security/intelligence organizations. The dramatic extent of that advantage was not revealed until the fall of Saigon in 1975, when events disclosed how thoroughly the enemy had penetrated the society of South Vietnam—including some American offices there.

Recognition of VM/VC determination to try to meet South Vietnamese and US escalation, and willingness to suffer great damage, if necessary, in order to win eventual victory. CIA analysts widely appreciated the fact that the enemy saw its battle as a long-range conflict and was prepared to go the distance. To sustain VM/VC morale, Hanoi repeatedly invoked past victorious Vietnamese heroes, even ancient ones who for nearly a thousand years had fought Chinese pressures to dominate Indochina. Like those heroes, Hanoi was confident that its many advantages in the field and the power of its forces to endure would in time frustrate more powerful, less patient outside powers and cause them eventually to quit. For decades, CIA analysts again and again told policymakers that the enemy would doubtless persevere, counterescalate as best it could, and do so despite suffering heavy damage.

Such Agency analysts' doubts were especially marked during the months in 1964 and 1965, when President Johnson's administration was stumbling toward carrying the war to North Vietnam and committing US combat forces in the South. During that time, and in the face of pressures to "get on the team," CIA analysts (as well as intelligence officers from other agencies) repeatedly warned decisionmakers that such US military escalation would not in itself save South Vietnam unless it were accompanied by substantial political-social progress in Saigon and especially in the villages of South Vietnam, where virtually all CIA officers at all levels had long

> **"**
> **CIA analysts (as well as intelligence officers from other agencies) repeatedly warned decisionmakers that such US military escalation would not in itself save South Vietnam unless it were accompanied by substantial political-social progress in Saigon and especially in the villages.**
> **"**

maintained that the war had to be won. Agency officers made this point to policymakers through clandestine service reports, DDI and ONE memos, National Intelligence Estimates (NIEs), participation in JCS war games and in NSC-sanctioned working groups, and, in the end, warnings by DCI John McCone. But no one in the administration wanted to listen. It was not until about 1966 that frustrations in the field caused certain previous senior true believers to begin defecting in place, especially Secretary of Defense McNamara, whose *In Retrospect* now holds that CIA warnings had been correct all along and that he and his policymaking colleagues had been "wrong, terribly wrong."

Recognition of the great difficulties French and American military measures encountered in trying to combat VM/VC political-military warfare. Virtually all CIA Vietnam officers, in the field and in Washington, remained strongly influenced by the French defeat in Indochina. They recognized how ill-suited French military tactics had been for fighting the enemy; how the VM had chewed up elite French military units; and how the enemy had stunned the world by overwhelming the French forces at Dien Bien Phu. Because Agency officers were not burdened with the operational task of training and developing South Vietnamese armed forces, they were much freer of certain views more prevalent among US military personnel, such as disdaining the French experience, maintaining that US military know-how could prevail, and trying to impose upon Saigon governments US military tactics that were better suited to European battlefields.[5] Such appreciation by CIA officers found reflection both in the field and at Headquarters: in CIA counterinsurgency measures that lost their effectiveness when later taken over by the US military, and in numerous Headquarters analyses that judged that US military tactics were not substantially reducing the enemy's ability and determination to continue the war.

Moreover, many Agency analysts were sensitive to the geographic and terrain features in Indochina that shielded enemy supply lines from outer view and helped enemy guerrilla tactics but impeded US mechanized forces. CIA analysts long at Indochina assignments recalled how reluctant the JCS and the US Army had been in 1954 to try to bail out the French militarily at Dien Bien Phu, in part because US military studies had concluded that Indochina's location and terrain were not suited for ready supply or effective US military action. These analysts also recalled, as most policymakers by the early 1960s seemingly did not, how reluctant US Army leaders had been to become engaged in war in Indochina, and how at the time the JCS had held that "From the point of view of the United States, with reference to the Far East as a whole, Indochina is devoid of decisive military objectives, and the allocation of more than token US armed forces to the area would be a serious diversion of limited US capabilities."[6]

Similar views following US expansion of the war to the North in 1965, together with available positive evidence, led most CIA—and DIA—analysts to conclude that, despite US bombing efforts, the level of Hanoi's arms shipments to the VC were continuing to rise. Subsequent accounts by Johnson administration decisionmakers confirm that those reports had a definitely depressing influence upon their earlier certainties, and, in some cases, were instrumental in causing some of those policymakers to lower their previous enthusiasm about the war's prospects.

Rejection of official claims that Moscow and Beijing were directing the enemy war effort and that international Communism was a monolith. Many senior policymakers judged for years that the enemy's war effort in Vietnam was being run by "the Communist bloc." One such example: Gen. Lyman Lemnitzer, at the time JCS Chairman, stated in 1962 that Vietnam's fall was "a planned phase in the Communist timetable for world domination" and that the adverse effects of Vietnam's fall would be felt as far away as Africa.[7] By contrast, virtually all CIA officers held that available evidence clearly indicated that, although the USSR and Communist China were giving Hanoi defense assistance, the Vietnam war was Hanoi's show and had been from the outset. Moreover, with the exception largely of one CIA office, Agency analysts had been way ahead of the rest of the IC in pointing out—for years without

> **We do not believe that the loss of South Vietnam and Laos would be followed by the rapid, successive communization of the other states of the Far East....**

much impact—that the Sino-Soviet alliance was coming apart at the seams; that the USSR and China were competitive with respect to the Vietnam war; and that their developing estrangement offered US administrations an exploitable opportunity. The principal exceptions to these views within CIA were largely confined to certain counterintelligence officers who, even *after* the Sino-Soviet firefights that occurred along the Ussuri River border in 1969, continued to maintain that the Sino-Soviet estrangement was a plot to deceive the West.[8]

Those CIA analysts who rejected the official view that Moscow and Beijing were largely running the Vietnam war effort based their skepticism on several sources. One was appreciation of the degree of independence from outside Communist control Ho Chi Minh's movement and fledgling government had enjoyed all along. Another was the fact that, following the French defeat at Dien Bien Phu, Moscow and Beijing could have given Hanoi more support at 1954's Geneva Conference than they did. There also was evidence that all along the Soviets had less interest in promoting Communist aims in Indochina than in buttressing Communist Party fortunes in France and Western Europe. Most CIA analysts held that the various Communist movements in Southeast Asia each contained conflicting nationalistic elements—as the later wars of Communist China versus Communist North Vietnam and Communist Cambodia versus Communist North Vietnam illustrated.

These judgments contributed to the doubts held by certain CIA analysts, especially within ONE, that the loss of Vietnam would inexorably lead to the loss of all Southeast Asia and the US defense position in the far Pacific. The doubts went unvoiced for years in the face of repeated embraces of the domino thesis by senior officials of the Truman, Eisenhower, Kennedy, and Johnson administrations. Then, when finally asked by the White House in mid-1964 for its view of the domino thesis, ONE replied heretically that "We do not believe that the loss of South Vietnam and Laos would be followed by the rapid, successive communization of the other states of the Far East..."[9] The impact of those doubts on policymakers was ni

Recognition of the fact that South Vietnam remained a fragile entity whose ability to cope effectively with the VC should not be overestimated. These views, held widely among CIA analysts, if less so among CIA operations officers, for years ran headlong into repeated assertions by successive US administrations that Saigon's military effectiveness was rising. Subsequent events validated such CIA judgments: former NSC staff officer Chester L. Cooper, for example, later recorded that, as of 1962, "The fact was that the war was *not* going well, the Vietnamese Army was *not* taking kindly to American advice, and Diem was *not* following through on his promises to liberalize his regime or increase its effectiveness."[10] In addition, over the years much field reporting underscored the fact that President Diem's government did not enjoy wide support in Vietnam's villages. His government was a minority Catholic one in a predominantly Buddhist country.[11] Diem was not a dynamic leader, and he could not compete with the widespread popularity Ho Chi Minh enjoyed. He was remote from the people, as attested even by Lyndon Johnson in early 1961 while still Vice President:

A final indication of the danger is the fact that the ordinary people of the cities [of South Vietnam] and probably even more of the rural areas are starved for leadership with understanding and warmth. There is an enormous popular enthusiasm and great popular power waiting to be brought forth by friendly personal political leadership. But it cannot be evoked by men in white linen suits whose contact with the ordinary people is largely through the rolled-up windows of a Mercedes-Benz.[12]

Subsequently published documents indicate that MACV and Mission officers occasionally voiced despair at the Government of South Vietnam's (GVN) lack of military and political progress, but tended to confine their doubts to official, classified channels. Public official admission of serious GVN shortcomings was rare. Even more so, senior US military figures, at home and in the field, were almost always reluctant to admit that for years South Vietnamese military units (the ARVN), usually much better armed than the enemy, were no match for the VC. Criticisms of ARVN shortcomings were especially off limits, lest there be an implication that US military advisers were not

> **"For years, CIA's messages did not find ready response downtown because they were up against fearful odds"**

doing a good job of converting the ARVN into an effective fighting force.

Such sensitivity was particularly registered in early 1963, when DCI McCone, the JCS, CINCPAC, MACV, the US Embassy in Saigon, and other policymakers took umbrage at a draft NIE which ONE and the IC's working-level officers had agreed upon. It held that among Vietnam's "very great weaknesses" were a lack of "aggressive and firm leadership at all levels of command, poor morale among the troops, lack of trust between peasant and soldier, poor tactical use of available forces, a very inadequate intelligence system, and obvious Communist penetration of the South Vietnamese military organization."[13]

Those criticisms by Community analysts raised a firestorm of protest among the policymaking officers. They brought such pressure on DCI McCone and ONE that the latter caved in and agreed to a rewritten, decidedly more rosy NIE (53-63), in which the earlier criticisms of the ARVN were muted and the tone of the Estimate changed: the first sentence of the revised NIE now read, "We believe that Communist progress has been blunted [in South Vietnam] and that the situation is improving."[14] This was not one of CIA's proudest moments. And less than four weeks later, serious riots began in Hue which introduced the chain of events that culminated in the self-immolation of Buddhist monks and the murder of President Diem.

Areas of Doubt

These, then, were the principal areas of doubt that for years lay behind so many CIA analyses of the outlook in Vietnam. Except for those occasions where Agency officers produced flawed accounts or rosied up their judgments to meet pressures from above, the areas of doubt translated into the following fairly stark messages to successive policymakers:

1. Do not underestimate the enemy's strength, ruthlessness, nationalist appeal, and pervasive undercover assets throughout South Vietnam.

2. Do not underestimate the enemy's resilience and staying power. He is in for the long run and is confident that US morale will give way before his will. He will keep coming despite huge casualties. If we escalate, he will too.

3. Do not overestimate the degree to which airpower will disrupt North Vietnam's support of the VC or will cause Hanoi to back off from such support.

4. Do not overestimate the military and political potential of our South Vietnamese ally/creation.

5. The war is essentially a political war that cannot be won by military means alone. It will have to be won largely by the South Vietnamese in the villages of South Vietnam.

6. The war is essentially a civil war, run from Hanoi, not a Communist bloc plot to test the will of America to support its allies.

7. Winning the hearts and minds of the Vietnamese is a tough task. Most Vietnamese simply want to be left alone, and most do not identify with

Saigon. And many are either too attracted to the VC or too afraid to volunteer much information about the VC presence in their midst.

What CIA Analyses Were Up Against

For years, CIA's messages did not find ready response downtown because they were up against fearful odds. Outweighing intelligence facts and judgments were many views, factors, and forces which for years obtained widely among the best and the brightest of our decisionmakers:

1. World Communism is essentially monolithic, and the Vietnam war is part of a world conspiracy run from Moscow and Beijing.

2. Khrushchev and the Russians are testing us: if the United States does not fulfill its stated commitments in Vietnam, our credibility among our allies elsewhere in the world will suffer seriously.

3. Vietnam is the first domino. If it goes, the rest of Southeast Asia, as well as America's strategic position in the far Pacific, will crumble.

4. Top policymakers were receptive to the views of progress given them for years by senior military and Mission officers, views that in many cases were distorted, optimistic versions of more candid appraisals initially registered by more-junior officers in the field who were closer to the scene.

5. There was a profound hubris among top policymakers. They believed their made-in-America schemes would work in Vietnam, where similar schemes by the French

> " Perhaps *the* most potent hurdle for intelligence... was the fact that the decisions on what to do in Vietnam were not taking place within a vacuum but in a highly charged political arena. "

had not. We would succeed because of our superior firepower.

6. Top officials believed that sustained US bombing programs will disrupt North Vietnam's supply routes to the VC, and would cause Hanoi to back off for fear of losing such industrial development as it has achieved.

7. Many senior decisionmakers were confident that Vietnam's enormous complications could be reduced to systems analysis and statistical measures such as body counts—attitudes epitomized by Secretary of Defense McNamara's oft-cited assurance (1962) that "every quantitative measure we have shows we're winning this war."

8. Senior policymakers were too harassed and bogged down in their many day-to-day tactical responsibilities to give intelligence or the longer range consequences of US initiatives in Vietnam the careful attention those matters deserved.

9. There existed among senior policymakers what a US Army–sponsored history has since called "a massive and all-encompassing" American ignorance of Vietnamese history and society.[15]

10. Caught up by their commitments and operational enthusiasm, most senior policymakers did not want to hear doubts from below. They tended to ignore such views, especially those of more junior experts unknown to them. Witness McNamara's subsequently telling us that there were no experts on Vietnam.[16] And Gen. William E. DePuy (1988): "We did intervene on behalf of a very weak and dubious regime, albeit better than Communism, but very dubious in terms of political weight and meaning. But I don't remember anybody saying that. Do you? Nobody. Not even the experts, not even the scholastics and academics said that."[17] Or, at times, policymakers denounced dissenters for "not being on the team"; or froze out doubters, as President Johnson did with the dissenting DCI McCone; or sent doubters to new, Siberia-type assignments, as State did with Southeast Asia expert Paul Kattenburg.

11. Intelligence was only one of the many forces that crowded in upon policymakers. In addition, those decisionmakers were aware of dimensions of which intelligence officers were not. The record shows clearly that their chief concern was the US position in the world, not Vietnam per se, and that in their view Vietnam was so vital to broad US interests that we *had* to make a strong stand there.

12. Perhaps *the* most potent hurdle for intelligence, however, was the fact that the decisions on what to do in Vietnam were not taking place within a vacuum but in a highly charged political arena. For some years, the Democratic Party had been vulnerable for having "lost" China and having been "soft" in Korea. Presidents Kennedy and

Johnson repeatedly stated that they were not going to be the US Presidents who "lost" Vietnam and Southeast Asia.

Classic Analytic Hazards

In short, the often pessimistic intelligence judgments that CIA and other analysts gave our Vietnam decisionmakers over the years did not have much impact, except on those occasions where senior consumers could use intelligence to buttress their own arguments, or where they had come to question the more optimistic reports they had been receiving from other sources, or where they had begun to doubt their own earlier enthusiasms. There has indeed seldom been a better example than Vietnam of the eternal occupational hazards intelligence analysts face: that the judgments they deliver do not necessarily enjoy careful, rational study, but disappear into a highly politicized, sometimes chaotic process where forces other than intelligence judgments often carry the day.

This is what CIA and other analysts experienced during the long years of the war in Vietnam, breaking their lances in trying to penetrate policymakers' consciousness that the actual facts of life were more grim than those senior consumers generally appreciated. Even so, those analysts performed well in trying to produce candid appraisals—inasmuch as the principal calling for intelligence analysts at any one time is to try to tell it like it is, to remain a unique calling within a policymaking process overburdened with prior commitments, emotion, special pleading, and hubris.[18]

Yet analysts have to keep in mind that hubris is not a monopoly of policymakers. Vietnam analysts sometimes got locked into mindsets. This contributed to their being wrong on occasion. Sometimes very wrong—especially in not sounding clear alerts that the enemy was about to launch an unprecedented Tet offensive in early 1968, and in later underestimating the amount of North Vietnamese military support being funneled to the VC through Cambodia.

Not least, at all times analysts had a much easier time of it than did harried decisionmakers: analysts operated in a protected, quiet atmosphere, whereas policymakers were beset by a weak Vietnamese ally, a tough Vietnamese enemy, and a US public that could not stay the distance in what came to be regarded, correctly or not, as an unwinnable war.

* * * *

Illustrative Quotations

[CIA Intelligence Memorandum, 1950]: The Vietnamese insurgents are predominantly nationalists rather than Communists, but Communist leadership of the movement is firmly established. . . . These insurgents have long controlled most of the interior of Vietnam. Before 1954, they will probably have gained control of most, if not all, of Indochina.[19]

[General Bruce Palmer, Jr.]: The first national estimate on Indochina, NIE 5, 29 December 1950, "*Indochina: Current Situation and Probably Developments,*" . . . was a very pessimistic estimate. . . .[20]

[General Palmer]: During the period 1950–October 1964, ONE produced forty-eight (NIEs and SNIEs) . . . dealing with Vietnam . . . . In addition to estimates, ONE produced 51 Memorandums for the DCI concerning Vietnam over the same period. Indeed, ONE published more on Vietnam than any other single subject.[21]

[NIE 35/1, 1952]: Through mid-1952, the probable outlook in Indochina is one of gradual deterioration of the Franco-Vietnamese military position . . . . The longer term outlook is for continued improvement in the combat effectiveness of the Viet Minh and an increased Viet Minh pressure against the Franco-Vietnamese defenses. Unless present trends are reversed, this growing pressure, coupled with the difficulties which France may continue to face in supporting major military efforts in both Europe and Indochina, may lead to an eventual French withdrawal from Indochina.[22]

[NIE 91, 1953]: If present trends . . . continue through mid-1954, the French Union political and military position may subsequently deteriorate very rapidly.[23]

[(Senator) John F. Kennedy, 1954]: I am frankly of the belief that no amount of American military assistance in Indochina can conquer an enemy which is everywhere and at the same time nowhere, "an enemy of the people" which has the sympathy and covert support of the people. . . . In November of 1951, I reported upon my return from the Far East as follows: "In Indochina we have allied ourselves to the desperate effort of a French regime to hang on to the remnants of empire. There is no broad, general support of the native Vietnam Government among the people of that area . . . . [To try to win military victory] apart from and in defiance of innately nationalistic aims spells foredoomed failure."[24]

[Former CIA officer Joseph Burkhalter Smith]: I was stationed in Singapore then [1954], and British intelligence officers told me that they thought the United States was mad to prop up South Vietnam.[25]

[Gen. Bruce Palmer]: Overall, the situation in Vietnam inherited by the United States from France in 1955 was disadvantageous, if not hopeless. It is difficult to escape the conclusion that the United States in deliberately pushing the French out of the way and replacing them in Vietnam acted unwisely.[26]

[ONE Memorandum, 1960]: The catalog of public discontent [in South Vietnam] includes a widespread dislike and distrust of Ngo family rule . . . Diem's tightly centralized control and his unwillingness to delegate authority . . . the growing evidence of corruption in high places; the harsh manner in which many persons, particularly the peasants, have been forced to contribute their labor to government programs . . . and the government's increasing resort to harsh measures as a means of stifling criticism.[27]

[Gen. William E. DePuy]: Well, there wasn't a Vietnamese government as such. There was a military junta that ran the country. Most of the senior Vietnamese officers, as you know, had served in the French Army. A lot of them had been sergeants. Politically, they were inept. The various efforts at pacification required a cohesive, efficient government which simply did not exist. Furthermore, corruption was rampant. There was coup after coup, and militarily, defeat after defeat. . . . The basic motivation of the ARVN seldom equaled the motivation of the VC and the NVA [North Vietnamese]. . . the ARVN was losing the war just the way the French had lost the war, and for many of the same reasons.[28]

[Former Director of the CORDS program in South Vietnam, Amb. Robert W. Komer]: In the first analysis, the US effort in Vietnam failed largely because it could not sufficiently revamp or adequately substitute for a South Vietnamese leadership, administration, and armed forces inadequate to the task. . . . As George Ball put it in his well-known 1964 memorandum on "Cutting Our Losses in South Vietnam," "Hanoi has a government and a purpose and a discipline. The 'government' in Saigon is a travesty. In a very real sense, South Vietnam is a country with an army and no government."[29]

[The authors of *The Pentagon Papers*]: In this instance, and as we will see, later, the Intelligence Community's estimates of the likely results of US moves are conspicuously more pessimistic (and more realistic) than the other staff papers presented to the President. This SNIE [October 1961] was based on the assumption that the SEATO force would total about 25,000 men. It is hard to imagine a more sharp contrast between this paper, which foresees no serious impact on the [VC] insurgency from proposed intervention, and Supplemental Note 2, to be quoted next . . . "the JCS estimate that 40,000 US forces will be needed to clean up the Viet Cong threat."[30]

[ONE Memorandum, 1962]: The real threat, and the heart of the battle, is in the villages and jungles of Vietnam and Laos. That battle can be won only by the will, energy, and political acumen of the resisting governments themselves. US power can supplement and enlarge their power, but it cannot be substituted. Even if the US could defeat the Communists militarily by a massive injection of its own forces, the odds are that what it would win would be, not a political victory which created a stable and independent government, but an uneasy and costly colony.[31]

[Judgment by the intelligence panel of an NSC interagency working group, March 1964]: It is not likely that North Vietnam would (if it could) call off the war in the South even though US actions [systematically bombing North Vietnam] would in time have serious economic and political impact. Overt action against North Vietnam would be unlikely to produce reduction in VC activity sufficiently to make victory on the ground possible in South Vietnam unless accompanied by new US bolstering actions in South Vietnam and considerable improvement in the government there.[32]

[NSC Action Memorandum 288, 17 March 1964]: We seek an independent non-Communist South Vietnam. . . . Unless we can achieve this objective in South Vietnam, almost all Southeast Asia will probably fall under Communist dominance . . . accommodate to Communism so as to remove effective US and anti-Communist influence . . . or fall under the domination of forces not now explicitly Communist but likely then to become so . . . . Even the Philippines would become shaky, and the threat to India on the west, Australia and New Zealand to the south, and Taiwan, Korea, and Japan to the north and east would be greatly increased.[33]

[ONE Memorandum for the Director, June 1964]: We do not believe that the loss of South Vietnam and Laos would be followed by the rapid, successive communization of the other states of the Far East. . . . With the possible exception of Cambodia, it is likely that no nation in the area would quickly succumb to Communism as a result of the fall of Laos and South Vietnam. Furthermore, a continuation of the spread of Communism in the area would not be inexorable, and any spread which did occur would take time—time in which the total situation might change in any of a number of ways unfavorable to the Communist cause. . . . [Moreover] the extent to which individual countries would move away from the US towards the Communists would be significantly affected by the substance and manner of US policy in the area following the loss of Laos and South Vietnam.[34]

[CIA officers' comment on JCS wargame, April 1964]: Widespread at the war games were facile assumptions that attacks against the North would weaken DRV capability to support the war in South Vietnam, and that such attacks would cause the DRV leadership to call off the VC. Both assumptions are highly dubious, given the nature of the VC war. . . . The impact of US public and Congressional [and world] opinion was seriously underestimated. . . . There would be widespread concern that the US was risking major war, in behalf of a society that did not seem anxious to save itself, and by means not at all certain to effect their desired ends in the South. In sum, we feel that US thinking should grind in more careful consideration than has taken place to date. This does not mean that the United States should not move against the DRV, but that . . . we do so only if it looks as if there is enough military-political potential in South Vietnam to make the whole Vietnam effort worthwhile. Otherwise, the United States would only be exercising its great, but irrelevant, armed strength.[35]

[The authors of *The Pentagon Papers*]: However, the intelligence panel [of an NSC interagency working group, November 1964] did not concede very strong chances for breaking the will of Hanoi [by instituting a program of sustained US bombing of North Vietnam]. They thought it quite likely that the DRV was willing to suffer damage "in the course of a test of wills with the United States over the course of events in South Vietnam.". . . . The panel also viewed Hanoi as estimating that the United States' will to maintain resistance in Southeast Asia could in time be eroded—that the recent US election would provide the Johnson administration with "greater policy flexibility" than it previously felt it had.[36]

[ONE officer memorandum of April 1965, written shortly after President Johnson's decision to begin bombing North Vietnam and committing US troops to combat in the South]: This troubled essay proceeds from a deep concern that we are becoming progressively divorced from reality in Vietnam, that we are proceeding with far more courage than wisdom—toward unknown ends . . . . There seems to be a congenital American disposition to underestimate Asian enemies. We are doing so now. We cannot afford so precious a luxury. Earlier, dispassionate estimates, war games, and the like told us that the DRV/VC would persist in the face of such pressures as we are now exerting on them. Yet we now seem to expect them to come running to the conference table, ready to talk about our high terms. The chances are considerably better than even that the United States will in the end have to disengage in Vietnam, and do so considerably short of our present objectives.[37]

[Gen. Bruce Palmer]: [In late 1965] W. W. Rostow requested an analysis of the probable political and social effect of a postulated escalation of the US air offensive. CIA's somber reply was that even an escalation against all major economic targets in North Vietnam would not substantially affect Hanoi's ability to supply its forces in South Vietnam, nor would it be likely to persuade the Hanoi regime to negotiate. Similar judgments were to be repeated consistently by CIA for the next several years.[38]

[General Palmer]: With respect to Vietnam, the head of the CIA was up against a formidable array of senior policymakers . . . all strong personalities who knew how to exercise the clout of their respective offices . . . . [But] McNamara was not entirely satisfied with his intelligence from the Defense Department and beginning in late 1965, relied more and more on the CIA for what he believed were more objective and accurate intelligence judgments.[39]

[Former NSC staff officer Chester L. Cooper]: It is revealing that President Johnson's memoirs, which are replete with references to and long quotations from documents which influenced his thinking and decisions on Vietnam, contain not a single reference to a National Intelligence Estimate or, indeed, to any other intelligence analysis. Except for Secretary McNamara, who became a frequent requester and an avid reader of Estimates dealing with Soviet military capabilities and with the

Vietnam situation, and McGeorge Bundy, the ONE had a thin audience during the Johnson administration.[40]

[From a US Army-sponsored history (1985)]: Added to this propensity to try to make something out of nothing was an American ignorance of Vietnamese history and society so massive and all-encompassing that two decades of federally funded fellowships, crash language programs, television specials, and campus teach-ins made hardly a dent.... If there is any lesson to be drawn from the unhappy tale of American involvement in Vietnam.... it is that, before the United States sets out to make something out of nothing in some other corner of the world, American leaders might consider the historical and social factors involved.[41]

NOTES

1. Editor's Note: The author of this study drafted his first National Intelligence Estimate on Indochina in 1952, and subsequently had Vietnam-related duties as staff chief of CIA's Office of National Estimates and as a CIA representative to certain interagency working bodies. Since retiring from CIA in 1986, when he was Acting Chairman of CIA's National Intelligence Council, he has prepared classified studies on Vietnam for CIA's History Staff.

2. OSS (Secret Intelligence Branch), "Political Information [from Swift]," 17 October 1945; Appendix to *Causes, Origins, and Lessons of the Vietnam War*, Hearings Before the Senate Committee on Foreign Relations, 92nd Congress, 2nd Session, 9, 10, and 11 May 1972 (USGPO, 1973), p. 319.

3. There were a few occasions where certain Directors of Central Intelligence (DCIs) brought pressure on Agency officers to make their Vietnam analyses more palatable to policymakers. In addition, numerous authorities attest that George A. Carver, who was CIA's Special Assistant for Vietnam Affairs (SAVA) for several years following 1966 and who enjoyed remarkable entree among the USG's top decisionmakers, fairly regularly gave them more optimistic judgments than CIA's analysts were holding at the time.

4. Report of NSC meeting of 4 February 1954. *Foreign Relations of the United States, 1952-1954*, Volume XIII, *Indochina*, Part I, p. 1,014. (Hereafter, *FRUS*.)

5. As of 1959, for example, CIA's Saigon station officers were distraught because the US military advisory group was bent upon training the nascent South Vietnamese armed forces in corps maneuvers, rather than in effective small-unit counterinsurgency tactics. (This observation is from the author's personal experience.)

6. JCS Chairman Adm. Arthur Radford, Memorandum to the Secretary of Defense, 20 May 1954. *FRUS, 1952-1954*, Volume XIII, *Indochina*, Part 2, p. 1,591.

7. Lemnitzer, Memorandum for the Secretary of Defense, 13 January 1962. US Department of Defense, *United States-Vietnam Relations, 1945-67 (The Pentagon Papers)*, Book 12, "US Involvement in the War, Internal Documents, The Kennedy Administration: January 1961-November 1963," Book II, pp. 449, 450.

8. The author's personal experience. In holding their dissenting views, these counterintelligence officers and their boss, James Angleton, had been heavily influenced by the testimony of a defecting Soviet officer. By contrast, other offices of CIA's clandestine service had for a decade before 1969 been doing a superb job of reporting serious backstage rifts in the Sino-Soviet relationship.

9. Memorandum to DCI John McCone, 9 June 1964. *FRUS, 1964-68*, Vol. I, p. 485. See fuller quotation in Illustrative Quotations section. Without quoting that part of this memorandum, Robert McNamara claimed that ONE *supported* the domino thesis. *In Retrospect: The Tragedy and Lessons of Vietnam* (New York: Times Books, 1995), pp. 124-125.

10. Cooper, *The Lost Crusade: America in Vietnam* (New York: Dodd, Mead & Co., 1970), p. 196. (Emphases in the original).

11. "[Because most of the people of Vietnam were Buddhists, President Eisenhower] asked whether it was possible to find a good Buddhist leader to whip up some real fervor.... It was pointed out to the President that, unhappily, Buddha was a pacifist rather than a fighter (laughter)." Report of NSC meeting of 4 February 1954. *FRUS, 1952-54*, Volume XIII, *Indochina*, Part I, p. 1,014.

12. Trip Report by the Vice President, May 1961. *FRUS, 1961-63*, Vol. I, p. 154.

13. Harold P. Ford, "The US Decision to Go Big in Vietnam," *Studies in Intelligence*, Vol. 29, No. 1 (Spring 1985), p. 3. (Originally Secret, declassified 27 August 1986).

14. CIA was not the only recipient of such policymaker wrath. Eight months after the above episode, INR issued a sharp critique of claimed ARVN military progress which "evoked a monumental outcry" from Secretary McNamara and Gen. Maxwell Taylor. McNamara phoned Secretary Rusk, denouncing INR for second-guessing military

analysis; Rusk apologized to McNamara. Thomas L. Hughes (who had been INR's chief at the time), "Experiencing McNamara," *Foreign Policy*, No. 100 (Fall 1995), pp. 161-162.

15. Ronald H. Spector, *Advice and Support: The Early Years of the United States Army in Vietnam, 1941-60*, rev. ed. (New York: The Free Press, 1985), pp. x, xi.

16. *In Retrospect*, (passim).

17. Statement made 1 August 1988, to William C. Gibbons, principal author of *The US Government and the Vietnam War: Executive and Legislative Roles and Relationships*, Part III, January-July 1965, prepared for the Senate Committee on Foreign Relations by the Congressional Research Service, Library of Congress, (USGPO, 1988), p. 455. General DePuy had been J-3 of General Westmoreland's MACV, and later commanded the 1st Division in Vietnam.

18. See the Illustrative Quotations section.

19. Intelligence Memorandum No. 271: "Initial Alignments in the Event of War Before 1954," 24 March 1950. (Initially Secret, declassified 4 January 1978).

20. "US Intelligence and Vietnam," *Studies in Intelligence* (special issue, 1984), p. 14. (Initially Secret, subsequently declassified). General Palmer had been General Westmoreland's Deputy in Vietnam and Army Vice Chief of Staff. After retiring, he was a member of the DCI's Senior Review Panel.

21. "US Intelligence and Vietnam," p. 12.

22. "Probable Developments in Indochina Through Mid-1952," 3 March 1952. *FRUS, 1952-54*, Vol. XIII, pp. 54, 55.

23. "Probable Developments in Indochina Through Mid-1954," 4 June 1953. *FRUS, 1952-54*, Vol. XIII, p. 594.

24. *Congressional Record - Senate*, 6 April 1954, p. 4,673.

25. "Nation-Builders, Old Pros, Paramilitary Boys, and Misplaced Persons," *The Washington Monthly*, February 1978, p. 25.

26. "US Intelligence and Vietnam," p. 23.

27. Memorandum for the DCI, "Approaching Crisis in South Vietnam?," 28 July 1960. (Originally Secret; declassified 6 November 1980).

28. Lt. Cols. Romie L. Brownlee and William J. Mullen III, *An Oral History of General William E. DePuy, USA, Retired* (Carlisle Barracks, Pennsylvania: United States Military History Institute, n.d.), p. 123.

29. Robert Komer, *Bureaucracy at War: US Performance in the Vietnam Conflict* (Westview Press, 1986), p. 21.

30. (Gov't ed.), Book II, pp. 82, 83.

31. Memorandum for the Director, "The Communist Threat in Southeast Asia," 24 May 1962. (Originally Confidential; declassified 25 June 1980).

32. As quoted in *The Pentagon Papers*, Gravel, ed. (Boston: Beacon Press, 1975), Vol. III, p. 156. The author of this article was a CIA member of that working group.

33. As quoted in *The Pentagon Papers* (New York: Bantam/New York Times, ed., 1971), pp. 283, 285. That portion of NSC 288 repeated, verbatim, a text which Secretary of Defense McNamara had written the day before. McNamara, Memorandum to the President, 16 March 1964. *FRUS, 1964-68, Vietnam*, Vol. I, p. 154.

34. As quoted in *FRUS, 1964-68*, Vol. I, p. 485.

35. Memorandum for the Record sent to the DCI [by an ONE analyst and an FE operations officer], "Comment on the Vietnam War Games, SIGMA 1-64, 6-9 April, 1964," 16 April 1964. As quoted in Ford, "The US Decision to Go Big in Vietnam," pp. 7-8.

36. Gravel, ed., Vol. III, p. 213. The author of this article chaired that intelligence panel.

37. Memorandum sent to the DCI, "Into the Valley," 8 April 1965, as cited in Ford, "The US Decision to Go Big in Vietnam," pp. 10, 11.

38. "US Intelligence and Vietnam," p. 43.

39. Palmer, *The 25-Year War: America's Military Role in Vietnam* (New York: Simon & Schuster, Inc., 1984), p. 166.

40. Cooper, "The CIA and Decision-Making," *Foreign Affairs*, January 1972, p. 227.

41. Ronald H. Spector, *Advice and Support: The Early Years of the United States Army in Vietnam, 1941-60*, rev. ed. (New York: The Free Press, 1985), pp. x, xi.

Annotated Bibliography

Ford, Harold P. *C.I.A. and the Vietnam Policymakers: Three Episodes 1962-1968*. Ann Arbor: University of Michigan. 1998.

Halberstam, David. *The Best and the Brightest.* NewYork: Random House, 1972.
Halberstam's massive (665 pages) *The Best and the Brightest* has no chapter titles nor a Table of Contents. It does have however, separate bibliographies for sections of the book: On John Kennedy, the Kennedy circle and the Kennedy style, 15 titles; The History ofAmerican Involvement in Indochina, 23 titles; The China Era, 9 titles; The McCarthy Period, 3 titles; The Cold War Period, 10 titles; The Nixon Years, 2 titles; Military, 4 titles.

Herr, Michael. *Dispatches*. NewYork: Knopf, 1978.

Oberdorfer, Dan. *Tet: The Turning Point in the Vietnam War*. NewYork: Doubleday, 1971.
This North Vietnamese offensive was the point when America concluded the war was lost.

Moran, Christopher. *Company Confessions; Secrets, Memoirs and the CIA*. New York: Thomas Dunne Books / St. Martin's Press, 2015

O'Brien, Tim. *The Things They Carried*. NewYork; Houghton Mifflin, 1990.
Since their publication, *Dispatches and The Things They Carried* have been acclaimed as two of the most influential books about the Vietnam War—or any other American war.

Weiner, Tim. *One Man Against the World: The Tragedy of Richard Nixon*. New York: Henry Holt, 2015.
Perhaps the most negative biography of Nixon and the most hypnotic and persuasive.

Notes

Page

1 "Timeline of the Vietnam War," from www.Britannica.com and other sources.

4 "So long as ..." Principal Findings, Central Intelligence Agency-analysis, first section pages 19-20.

6 Rolling Thunder, in "Role of the United States in the Vietnam War," Wikipedia entry.

6 Nixon speech in Weiner, *One Man Against the World*, pp. 87.

7 List beginning "Do not underestimate ..." Harold P. Ford, "Unpopular Pessimism: Why CIA Analysts Were So Doubtful About Vietnam."

Harold P. Ford joined the Central Intelligence Agency shortly after its creation and became one of its most influential analysts. He was seen inside the agency as a master of the delicate art of interpreting ambiguous and contradictory intelligence reports and a dogged defender of the C.I.A.'s work from political pressure. His 1998 book, *C.I.A. and the Vietnam Policymakers: Three Episodes 1962-1968* argued that the pessimistic views of rank-and-file C.I.A. analysts on the war had proved accurate. The book received the George Pendleton Prize from the Society for History in the Federal Government. He died Nov. 3, 2010 at 89.
— "Harold P. Ford, C.I.A. Analyst, Dies at 89,"
The New York Times obituary, Nov. 11, 2010.

About Thomas Fensch

A native of Ohio, Fensch is the author or editor of 39 previous books, including:

The Kennedy-Khrushchev Letters, 2001;
The Man Who Changed His Skin, the only full biography of John Howard Griffin, who wrote the American classic *Black Like Me*, 2011 ;
Orwell in America, 2018.

Almost all of his titles are available on Amazon and elsewhere.

Fensch has a doctorate in print communication from Syracuse University and lives outside Richmond, Virginia, with three 27-inch Apple desktop computers, a working library of 700-plus books and a posse of four dogs who follow him everywhere.

www.ingramcontent.com/pod-product-compliance
Lightning Source LLC
Chambersburg PA
CBHW08003610052
44584CB00023BA/3225